The BRITISH CITROËN

The BRITISH CITROËN

By MALCOLM BOBBITT
Edited by ALAN TOWNSIN

© Malcolm Bobbitt and Mopok Graphics
1991

ISBN 086317 167 2

All rights reserved. Except for normal review purposes no part of this book may be reproduced or utilised in any form or by any means, electrical or mechanical, including photocopying, recording or by an information storage and retrieval system, without the prior written consent of the Publishers

> **Readers may find some confusion between English and French horse-power ratings as both are used throughout the text. A comparative table will be found in the Appendices on page 153.**

Typeset and produced for the Publishers by
Mopok Graphics, 128 Pikes Lane, Glossop, Derbyshire
Printed and bound in Great Britain

This book is dedicated to the memory of my late father who was responsible for my love affair with the motor car and Citroën in particular.

Contents

	Introduction	4
1.	One hundred cars a day	6
2.	Early days—Gaston's and Brook Green	13
3.	Arrival at Slough	24
4.	Comfort far beyond its price	32
5.	The great push	40
6.	The end of an era	54
7.	Pulling power	71
8.	Peace and the road ahead	86
9.	Two horses and a jewel	96
10.	The goddess	109
11.	The sun sets at Slough	128
12.	Tomorrow	130

Contents continued

Appendices
1. Citroen taxicabs — 148
2. Delivery of vehicles in and from Britain — 151
3. British and French model designations — 153
4. Production of Traction Avant cars at Slough — 154
5. Total production of Traction Avant cars — 155
6. Production of 2CV at Slough — 156

Index — 157

Acknowledgements — 159

Bibliography — 160

Introduction

Seldom in the history of the motor car has one marque created so much controversy, attracted such widespread attention and yet earned such respect as Citroën. From the beginning, the cars mirrored the charisma of André Citroën, founder and very much *le Patron* of what he insisted should leap into prominence as the greatest motor manufacturer in France, in the ceaseless quest for the logical advancement of technology.

From the modest beginning of the gear company which gave rise to the chevron emblem used to this day, and the daring venture set up by the still-unknown Citroën to produce artillery shells for the First World War at a rate thought impossible but achieved against all the odds, came the factory on the banks of the River Seine from which great advances in car design were to come. The original 10 h.p. Type A can be claimed as the first European 'people's' car and was a truly remarkable venture for a new name amid all the numerous concerns trying to break into the world of automobiles in 1919.

The Citroën car found favour with the British motorist, some 750 being sold in 1920, and from this healthy following sprang the decision to set up a British company, Citroën Cars Limited, complete with an impressive headquarters and service centre at Brook Green, near Hammersmith, London in 1923. Sales continued to rise but imported cars were handicapped by the import duties imposed on all foreign products and André Citroën became convinced that he should set up a manufacturing plant in the United Kingdom.

He was aware of the huge premises that had been used as a military vehicle repair depot during the war years in Slough, Buckinghamshire, for part of the land had been used for a large-scale demonstration of the Citroën Kegresse half-track vehicle. An attractive feature to the ever-publicity-conscious André Citroën was the fact that the main building was described as the largest factory building under one roof in the country. He took a lease on this, with an option on a further sixty acres of adjoining land and thus Citroën was among the first companies established on what had become the Slough Trading Estate, in 1926.

The aim of this book is to provide an account of the Citroën enterprise in the United Kingdom from the earliest days when Gaston Limited imported that original 10 h.p. model from Paris, through the formation of Citroën Cars Limited, the opening of the Slough Factory and such events as the establishment of what were claimed to be the most imposing car showrooms in the country at New Devonshire House, Piccadilly, as well as the story of the numerous models and body styles sold in Britain over the years, whether built at Slough or otherwise.

In order to give a proper perspective of the British operation, the story of what Citroën was achieving in its homeland is told in parallel, as well as indicating the ways in which a different approach was chosen for the business to suit national variations of taste. Citroën the man was the key figure on both sides of the Channel and so the unfolding of his career as a remarkable entrepreneur is woven into the chain of events. Arguably, his decision to pursue the concept of an entirely new type of car, combining front-wheel-drive and integral construction, two elements of car design which have become accepted world-wide in recent times, was his greatest legacy to automobile history. Yet the Traction Avant models that set so advanced a standard at their introduction in 1934 virtually broke the Company, and doubtless the financial problems and worries played their part in undermining the health of André Citroën himself, leading to his death in 1935.

Yet the fulfilment of his dream did follow, even if not until too late for him to see it. Tribute must be paid to Pierre Boulanger not only for his shrewd management of the business which allowed the flowering of the seed sown by the founder but also in showing a similar willingness to pursue the unconventional, most notably with the 2CV.

An idyllic village scene at Goodman's garage, South Kilsworth, Leicestershire **circa** *1933. A Citroen Twenty Seven-seater De Luxe Saloon is prominent in the foreground and an Austin Seven is parked near the Shell petrol pump.*

The British Citroën is examined in depth, detailing the cars that emerged from the Slough factory from 1926 and describing manufacturing methods and how they altered with successive generations of cars. The Traction Avant figures prominently as a matter of course, with an indication of the way in which the British versions differed from their French built counterparts, but the story of Slough production of the 2CV and of the stylish and complex DS is also told. Overall, the British Citroën factory played a valuable role in the motor industry of the United Kingdom, one that is all too apt to be forgotten. It played its part in the all-important export drive of the early post-war years, when cars built at Slough were sent to all corners of the Earth. Numbers of them, often many years old, can still be found providing sterling service, just as they can in this country.

Although the assembly of cars at Slough ceased in 1966, Citroën Cars Limited not only lived on but has lived to see expansion of sales as British car buyers became more receptive to the concept of the car that also appealed to the European market as a whole. Indeed, Citroën's flair for producing something 'different' has created markets of its own in a world where bland uniformity leaves less scope for individuality, not only with such models as the 2CV, far more successful in Britain in its later years than in the original ultra-low-powered form, but also the chunky-looking BX. Yet Citroën cars are still the subject of controversy, just as they have been since the beginning in 1919 — it is hard to believe that Andre Citroën would have wished it otherwise!

Malcolm Bobbitt
Uxbridge, 1991

André Citroën.....
This photograph of the Patron, signed by him, was taken in October 1928 when he was aged 50. Citroën was born in Paris on 5th February, 1878, the fifth child of a Paris diamond merchant. André's father suffered from extreme melancholy and committed suicide in 1883 by jumping from a window; his mother, Amelia, never overcame the grief of her husband's death and died in 1900 at the age of 46. Citroën left school at the age of sixteen and attended the Polytechnic, studying for a diploma in engineering.

Chapter one: One hundred cars a day

In terms of the early days of motoring, André Citroën's advent into the business of manufacturing motor vehicles was rather late. His contemporaries both in Britain and Europe had already experienced the pains of failure and ecstasy of success. Even though the motor car was but thirty years old it seemed that its design and future would follow a somewhat narrow and conservative route; only a few makers could envisage the motor car being made and marketed as a complete package; Henry Ford was one of them. The course that Citroën took to produce automobiles was an obscure one but nevertheless of great interest and a remarkable example of foresight, ingenuity and enterprise. André Citroën was, in the very truest sense, an entrepreneur.

The son of a Paris diamond merchant, André Citroën was born on the 5th February 1878 at the family home, 44 Rue Laffite. The home was not always a happy place. André's father, Dutch in origin, suffered from extreme melancholy and died in 1883 by falling from a window; his mother, who was Polish, never overcame the deep distress of her husband's death and died in 1900 at the age of 46. André Citroën proved to be a good pupil and fun-loving. He left school at the age of 16 in 1894 and entered the polytechnic to study for a diploma in engineering, leaving there in 1898. A major contribution to Citroën's success was the desire by his mother for him to achieve the best qualifications and obtain in life all that which had been denied her. Sadly, she was never to enjoy the contentment of witnessing that success.

The highlife and nightlife attracted Citroën. He enjoyed taking a risk and his dynamic personality took him to the gaming tables and nightclubs. His desire for adventure and competition would be with him for the rest of his life whilst his financial escapades would eventually be his downfall. Soon after the death of his mother, the young Citroën travelled to Poland visiting relatives he had never seen; the journey to Lodz was to have a major significance on the path in life that he was to eventually take.

While staying at Lodz, Citroën met a mechanic who was also something of an inventor. This man lived virtually as a recluse in a world of his own rarely having contact with civilisation outside the village. Laying on a bench in his workshop was a model that halted Citroën in his tracks; the mechanic had been experimenting with a gear drive but instead of the teeth being cut at right angles they were shaped in the form of chevrons. At once Citroën realised the potential of what was lying before him, it could without doubt revolutionise the engineering industry. The model had been constructed in wood; somehow a technique would have to be found to cut the gears in steel. Purchasing the patent, Citroën returned to Paris with certain ideas planted securely within his mind. Realising what future could develop from the concept of the chevron gear, it can be safely said that Citroën himself was effectively the inventor of the gear-drive using double helical teeth.

With the same drive and enthusiasm as he had shown during his education, Citroën set about putting his invention to use. Following the building of a prototype herringbone gear drive in steel, it was clear the idea was going to be a success; the gear proved to be most smooth and silent in operation, the future was set, Citroën decided to start his own engineering company. By 1912 his success was realised and he founded the Citroën Gear Company. In the time leading up to this momentous event in his life, some seven years had been spent working with much industriousness with two partners in the town of Essonnes where the three young men had opened an engineering workshop.

The Citroën Gear Company supplied an important service to industry. The invention of the chevron gear allowed many commercial businesses to expand; more efficient machinery could be built for use in mines and mills as well as other heavy industries. It was obvious that the founder of the gear company was not going to be satisfied to sit back on his laurels, in fact it made his ambitions even stronger. Always throughout his life he had great ideas in his head, now, he realised, was the time to really start putting them into practice. The dynamic and forward thinking André Citroën should soon look towards furthering his achievements and in the event it was not to be long before the opportunity arose.

Meanwhile, Citroën's elder brother, Hughes, had married the daughter of Monsieur Harbleischer, President of the board of Mors, the well-kwown French motor car. André Citroën joined the board of Mors shortly before the company went into deficit by £440,000, in 1907, and argued against closing it down. Some recovery was achieved and a small profit was made in 1910. Hughes had pressed for André's skill in management to be used, particularly as the threat from competitors, notably Peugeot, was looming larger. As conditions worsened Hughes again suggested that his dynamic brother be asked to take control but only when the situation became all but impossible in 1911 did Harbleischer agree to reconsider his earlier decision. André Citroën was called for and at once took swift action.

Mors were producers of fine automobiles; their output, however, was very limited at just four cars a week. Citroën set out to increase this figure and went about it in three ways: firstly to develop a luxury new car to dispel the bad rumours that were circulating about the the company; the

The Double Helical Gear. Citroën had realised the potential of such a gear when he saw a wooden model crafted by a mechanic at Lodz, in Poland, during a visit to the country as a young man. On his return to Paris, Citroën developed the idea and took out a patent for the gear design. It is clear, looking at the configuration of the teeth of the gear how the Double Chevron Citroën emblem materialised.

engineers managed, by installing a new engine, to obtain very impressive performance results which gave interest in the car and the company a considerable boost. Citroën's idea was successful and sales began to rise. A competitor of Mors, Theophile Schneider, heard of their plight and made an offer for the company in the sum of a million francs in order to swallow the opposition so he could market his own vehicle. Citroën saw his second chance and secured a loan for a matching sum from a multi-millionaire diamond merchant who had been a friend of his father and so kept the Mors company alive. Thirdly, the help of Georges-Marie Haardt was enlisted who assisted in the development of new models. Haardt remained a lifelong friend of André Citroën and together they were responsible for exploring new frontiers. Two new cars were launched, the 14 h.p. and the 20 h.p.; both models were completely successful and sales of Mors cars rose from 125 to 1200 a year.

Significantly, in 1912 Citroën went to America, where he was impressed with Henry Ford's production methods and even more so with the Model T. He managed to meet Ford and discuss his business ideals and, on returning to France, set about putting some of what he had learnt into practice, though other events intervened before this process could be taken very far within the Mors company. Mass production was to play a big role in the Citroën story but not in the way that might have been expected.

War was also on the horizon; when The Great War broke out in 1914 Citroën left his gear company and the motor cars of Mors to fight on the front lines as an artillery captain. France was unready for war, the country had little in the way of ammunition and the order of the day went out to economise on shells. Not bearing to witness France face defeat in the eyes of the enemy, Citroën rushed to the war office. He argued that production of shells must be increased, alas he was met with the reply that it was just not possible. Not being able to accept this lethargic response he put it to the director of artillery at the War Ministry that if given a license he could guarantee the manufacture of 50,000 shells a day. At first the offer was met with an air of almost disinterest. Not being put off, Captain Citroën pleaded again managing this time to convince the ministry he was able to supply the shells; success did not elude him and the authorisation for the license was granted. This was yet another turning point in the life of André Citroën.

Not a minute of time was wasted; immediately loans were assured and twelve hectares of land obtained near the banks of the River Seine in Paris at the Quai de Javel. It seemed that almost overnight Citroën's factory sprung up. The man's great energies were concentrated in this new venture, everything he ever stood for was reflected in the way floors were cemented, steel structures erected and machinery installed with such speed but yet deliberence. By the time the brick walls were built and the roof installed, the first shells were leaving the premises and on their way to the front lines. The targets set for production of ammunition were immense, critics of the French manufacturer delighted in telling the world this man was mad and to produce so many shells was a pure impossibility; the one man who was heard to shout the loudest was Citroën's later rival, Louis Renault, founder of the famous car maker and who was referred to by Citroën as the 'Bear of Billancourt', Billancourt being the place where Renault had established his huge car factory. Not concerned by the derogatory remarks Citroën forged ahead, he knew what had to be done and how he would do it. The answer, he assured himself, was in mass-production. From America the ideals of 'Taylorisation', in which Citroën totally sympathised, were implanted in the Javel works and enabled an ingot to enter a door at one end of the factory and come out as a completed shell at the other end. To do this Citroën installed the most modern equipment available from the other side of the Atlantic and such machinery appeared as electric trolleys and mechanical transporters. To the joy of France and the annoyance of his rivals it was soon evident that the target of 50,000 shells a day could be well achieved.

Whilst Citroën proved that he could bring mass-production to the engineering industry and accomplish what was considered the impossible, he did not lose sight of the people that had made it feasible, his employees. The concept of a modern factory was not allowed to stop at the end of the production line, his workers were to share exceptional conditions, showers were installed, a restaurant was provided where meals of the highest quality were served, drinking fountains were supplied and a social club inaugurated. Having built a factory with a capacity for large scale production the thoughts of the dynamic industrialist searched beyond the end of the war

Quai de Javel, Paris. André Citroën built his factory on the bank of the River Seine, originally to manufacture munitions for the Great War. Making 50,000 shells a day was the target Citroën had set himself, an aim that he surpassed. At the end of the War, Citroën turned his business over to the manufacture of motor cars and initiated the mass-production of vehicles with his plan to build 100 cars a day. In effect, the Type A, Citroën's first production car ready to be driven away from the production line, became the first European people's car.

Announced in the press during April 1919, by this advertisement, the Citroën 10 h.p. Type A was put into production in May, with the first car delivered on 4th June. Citroën's rivals doubted his claim that he would build 100 cars a day; Louis Renault, who had his motor car factory on the opposite side of the River mockingly asked who would buy these cars — Citroën replied "the whole world!" The wording used — 'the first French car in volume production' would be an idiomatic translation — was remarkably bold for a firm with a name not hitherto seen on any car, yet amply justified by subsequent reality.

which he knew must come before too long. With the apparatus available he could turn his machines to almost anything; he knew, however, the destiny that lay before him was the manufacture of motor cars, not the type the French had seen before where a costly chassis was supplied to a coachbuilder who then in turn would supply the vehicle often without essential accessories, but a motor car complete in every detail and finished to the highest standards that could be driven away immediately it had come off the assembly line. With the car would be a service network that avoided the owner having to resort to the services of an uncertain mechanic. Already Citroën announced that by the end of 1919 he would build one hundred cars a day. Again his critics laughed at him, including Louis Renault who was considered at the time to be the great car builder of France. Even he could not match anywhere near that figure. Citroën was asked who would buy these cars, he replied, "The Whole World"!

As envisaged, the war came to an end in 1918, with hostilities over Citroën saw the end of the production for ammunition. Had he not been so astute he may well have been left looking upon a completely deserted factory floor with all the great machines at rest. This indeed was not so, the production lines were still working but instead of shells waiting for despatch it was tools. Citroën needed to occupy his workforce and the machinery, therefore toolmaking was a good diversification whilst preparations were being made to establish a car manufacturing plant. It would take time to convert the works to produce automobiles and build a prototype model that he could base his future upon but on the 4th June 1919 Citroën's ambitions were realised; on that very day the first motor car

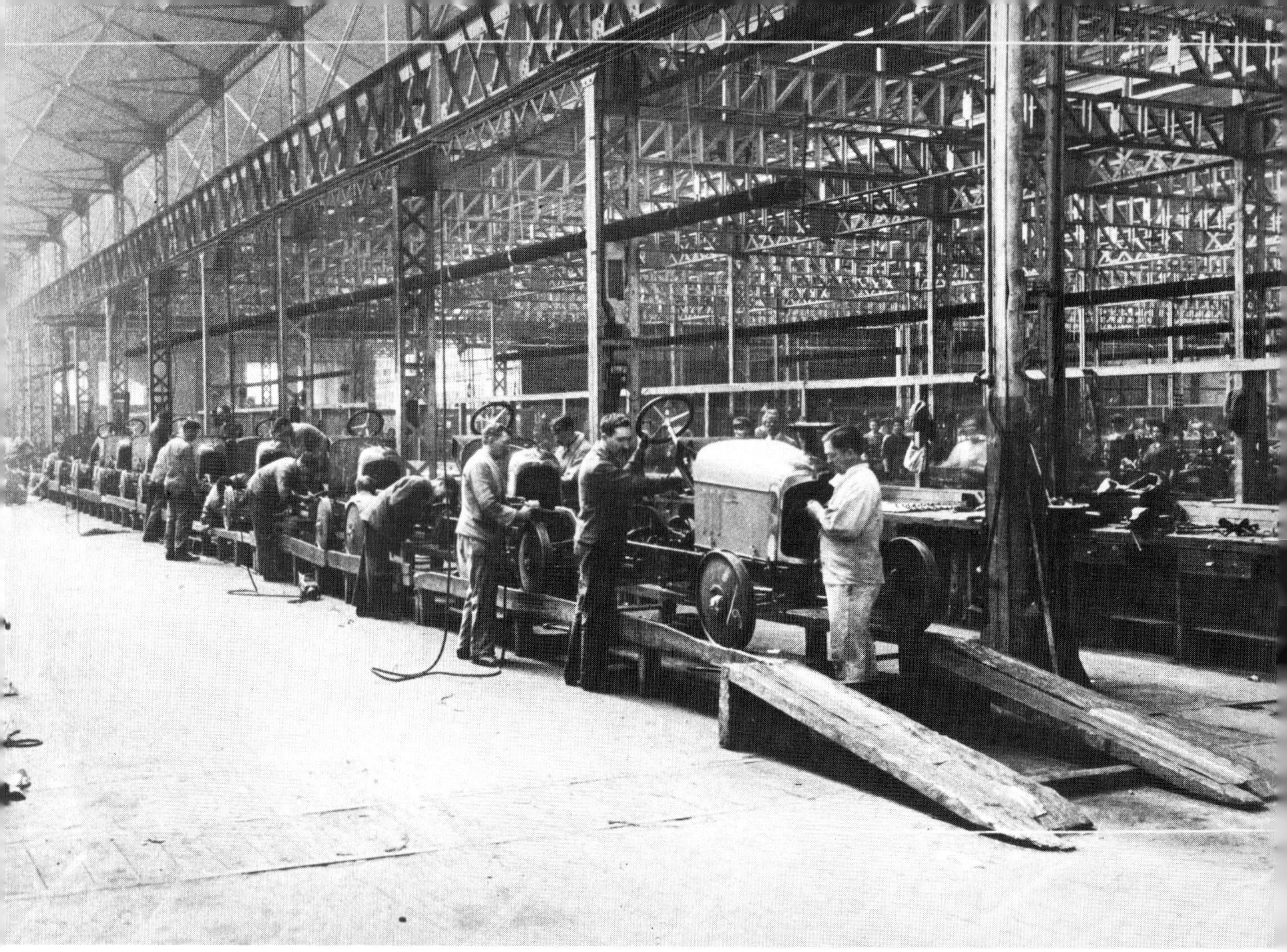

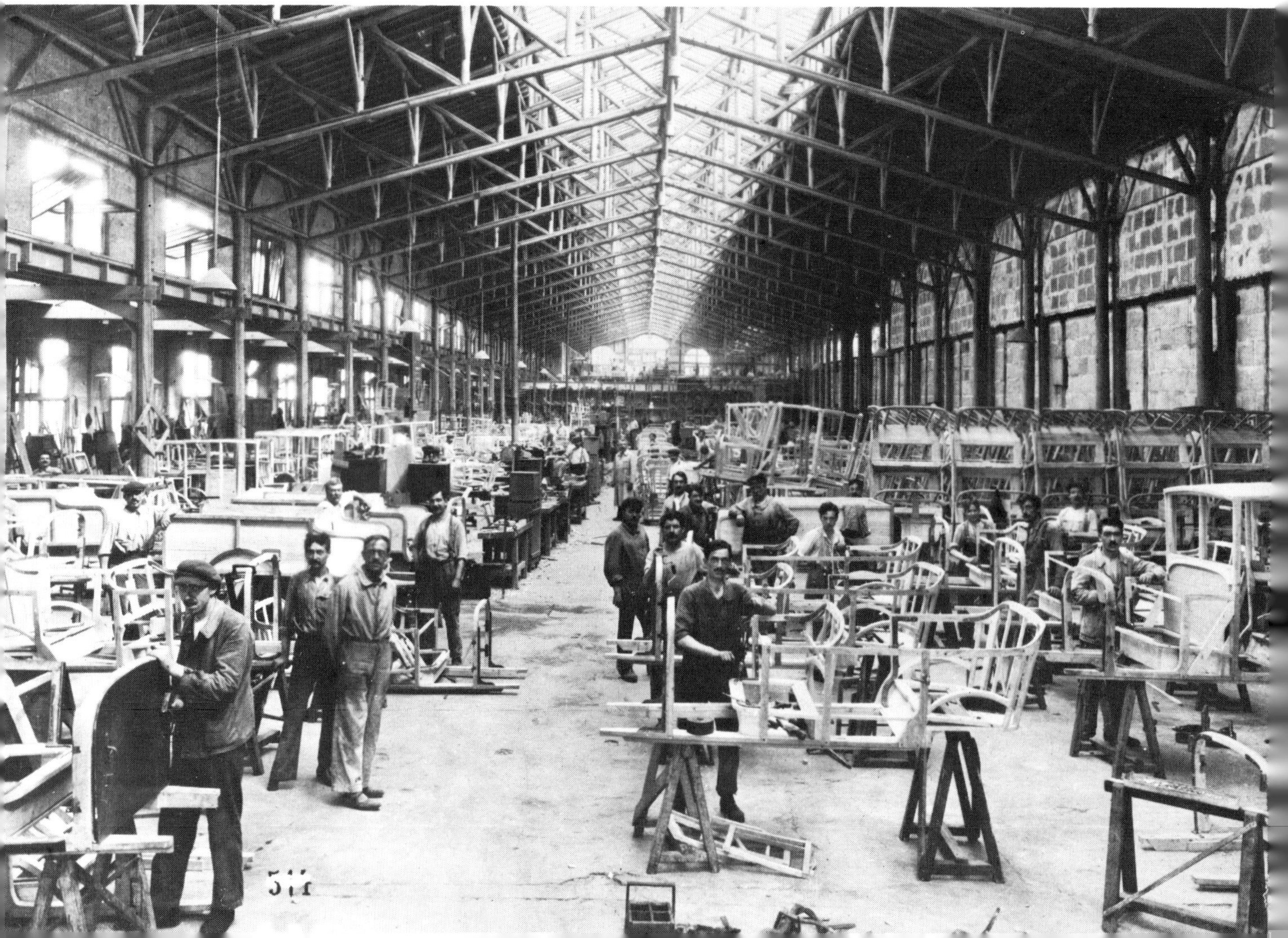

The production line for the Type A 10 h.p. Citroën at Javel, circa 1920. It would appear that the car in the foreground is right hand drive. Compressed air tools can be clearly seen in use; it is evident from the background of the photograph that a high proportion of female staff are employed operating machine tools. Citroën pioneered good working conditions for his staff and made available nurses, canteens and a social club. Note that the assembly 'track' is a simple wooden structure, evidently made in sections and already looking much worn.

bearing the name of Citroën was delivered from the factory and on the radiator cowling there was an emblem representing the double helical gear, The Double Chevron.

The factory on the Quai de Javel, standing where cabbages had once grown in market gardens, was now the producer of a unique motor car, one that was soon to be recognised as a 'peoples car', coming fully equipped with five wheels, horn, electric starter, electric lighting and a price tag of just 7950fr. For a time all went well, Citroën sold his cars, finding the very niche in the market he had envisaged, nevertheless, due to devaluation of the Franc and many internal crises of the government there began a slowing down of sales and profits. As a remedy Citroën knew that he would have to make his name synonymous with his products, thus said he started one of the most flamboyant and outrageous publicity campaigns ever witnessed in all time. At first there seemed little point in advertising the Citroën Car as the press and critics were doing it all for the company. The Paris motor show of 1919, the first for five years due to the Great War, was not as elegant as had been seen in previous days but yet, after five years of hardship and horror the Parisians were in a mood of extravagance; there was a new will to live and a new era lay ahead. Perhaps Citroën knew this better than anyone, here in the Salon was his new product, The Type A Citroën. This automobile brought to the people of France a fresh desire to forget the past and become once again a consumer nation.

Citroën's new product, the Type A, was announced in the national press in April 1919; five versions of the car were to be available, the four-seat 'Torpedo' together with a cheaper three-seat variant built on a shorter chassis, three-seater Doctor's Coupé, four-seat saloon and an attractive Coupé de Ville which was the most expensive of the cars at 9,800 Francs. Production of the Type A commenced during May and by mid-June thirty cars a day were leaving Javel. Between June and December 1919 2,500 cars were built and in 1920 Citroën produced 20,200 vehicles; cars rolled off the assembly lines in increasing numbers 1923 saw over 36,000 vehicles built with 67,200 cars the following year. No longer was the automobile a toy for the rich, Citroën's Type A placed the motor car in

The Eiffel Tower illuminated during Citroën's prestigious publicity campaigns. Over a quarter of a million light bulbs were required to achieve this impressive result. Parisians were used to Citroën's bizarre advertising methods; on one occasion aircraft were employed to write the Company's name in smoke in the sky. Citroën achieved his aim, over 36,000 cars were built in 1923.

Wooden frames for the Type A 10 h.p. Citroën being constructed at Javel. In the foreground can be seen frames for the 'Torpedo' open cars whilst on the right of the picture the frame for a Coupé de Ville is being assembled. As can be imagined by the number of cars built during the earliest years, the bodyshop is a hive of industry.

reach of almost everybody; large advertising posters were aimed to strike their message to the masses and made much of the low running costs of the car. By the end of 1919 Citroën had acheived his goal, out of the factory on the Quai de Javel came one hundred cars a day. Faced with opposition from Louis Renault, Voisin and Panhard together with many smaller manufacturers, Citroën took some very bizarre methods of publicity. Perhaps the most famous was in 1925 when the Eiffel Tower was used to broadcast the name of Citroën illuminated by over 250,000 light bulbs. Almost the entire tower was ablaze with lights, the lower sections carried the Citroën emblem at each corner while each of the four soaring sides of the ediface spelled out his name stretching out to some 650 feet. No doubt Renault fumed, he had already called Citroën the 'Little Jew of Javel'. On another occasion an aircraft etched the name of Citroën with smoke in the skies above Paris, every Frenchman gazed up at the spectacle. Parisians were getting used to being shocked in such ways, one morning the City awoke to find posters daubed at every conspicuous place displaying life-sized portraits of cars. During the 1923 Paris Salon André Citroën lined up 150 of his cars all of varying body styles in the Place de la Concorde. With each car a chauffeur attended, turned out in immacualte uniform, their job was to take prospective clients for a test drive along the Champs-Èlysées and the bank of the Seine, everywhere to be seen were Automobiles Citroën.

Not only in France was the Citroën car gaining in popularity; in that country it was already a household name. In Britain it was associated with quality and finesse; motoring magazines were excited about the new car from the other side of the Channel and suggested the British motoring public would be able to look forward to a style of leisure previously unknown except for the more prosperous classes and also, with the Type A, an advantage was that servicing was not out of the question for the owner. The *Light Car and Cyclecar Magazine* was the first motoring journal in Britain to review the Type A, it referred to it as a 'remarkable French production by a famous munition concern'; complimentary in its review, the magazine enthused over the car and described the engineering of the machine in some detail. In 1922, the same journal again wrote highly of the Citroën when it published: 'The Citroën is undoubtedly one of the most popular utility machines on the British Market of which ample evidence is provided by the number which may be seen on the road. Although essentially a mass-production job, the points needing attention from time to time are no more numerous than one would find on a much higher priced car.'

André Citroën had been successful in his native France, his cars had a good reputation which had spread abroad to the British shores. Faced with grim opposition from the many indigenous car makers, all of whom were clamouring for increased sales on the home market, Citroën was able to sell enough models to Britain to make it worthwhile having them fitted with right-hand steering. From the Quai de Javel, Citroën appointed a young man to look after the company's interest in Britain; his name was Monsieur d'Esparbes, he was despatched to London with an advancement of one thousand Francs and a suit of clothing in the manner that the British Gentleman would approve. No more was the name of Citroën to be quite so strange; the dynamic industrialist of the Chevron Gear fame was already gazing across the English Channel to the White Cliffs of Dover.

Citroën Type A chassis receiving attention before the fitting of bodies. This superb period photograph shows the Javel factory in Paris circa 1920 when production of Citroën's first motor car was in full swing. Note the varying stages of completion of the chassis lined up upon the shop floor; some cars are fitted with Michelin tyres whilst others stand on their disc wheels. Note on the far side of the workshop some completed cars including several Coupé de Ville models and a 'Torpedo' with hood up. Note also the clean, precise and orderly state of the factory, this together with the high standard of facilities offered to staff were amongst Citroën's ideals.

The Finishing Shop at Javel; various models receive final touches before being made ready for delivery. The Coupé de Ville in the foreground waits for a set of tyres whilst next to it a four-seat 'Torpedo' has engine adjustments. Note behind the Coupé de Ville (centre foreground) two right hand drive Torpedos await completion.

Chapter two:
Early days—Gaston's and Brook Green

The new mood in France had its effect upon the automobile industry; the target that André Citroën had set himself in 1919 of building one hundred cars a day had, by 1923, been superseded. Instead of producing 35,000 cars a year the demand was double that figure. Consequently, the factory on the Quai de Javel was working at full stretch and it was necessary to replace much of the equipment that had earlier been installed. This was an opportunity for Citroën to further exercise his beliefs in 'Taylorisation'; in addition to the Javel works two subsidiary factories were opened, at Levallois which was producing the 7.5 h.p. model often nicknamed the 'Cloverleaf' and at Suresnes where the foundries were situated and die-casting and drop-forging was carried out. It was at the latter premises the latest type of oil fired furnaces were installed and the whole of the factory floor laid in such a way to enable extremely high production levels.

The Javel factory was relaid and re-equipped during 1923; the task was immense but resulted in the works becoming the largest car producing factory in Europe. It was also the most modern. It has been said, and few would deny it, that Javel was the largest factory anywhere in Europe. From the outset the concern was with automation and the installation of the most modern machinery and techniques available. During 1923 the design had been laid down to unload railway wagons shunted into the works by an electro-magnetic process; this consisted of overhead conveyors connected to the main factory buildings and it was considered such a system would certainly reduce the unnecessary time wasted by unloading by hand. The mechanisation at Javel would have been enough for other car makers to take to their heels and there was still a feeling in France, as throughout the rest of the world with the exception of a very few

Front view of Citroën's first model produced. The Type A — known in Britain as the 10 horse power - was manufactured at the factory at Quai de Javel and imported to Britain by Gaston's who were, until Citroën Cars Ltd. were formed, the sole concessionaires for Citroën. This particular car is amongst the earliest to survive and was pictured at the Motoring 100 celebrations, Silverstone, May 1985. The 1327 c.c. (65 x 100 mm) engine was rated at 10.4 h.p. in Britain but was quoted as developing 18 h.p. at 2,100 r.p.m. This modest output was assisted in giving adequate performance by the light weight of the car - 13½ cwt. with four-seat body.

Manufactured in 1921, this 10 h.p. which is in beautiful condition was amongst 1700 cars imported via Gaston's during that year. The four seater cost £395 when new; specification included head, side and tail lamps, self starter, electric lighting set, five Michelin disc detachable wheels together with a kit of tools. The hood and side curtains were provided on open models. A noteworthy feature was the use of Citroën patent chevron gears for the rear axle bevel final drive.

manufacturers, that the motor industry should remain as solid an establishment as it had been when automobiles were considered only for the rich and not the peopled masses. When unloaded from the conveyor system, the contents of various materials from the railway trucks were placed in smaller wagons on a moving track and despatched to their different destinations around the works. Sheet metal of differing gauges would find its way to the correct shop where it was marked out before being fed into guillotines which cut the sheet to correctly sized segments and these in turn eventually found their way onto the chassis and body production lines; in a short space of time those segments would be part of a finished car. Little material was purchased ready-made from outside sources; practically the entire car was built at Javel by Citroën workers.

The factory at Javel was of such a huge scale that one person reported it took two days to inspect the whole works and involved many miles of walking. On such a journey, however, the onlooker would have witnessed many strange sights which seventy years later would be quite commonplace. At the end of a production line the chassis was placed upon a rolling road where the brakes, steering, gearbox and transmission were tested before the

The Type A as shown in Gaston's catalogue published mid 1921. The Open 4-Seat Tourer which, in France, was known as the Torpedo, sold at the same price as the 2-Seat Touring Car which had the facility of an extra single folding seat that could be stored when not in use in a small locker at the rear of the driver's seat. The 4-Seat Open Tourer was the standard model designed for normal business and pleasure purposes.

supervisors were completely happy about the product. Citroën had caught the imagination of the nation and of car-buyers throughout the continent. No wonder car production was the highest of any manufacturer in Europe. Cars designated for the United Kingdom were built in the Paris factory; these were supplied with right-hand steering and special bodies, the general opinion was that for export a more suitable body was called for than the type normally fitted to home market cars. The Type A of 10 horse-power was followed by an 11.4 h.p. and a smaller 7.5 h.p. car, all three were well received by British critics. The main problem was the organisation of transportation from Paris and moreover, once upon British soil, the distribution to the concessionaires and their agents. Cars in the early days were taken from Javel, packed into special cases and loaded onto railway wagons to be delivered to the Channel ports. Citroën had devised a special scheme with the transport companies which avoided the normal delays and congestion on French railways and at the quayside. The packed cars were then despatched across the Channel, along the Thames Estuary to arrive at London Docks.

From the commencement of sales of Citroën Cars in Britain, the transactions were undertaken by the sole concessionnaires, Gaston Limited, who had showrooms at 212-214 Great Portland Street, London, W.1. In addition to the London Showrooms, Gaston's had sales and servicing premises at 99, Boston Road, Hanwell, London W.7 and at Larden road, Acton, a few miles away in W.3. During the first year of manufacture, Citroën exported 750 cars to Britain from Javel which were handled by Gaston's and by the end of 1921 sales totalled 2451 vehicles, showing that 1701 cars were imported during the second year. This was in sharp contrast to Austin who, in 1919 managed only to produce 200 cars. Following unloading at London Docks, Gaston had an arrangement with a local transport company, L.E.P. Transport, which has now developed into a national concern, to deliver the new cars to their storage yard at River Wharf, Chiswick to await delivery to the distributing and conditioning depot at Ashford in Middlesex a few miles west.

LEP had specialised in the import and export of motor vehicles into and from Britain and practically held the

All-weather COUPÉ (closed).
Price £495 complete.

All weather COUPÉ (open).

Saloon-type COUPE (permanently closed)
Price £495 complete.

The Coupé — often referred to as The Doctor's Coupé because of its luxury and distinctive trim designed as being suitable for 'professional people'. Gaston's claimed this car was ideal for Doctors and Surgeons. The car was available in two models, Coupé with a folding head and a permanently closed version. The Coupé shared the level of trim with the Town Car and both were specified with Bedford Cord upholstery and mahogany panels. At £495 the car was not considered expensive.

The 2-Seater Type A 10 h.p. Touring Car could be specified with an 'occasional' third seat. The passenger was positioned further back from the driver and the extra folding seat, often known as a 'truffy seat' could be placed in front of the passenger enabling three people to be carried. At £395 the Citroën was £20 more expensive than the Morris Cowley, the price of which had been slashed by £90. The 10 h.p. was reckoned to be economical with a fuel consumption of a full 38 miles to the gallon.

monopoly of the trade. Their early connections with the motor industry included the winning of a contract to handle 100 Renault taxicabs for the British Motor Cab Company at Brixton in South London. At their River Wharf storage complex which covered an area of some eight acres, LEP were able to offer motor manufacturers a complete service in the exportation of cars which included the specialised task of packing the chassis in wooden crates. Likewise, LEP specialised in the importation of cars and were able to keep vehicles in bonded warehouses until required. As part of their manifesto, LEP also offered an assembly service where importers of cars specifically required this.

Later, Gaston's moved their showrooms from Great Portland Street to 60, Piccadilly. On packing the cars in Paris, the Michelin-tyred road wheels were replaced with special wooden disc wheels for shipping purposes and the normal wheels despatched separately to Gaston's who arranged for them to be refitted on arrival at Chiswick. A number of the vehicles were imported as chassis only and these were sent to such companies as Weymann and Short Brothers who specialised in the coachbuilding of special bodies.

Gaston's marketed the car well and published a comprehensive catalogue describing both the car and manufacturer in some detail and reported on the French motor trials at Le Mans during 28th-31st October 1920 when it was announced that the 10 h.p. model was officially recognised as the most economical car in the world. It appears that 72 cars and trucks of all makes competed in the event and the Citroën team, which was composed of seven ordinary cars belonging to private owners had four cars placed amongst the first eleven cars in the general classification. The Citroën car took both first and second places in its own class, it covered a distance of 112 miles and 1233 yards on 1.85 gallons of petrol, that is to say over 60 miles per gallon! *The Light Car and Cyclecar* magazine in December 1921 tested the 5CV model, observing that although the car was fitted with right-hand steering, the driver's door remained on the opposite side of the vehicle. The writer went on to report: 'It is certainly a remarkable proposition for 250 guineas especially when it is remembered that this includes five wheels, hood, screen, electric starter and lamp etc. The well known 10 h.p. model has gained for itself an enviable reputation for reliability, and we see no reason why this latest production should also not share the laurels in this direction.'

With the furthering of popularity of Citroën cars in France, it is little wonder that in Britain increasing numbers of these cars were being sold. Harrods, the eminent London store, for example, staged an exhibition by lining Citroëns up outside their premises and took customers on a free trip into the Capital. Monsieur Citroën, still very much his dynamic self, had a publicity stunt up his sleeve that would attract the attention of the world's press to his company and his cars. For some time he had become acquainted with a young engineer, Kegresse, who had proved that a vehicle equipped with special creeper or caterpillar tracks fitted to the rear axle could enable it to more easily traverse difficult obstacles such as snow and ice, sand, mud and a variety of surfaces not normally encountered during average driving conditions. Citroën was keen to exhibit this type of machine and had the device fitted to a number of his cars; he was very pleased

For 1923, the little 7.5 h.p. Two-Seater and Coupé cost £195 and £245 respectively. Its 855cc (55 x 90) engine could propel the car to 40 m.p.h. — considered to be quite adequate for the time. The 7.5 h.p. Citroën, known as the 5CV in France, had been claimed as the most successful small car of the year. The single door of the car was on the passenger side and not the driver's side. The car sold in large numbers and over 3,000 Citroëns were imported during the year.

Harrods, the world-famous London store, staged an impressive event to publicise the sales of Citroën cars by arranging, through Gaston's, to supply a number of chauffeur driven Type A 10 h.p. models to convey their customers to the City and to railway stations following a shopping trip. Little is known as to the success of this venture but it certainly created an awareness of Citroën. It is thought that the picture dates from some time during 1920; the cars have successive numbered registration plates and the cars used by Harrods and Gaston's are the four-seat Tourers.

with the result and at once was anxious to demonstrate to the world this development of cross-country traction, even more so that it be on a car bearing his name. Plans were drawn up for an expedition to cross the Sahara Desert, the first time such an attempt was to be made by a motor vehicle. Known as half-tracks due to the caterpillar style of traction restricted to the rear axle only, the vehicles left Touggourt in North Africa on 17th December 1922; by the 4th January 1923 the expedition had reached the River Niger and on the morning of 7th January the crossing was successfully achieved, the last section consisting of twenty-seven hours carried out non-stop. The total distance covered was 2000 miles and completed in twenty-two days. It was reported that all vehicles arrived at their destination at Tibuctoo in first class condition. André Citroën had scored yet another striking success over his rivals.

Citroën and Kegresse were anxious to demonstrate the principle of cross country transport elsewhere in Europe and what better place than in Great Britain where the country was struggling to get back on its feet after the war. Both farmers and industrialists would no doubt relish such a vehicle that Citroën had to offer. A suitable site had to be located for the demonstration, one was soon found, a huge munition dump at Slough, just twenty miles west of London, which had been taken over by the Slough Trading Company. Gaston's arranged for the trials and exhibition to take place and a large number of guests were invited to the event; there was great interest in the trials especially in view of the recent Sahara expedition. The large audience present at the trials witnessed some astonishing feats. From one car a rope was attached to two railway trucks filled with spectators, moving alongside the railway track the Citroën Kegresse pulled the wagons with ease, moreover, the vehicle was moving over a ploughed surface. Further tests were carried out, the cars were made to ascend and descend the banks of a disused gravel pit, the incline being almost sheer in places.

At the time of the experiment the weather was wet and the banks covered in deep weeds which did little to enhance the situation; the cars made extremely light work of their task and received a lot of attention and admiration from the enthusiastic gathering. There were times when, due to the incline, the front wheels were raised completely from the ground with the cars moving up the incline on their crawler tracks only. As they neared the top of the embankment and the rate of incline somewhat reduced so the leading axle was able to make contact with the ground

Cross country — Citroën style. A Citroën Kegresse proves its worth over rough terrain. The left hand drive vehicle shown demonstrates the vehicle's ability to climb and descend the very worst conditions utilising the creeper tracks on the rear axle. It was similar vehicles to this that were demonstrated at the ammunition dump at Slough, the demonstration being jointly organised by Gaston's and Citroën. Following the exhibition of the vehicle's capabilities, some 200 cars were sold.

The Type A Saloon at £645 represented Citroën's flagship to their range of cars. Luxuriously appointed in the same manner as the Doctor's Coupé and Town Car, the saloon had three doors — two on the kerb side and one on the driver's side.

The Coupé de Ville, otherwise known as the Light Limousine or Town car. For customers who had the services of a chauffeur, this was claimed to be the ideal car. Upholstery and interior trim was finished in grey Bedford cord whilst the doors and panels were finished in mahogany. The Doctor's Coupé was finished in similar style but were 2-Seaters whereas the Town Car had four seats.

again. At times the Citroën Kegresse cars appeared to be about to topple backwards but this was made impossible as special locking devices were fitted to the tracks to prevent the occurrence happening. Whilst being ideal for cross country work, the Citroën Kegresse was equally happy on the firm road, this enabled the farmer to travel from field to field and from farm to farm. On another test, one of these vehicles was driven on the road from London to Cambridge; it attained an average speed of twenty miles per hour. Following the trials it was anticipated there would be a demand for the half-track vehicle and it was intended models for the British market would be available at an early date. Gaston's arranged to handle the enquiries and in total something over 200 Kegresse models were sold.

By 1923 there were over 60,000 models of Citroën Cars in service and during 1922 sales of Citroën cars to the United Kingdom numbered 889 vehicles; for three successive years, 1920, 1921 and 1922, Citroën had won the Official French Fuel Economy Tests at Le Mans against all other competitors. With the expansion of business in France it followed that more and more cars were finding markets in other countries and Britain was no exception. With the number of Citroën cars being sold to the United Kingdom it was becoming almost impossible for Gaston's to continue their operation as they had done since the outset in 1919. Aware of the market potential in Britain, André Citroën decided that Citroën Cars Ltd. should take over the sales and service of their cars and gave instructions that suitable premises be obtained to open a company office in London. The acquisition took place of a large building at Brook Green, near to Hammersmith in West London and only a short distance from where Gaston's had provided Citroën service for four years. The move to Brook Green by Citroën Cars stands as a landmark in the history of the company as the acquisition of the premises was the most important step it had so far taken in the development of sales of new cars to Britain. The Citroën Building, as it was then known, still stands today. Citroën cars gave up the premises many years ago and it became occupied by the United Kingdom Government for the Central Office of Information. With the creation of Citroën Cars Ltd. sales of new Citroëns dramatically increased, during 1923, 3009 cars were imported, this figure increasing to 3080 for 1924.

When opened, Citroën justly boasted their new headquarters to be the largest motor car service station in the world. It occupied a prime site near to central London and close to public transport connections. Just as Citroën's factories in France were equipped with the latest in technology, so the Citroën building was fitted out with the most modern machinery and servicing equipment. The building consisted of a floor space of 100,000 square feet spread over three storeys. The organisation of the works was a model of efficiency and mirrored the fine reputation Citroën had established in France. The entire operation of Citroën Cars centred around the Brook Green Building; it housed under one roof spacious showrooms on the ground floor that allowed customers to peruse the complete range of vehicles in a relaxed atmosphere, behind the showrooms the delivery bay was situated which included petrol pumps and a car-wash. In a separate section the spares department carried over 3000 items which could be

The opening of Brook Green as a Service Station marked the establishment of Citroën Cars Ltd. in Britain. The Citroën Building handled all sales of the car, taking over the operation from Gaston's who had been responsible for selling Citroën cars since the Company's venture into manufacturing began in 1919. The opening of Citroën's headquarters was a landmark in the development of sales of the car. Brook Green was the largest motor service station in the world and occupied an area of almost 100,000 square feet over three storeys.

First floor reception hall for visitors to Citroën's executive offices. The reception area and offices were appointed with luxury and dignity.

Showrooms on the ground floor at Brook Green allowed the customer to be able to choose a car in relaxed surroundings where all models could be displayed. Note the vehicle in the foreground is a chassis only; as well as being able to study the mechanical design, customers would have been able to specify a special coach-built body if desired. The car in the background appears to be an 11.4 h.p. with English body.

Works delivery bay, petrol store and car-wash facilities were provided on the ground floor at the rear of the Brook Green showrooms. Electric lifts to all floors enabled cars and materials to be quickly transferred to other parts of the building.

The top floor at Brook Green housed a huge repair and machine shop, with lathes and other essential equipment. There was also a varnish and paint room so that all types of service and repairs could be carried out quickly and efficiently.

obtained by owners and trade alike 'over the counter'. New cars were delivered to Brook Green by railway; sidings from the Metropolitan and London and South Western main line terminated in a loading platform at the rear of the building and a special crane and gantry facilitated the unloading of cars. A purpose-built lift was installed to take cars up to the first floor where pre-delivery inspections were carried out and to the top floor where servicing and repairs to customers, cars were undertaken. The Company's offices were situated on the first floor in a wing adjacent to the conditioning shop together with the handsome reception area and executive quarters.

The facilities at Brook Green were the envy of every other car manufacturer. The building had excellent standards of lighting and heating; there were fire precautions with sprinklers abounding; telephones linked all the departments; a ventilating system had been installed to remove the exhaust fumes of the cars from the building and a compressed-air and vacuum plant assisted driving of machinery, inflating tyre pressures and cleaning both the premises and the cars. The machine shop was fitted out with lathes and jigs, a paint shop and supply of all necessary tools in order that any job could be carried out. The staff were well looked after with a good canteen and the provision of a first-aid unit. Citroën was proud of the Brook Green works which was in itself an outstanding advertising feature of the company's cars. Although Citroën left Brook Green many years ago, still in evidence is the large rear courtyard where customers collected their vehicles together with the ramps and doors leading to the reception and 'quick service' area.

As the Citroën Car grew in popularity so there was the need to extend the stores at Brook Green. Replacement parts were dispatched from here to the Citroën Agents that were being established throughout the country, the first of which was Worthing Motors in Sussex. At one time there was need of twenty storemen. The existing storage areas for new cars delivered to the United Kingdom which had been organised by Gaston's were by now totally outgrown by demand and a new site at Feltham in Middlesex was acquired which had a capacity of between 400—500 cars at any one time.

Events during the years immediately following the opening of the Citroën building at Brook Green in 1923 gave rise to the speculation that André Citroën was considering building cars in Britain. Firstly, Herbert Morris announced he intended opening a factory in France at Bollée; straight away Citroën was being asked the question as to when he might open a manufacturing plant in Britain. It was rumoured this was under serious consideration, not because Hebert Morris might open in France, but due to an impending tax to be levied on imported cars and known as the McKenna Duties. This was a swingeing tax at the rate of 33.3% payable on all foreign cars imported from abroad already fully assembled. It presented a damaging threat to sales of Citroën cars in this country as well as contemporary manufacturers such as André Citroën's arch rival, Renault. It seemed, therefore, most appropriate to establish a factory in the United Kingdom. Moreover, there were other factors significant to the building of cars in Britain, the factory at Javel was running at full capacity, cars manufactured for the British markets had to be transported long distances which, in itself, was a costly enterprise. Furthermore, the United Kingdom had valuable trade links with its colonies all over the world, cars produced in Britain would find markets in Australia, New Zealand and South Africa, in fact, wherever there were British Colonies or Empire territory.

The seeds had already been sown for future Citroën activities within Britain when the trials of the Citroën Kegresse took place at Slough. The site was admired by Citroën and on September 11th, 1925, it was announced that negotiations had taken place with Messrs. Hampton and Sons of St. James' Square, London, for the lease of property and land owned by the Trading Company at Slough in Buckinghamshire. A press release stated that one building taken over consisted of eight acres under one roof, another, adjacent, of some five acres together with ample land for future extension. In the same newspaper, the story was reported with a lot of enthusiasm as the problems of Slough, it felt, could well be reduced, if not overcome with the opening of the French Motor Car Works.

The Citroën Light Delivery Van was based upon the 10 h.p. Type A chassis, being the vehicle supplied complete as with the cars. The price of £335 reflected an exemption of import duty and as such offered unquestionable value. The Light Delivery Van had a pay-load of between 5-6 cwt.

The Scottish Cup, for the vehicle with the most economical performance during the 1922 Six Days Scottish Reliability Trial over difficult roads in mountainous country, was awarded to this standard 11.4 h.p. Citroën, registered XF 8528, carrying four people and averaging 36.8 miles per gallon over 1,020 miles. The 11.4 h.p., with 1452 c.c. (68 x 100 mm) engine, also known as the B2, had been introduced in 1921 and had a slightly higher bonnet line than the Type A.

Much was made of the English coachwork option available on 11.4 h.p. cars, which altered the appearance considerably, giving a more conservative look than the French-bodied cars, largely due to the style of mudguard. This page from the Gaston's catalogue of May 1923 conveys the character of the four-seater version.

The choice of the location is quite interesting if not ironical. The factory was to be built on land used as a munition dump following the First World War; had not André Citroën himself been a manufacturer of ammunition during the same war on the very site that was later to become the Citroën factory in Paris upon the banks of the River Seine, the Quai de Javel? During the war the land owned by the Trading Company at Slough was used as an ordnance depot, part of the site was also made to house a prisoner of war camp. However, at the end of hostilities the area was used as a huge lorry dump, from which numerous ex-military vehicles were sold for civilian use.

The land at Slough appeared to be quite convenient for the factory, indeed it attracted a number of other companies who were seeking a suitable location in which they could expand. In the years to follow, Slough Trading Estate as it was to become known, grew to be the largest trading estate of its kind in the country. The site was served extremely well with transport facilities, the Great Western Railway built a branch from the main West of England line that passed through Slough into the Trading Company area and sidings terminated in the factories; a spur from the Grand Union Canal had been constructed allowing access to the main artery of the British Waterway system and last but not least, the main London to Bath trunk road, the A4, skirted the boundary of the estate. The munition dump was piled high with army vehicles now redundant from the 1914-18 War and the intention had been that all the vehicles should be repaired and sold as Ministry of Defence surplus. The Slough Trading Company had purchased the land in April 1920 from the War Office, the masses of lorries, cars and motor cycles in condition varying from quite serviceable to mere wrecks were sold as part of the contract. At one time 8000 people, then equal to half the population of Slough, worked in connection with the renovation of the vehicle grave yard which gained the nickname by local inhabitants as 'The Dump'. Over thirty buildings had been erected by the Trading Company, some of them no small size. One set of these huge buildings was later to become the premises leased by The Citroën Company. Gradually, the land was cleared to make way for the new wave of industry.

During the years immediately following the First World War, there had been a rush of companies establishing a stake in the car manufacturing business. Many of these failed very quickly and some never progressed further than the stage of producing a catalogue but there were a number who experienced success even if, in some cases, it was relatively shortlived. In respect of numbers of cars sold in Britain, Citroën's position as a major supplier of vehicles was considerably boosted in 1925 when 6635 cars were imported. Clyno, a British manufacturer reformed in 1922 out of a motor cycle business, reaching the dizzy heights of success until its sudden demise in 1929, sold 4849 cars the same year which was considered to be one of its most successful trading periods.

By the end of October 1925 there was much activity at the premises taken over by Citroën and it was anticipated that production of cars would be starting in the near future. However, to dampen down over-enthusiasm and avoid unnecessary speculation, an announcement was made that it was not envisaged that production of cars would get into full swing during 1926 but great advancements to the schedule could be expected in the following year, 1927. Initially, it seemed the numbers of persons employed at the works would be relatively small, no more than fifty or sixty, but as soon as car manufacture was under way there was no doubt the figure would rise dramatically. Slough, like most towns was reeling on its feet with the after-effects of war and any news in which some consolation could be gained regarding unemployment was good news indeed; the prospect of a large car building plant went a long way to achieve this aim. The population of Slough had good reason to rejoice, such a venture as being

Gaston's used Citroën's successful expedition across the Sahara to publicise the 7.5 h.p. car. This particular advertisement dating from June 1923 shows the little car to good effect, the wording also being intended to underline its different concept from the crudely constructed cyclecars of the day. At £195, the 7.5 h.p. was very affordable and became noted as being especially suitable for lady drivers. The car was certainly marketed in France with them in mind and several advertisements appeared with attractive young ladies at the wheel. The style of lettering used for the Citroën name set a pattern followed for many years.

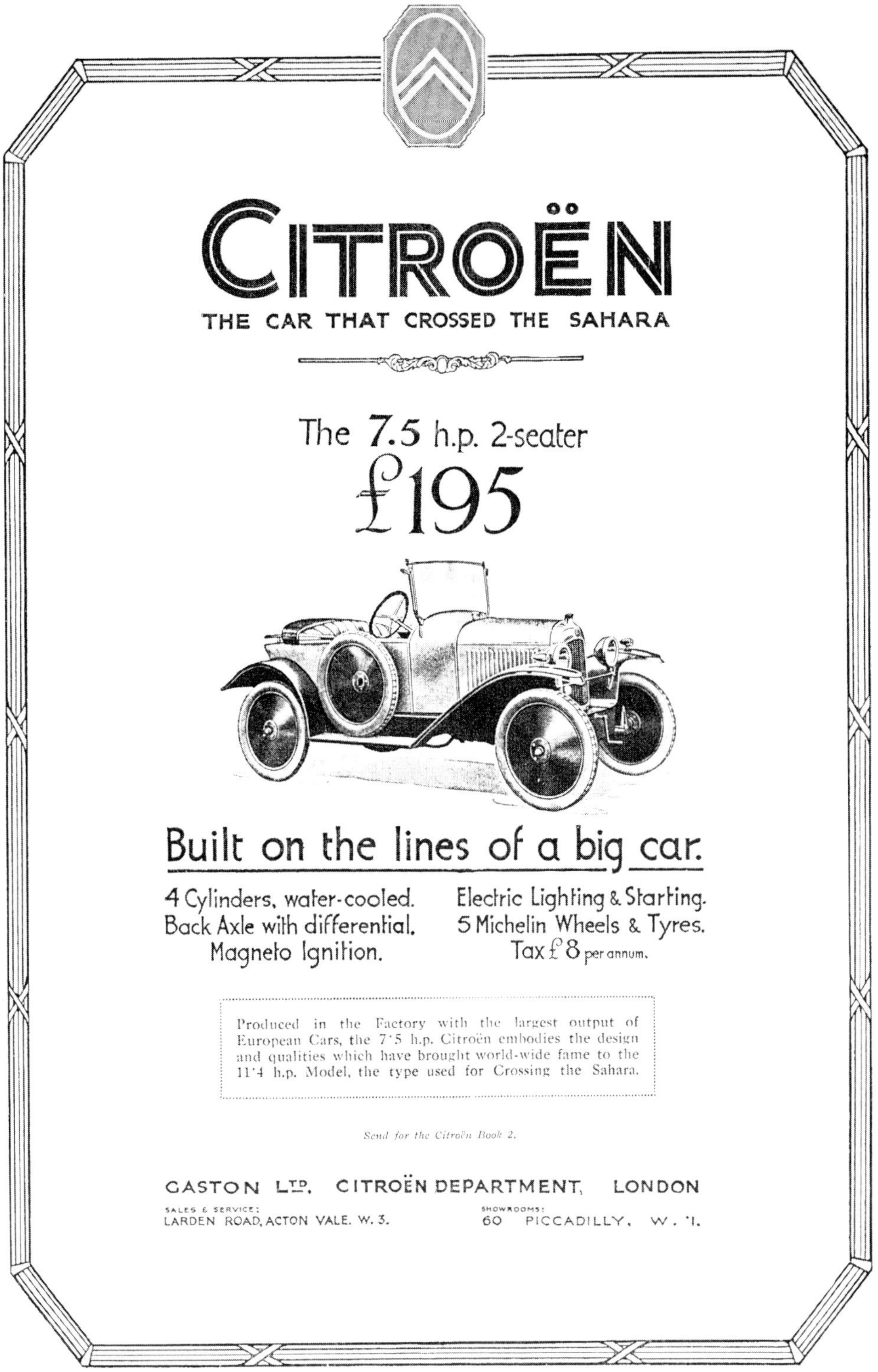

CITROËN
THE CAR THAT CROSSED THE SAHARA

The 7.5 h.p. 2-seater
£195

Built on the lines of a big car.

4 Cylinders, water-cooled.   Electric Lighting & Starting.
Back Axle with differential.   5 Michelin Wheels & Tyres.
Magneto Ignition.   Tax £8 per annum.

Produced in the Factory with the largest output of European Cars, the 7·5 h.p. Citroën embodies the design and qualities which have brought world-wide fame to the 11·4 h.p. Model, the type used for Crossing the Sahara.

Send for the Citroën Book 2.

GASTON LTD. CITROËN DEPARTMENT, LONDON
SALES & SERVICE: SHOWROOMS:
LARDEN ROAD, ACTON VALE. W. 3.   60 PICCADILLY, W. 1.

---

presented to them would almost without doubt bring extra employment and prosperity to the area. Already at the announcement of Citroën's plans there was talk of extra housing being required to accommodate the influx of workers, this had a snowballing effect as there would have to be increased labour in the town to build the houses and to supply the enlarged transport demands; immediately there were discussions on farmers catering for the additional supplies of meat, dairy and vegetable produce, bakeries installing larger capacity ovens and shop-keepers preparing to stock higher levels of provisions. When production at the car factory reached full capacity it was estimated the workforce would rise to 5000, this meant that an overall expansion of population of the town was forecast to an eventual twenty thousand inhabitants. Although it was going to take about nine months to get the premises anywhere near operational there were rumours that bodies of Citroën cars were already being transported to the works in readiness for early production.

Chapter three: Arrival at Slough

The tenure of lease had been settled. At last André Citroën had his factory in Britain. There was good reason indeed for British car manufacturers to take note of the Frenchman who was transferring some of his business to these shores. Not only did he own the largest car factory both in France and Europe but at Slough he had opened one of the largest car factories in the United Kingdom. It was generally considered that at the time the main shop constituted the largest factory building under one roof anywhere in Britain. Now that Citroën had control of the premises it was understandable that he wanted car production to start as soon as possible, but newspaper reports at the time suggested that it would be at least nine months before the first car rolled off the assembly line. The observers had of course not accounted for Citroën's demands, personality and dynamic methods of getting a job finished; they could have done well to remember the speed at which he started production of shells at Javel.

As soon as the contracts for the premises had been signed, The Slough Trading Company undertook to clear the factory space of all remaining spoils of war, the accumulation of broken vehicles made way for the new era of fine modern motor cars that would advance to lead the world. André Citroën was determined to see the most modern machinery installed at the new works, they were to be on the same principle as the Quai de Javel and were to adopt his futuristic ideals in mass production methods. For the initial planning and layout of the works Citroën sent over his specialists from Paris; they supervised all the work in the fitting out of the factory together with the complex installation of a system of conveyor belts and overhead tracks. Some 500,000 square feet of floor space was available for car production and in addition there was considerable space for expansion if required. In total, Citroën had leased sixty acres of land. So stringent were Citroën's instructions concerning the installation of the most modern ideas and equipment that, when completed, it was claimed to surpass even the latest American car manufacturing plants.

During the time the factory under was preparation, the Citroën Building at Brook Green were dealing with ever increasing sales of new cars. It was customary in the motor vehicle trade for sales of new cars to increase during the spring months, the new owner having the better weather of the spring and summer to acquaint themselves and to enjoy to the best advantage their recently purchased car. Citroën was no exception to the rule in finding this fact; in order to spread the load of production throughout the year instead of having to gauge for demand, press releases encouraged the prospective buyer to take delivery of the car at an early date — even before Christmas. Taking delivery of a new car early in the season would enable the purchaser to obtain the exact model, choice of colour and body style that might not otherwise be available.

The models for 1926 available in Britain consisted of the 7.5 h.p. two-seater, Cloverleaf and Coupé; the 11.4 h.p. fitted either with English or French body and supplied in two or four seater options in coupé or 'all-weather' guises including a fully closed version; in addition a splendid Landaulette was specified which claimed to be the smartest town carriage of moderate size available — 'an ideal car for those who require a smart but inexpensive chauffeur-driven carriage'. The cars were equipped with more efficient brakes, aluminium pistons and improved steering; advertising of the day assured the would-be owner there were over 200,000 Citroëns in service around the world, however, even with this high figure the car managed to retain its individual and distinctive appearance. To ensure an even distribution of cars, a network of agents had been formed, local agents performed an important link in the Citroën chain as not only did they enjoy the sale of new cars, but offered a maintenance service so there was no need to entrust the car to a mechanic not fully educated to the workings of the Citroën car. After Worthing Motors, other garages took on an agency for Citroën cars and soon a comprehensive network of dealers numbering 300 were formed around the country.

Work on the fitting-out of the Slough Factory proceeded with the greatest of speed. The assembly lines were installed in the various shops that would build the chassis and bodies; most of the equipment required in the factory such as stove enamelling, chromium plating, upholstery and finishing as well as heavier manufacturing gear, had the advantage of being brought directly into the works by rail which facilitated easier construction. It was no wonder that by the end of 1925 it was possible to start the manufacture of the first Citroëns at Slough. As one area at a time in the factory was being completed so it was put into operation. Initially, production lines for the chassis were commissioned which made it possible for vehicle bodies to be brought to the works from coachbuilders for assembly, the bodies arrived by both road and rail transport as were the engines which were still being built in Paris and would be for a little time to come. When in full operation it would be possible to build a chassis in a mere two hours from the laying-down of the rigid steel sections to the emergence of the completed frame. It was planned that at the end of the conveyor system it was to be feasible to run a car off the assembly lines every ten minutes, each car being finished and ready for the road ahead. At the outset of planning it was intended that the major part of each car would be made in Britain using British workforce and materials. The railway spur into the works allowed manufacturing materials to be delivered and the finished products despatched with the same ease. The conveyor systems and revolutionary machinery were the envy of other manufacturers; mass production in its most up-to-

The immortal Citroën 5CV, listed in the British catalogue as the 7.5 h.p. In France, the little car was often nicknamed Le Petit Citron (Little Lemon) due to its unusual bright yellow paintwork. This particular car was owned by the late John Poxon of Worthing Motors, Britain's oldest established Citroën Agent. John was also Vice-President and a founder member of the Citroën Car Club formed over 42 years ago. The 5CV Cloverleaf did much to put France on the road and it was marketed to appeal especially to lady drivers. It was a huge success in its native France, it was easy to drive and easy to handle, returned 40 m.p.g. and managed a top speed of almost 40 m.p.h. The little Citroën arrived on the market during the era of the 'light car'; it had competition from the Austin 7, Peugeot's Bebe, the 9/15 Renault and Fiat's type 501 and 509. A tribute to the success of the 'Little Lemon' is the surprising number of examples that have survived.

The smartest car in town. The 11.4 Landaulette was a car for all seasons. Chauffeur driven passengers could enjoy the benefits of the closed car — and an open car — both at the same time. Priced at £295 for 1925/26, this car represented luxury at low cost with specification including Bedford Cord upholstery and mahogany panels, a vanity case for lady passengers and a clock to ensure arrival for appointments were strictly punctual. A speaking tube was provided for communication with the chauffeur and specially designed artistic carriage lamps gave the necessary finish to an aristocratic model.

A splendid example of the 11.4 h.p. dating from 1925/6. In France this car would have been designated the B12. SF2232 is shown in two guises with the photographs taken on different occasions. The car is shown as an open tourer and later it was seen with the side curtains fitted to afford protection for passengers from the elements. The price of the open tourer in 1926 offered excellent value at £165; an All-Steel Saloon was also listed in the catalogue. On the occasion of the photograph of the car in open form (left), this 11.4 h.p. was painted dark blue, on the occasion with the side curtains mounted (below), it had changed to maroon! Note the pre 1939 Light 15 Roadster in the background, a successor to the 11.4 h.p.

11.4 h.p.
3-SEATER
COUPÉ

The 11.4 h.p. Coupé had a folding hood which quickly converted this neat car into an open tourer. Often referred as a Doctor's Coupé, the car was elegantly furnished and considered completely suitable either for the doctor or professional businessman. The split vee-shaped windscreen had two opening upper-halves and gave the car a distinguished appearance. Ample storage space was provided behind the driver and in the boot, access being gained through the hatch behind the hood. The car was well equipped with door panels finished in mahogany; side windows were winder operated so that they could be raised or lowered easily and when left in the up position formed a windscreen extension giving added protection when the hood was lowered.

date form had been brought to Slough and the United Kingdom by André Citroën.

Initial production showed two types of car coming off the assembly lines, the Cloverleaf 7.5 Horsepower and the new 11.4 Horsepower, the latter being available in two body styles, Open Tourer and 'Tout Acier'—All Steel Saloon. Regarding the latter model the Citroën sales brochure for 1925 emphasised the advantages of the all steel body as against the usual wooden bodies found on other makes of car. The brochure quotes -:

'FREEDOM FROM RATTLE—There is no body assembling or jointing, all the pressed steel sheets compromising the body being rigidly electro-welded together joint by joint, and this welding is indestructible. There is thus an entire absence of body rattle.
NO DISTORTION—The body being of one-piece construction, will not warp and defies all weather conditions.
LIGHT WEIGHT AND COMFORT—Steel being much lighter than wood, a body of the same weight gives much more room and is consequently more comfortable.
ELEGANT APPEARANCE—Steel is more easily moulded into harmonious lines.
ECONOMY—An all-steel body means long life for the car and economy of petrol and tyres. The cushions, seats and inside fittings being detachable, the car is easier to clean and repair. The body can very easily be removed from the chassis.'

In addition to the convincing statements about the all-steel body, the manufacturers were keen to demonstrate the equipment and comfort aspects of the car. The brochure announced that the car was fitted with exceptionally wide doors and offered very commodious and comfortable seating for four people, that the upholstery was of the finest quality and windows could be opened by means of a winder. Carpets were laid on the floor, a rug rack on the rear of the front seats, armrests and silk blinds for the rear windows. For the year, the equipment was superb, it included electric lighting, self-starter, sun-shield, interior lighting, non-rattle door locks, bonnet fasteners, fascia panel lamp, driving mirror, license holder, adjustable windscreen and windscreen wiper, ventilation shutter, inspection lamp, tool kit housed in a special box underneath the front seats, 'comfort' tyres, electric horn and exterior lighting that surpassed comparable cars of the time with five lamps—head, side and tail. It is interesting to compare a Citroën advertisement with that of a Peugeot of the same period; whilst Citroën describe their car in detail Peugeot portray a family scene with the car standing in the background and much being made on how to pronounce the name Peugeot—'Pur-jo'!

The Citroën Factory was officially opened on Thursday February 18th 1926. It was a gala day for the town, flags of France and Britain were to be seen all around the streets and hundreds of red, white and blue posters directed the throngs of visitors to the Factory on the Trading Estate. The Town was alive with people who had travelled from miles around by car, trains and charabanc. There were of course fleets of Citroën cars ferrying important visitors to and fro as well as adding to the general advertising of the occasion. From London came Members of Parliament, officials from a multitude of organisations and, needless to say, journalists from all newspapers, magazines and motoring journals of the time. The Great Western Railway operated extra trains during the day, many of which were especially terminated at Slough on a shuttle service from Paddington. During the morning local dignitaries were escorted around the factory and were shown the production lines with workers assembling the cars. It was easy to see that with the advanced methods of construction, André Citroën's forecast of up to two hundred vehicles leaving the works a day was no idle dream.

With all the prominent people arriving at Slough that day and making their way to the Trading Estate, there was one party that created more interest than almost any of the others—that which included André Citroën himself. Just after midday, Citroën, who had spent the morning talking to journalists and fellow industrialists as well as the Mayor of Slough and the local councillors, attended a special luncheon at the factory. A marquee had been especially erected for the purpose at one end of the works, this was a

The 11·4 H.P. All-Steel Saloon

Supreme Value

IN CLOSED CARS

Comfort and Luxury at Low Cost

COACHWORK—This new Saloon Model has exceptionally wide interior dimensions and offers very commodious and comfortable seating accommodation for four persons. It is beautifully upholstered throughout. There are four doors, with sliding windows opened or closed by means of winders.

The body, composed of steel panels electro-welded together forming a very light jointless construction, is fitted with detachable upholstery and seats. Silk spring blinds for the rear windows, arm-rests fitted to nickel-plated rods, rug strap on back of front seat, and carpeted floor are items which indicate the luxury of the fittings and finish.

EQUIPMENT is exceptionally complete, including electric lighting and starting, 5 lamps—head, side and tail—electric horn, 5 detachable disc wheels and 5 'Comfort' tyres (spare wheel is carried at rear), adjustable wind screen, wind-screen wiper, shock absorbers, ventilator shutter which also gives access to petrol tank filler and can be operated from interior of car, kit of tools in tool-box under front seat, dashboard clock, speedometer, Boyce motometer, driving mirror, Ice cc holder, special type non-rattle door locks and bonnet fasteners, dash lamp, inspection lamp, grease gun chassis lubrication, interior lighting, and sun shield.

OVERALL DIMENSIONS.—Length, 13-ft 1-in. Width, 4-ft 8-in. Height, 6-ft. 2¼-in.

CITROËN is the first European Maker to realise the proven advantages of ALL-STEEL Coachwork, and to lay down a complete factory, with unique machinery, for its production. The acknowledged leader in all recent developments in the industry he has again proved himself to be without question the most progressive car manufacturer in Europe.

Steel has rapidly replaced the use of wood in modern mechanical practice. Bridges, buildings and ships are now constructed almost entirely of steel, and the principle is being extended to tram and railway coaches.

The body of a motor car, as well as the chassis, is subject to severe strain due to speed and the inequalities of the road. This stress is best withstood by a metal structure.

All-steel coachwork is therefore a logical and vital development. Its manufacture is the most important step yet taken in the progress of motor car body building.

It is fitting that this development should be in the hands of the Citroën organisation, which has the largest output of cars in Europe. 200,000 Citroëns are now in service.

In addition to the advantage of greater safety mentioned overleaf, all-steel coachwork has the following further points in its favour

Freedom from Rattle. There is no body assembling or jointing, all the pressed steel sheets comprising the body being rigidly electro-welded together joint by joint, and this welding is indestructible. There is thus an entire absence of body rattle.

No Distortion. The body, being of one piece construction, will not warp and defies all weather conditions.

Light Weight, and Comfort. Steel being much lighter than wood, a body of the same weight gives more room and is consequently more comfortable.

Elegant Appearance. Steel is more easily moulded into harmonious lines.

Economy. An all-steel body means long life for the car and economy of petrol and tyres. The cushions, seats and inside fittings being detachable, the car is easier to clean and repair. The body can very easily be removed from the chassis.

The Saloon Car is rapidly gaining in public favour, because of its warmth and comfort in winter, its coolness and airiness in summer. The All-Steel Saloon will undoubtedly become a vogue.

'Supreme value in closed cars' — Citroën's claim for the 11.4 h.p. 'Tout Acier' or 'All Steel' Saloon, the first of its type to be offered by a European manufacturer. In 1925, this four-door saloon presented comfort and luxury at low cost; the all-steel coachwork, based on the latest methods as developed by the Budd concern in America, gave freedom from rattle whilst at the same time saving on body weight and affording more interior space. The well-appointed interior had upholstered door panels, interior lighting and an opening windscreen. Further luxuries included silk spring blinds for the rear windows, arm rests and a rug strap on the back of the front seat as well as a fully carpeted floor.

This aerial view of the Citroën factory at Slough gives an indication of its nature — the main shop was the largest factory building under one roof in the country. The single-storey layout on a level site facilitated the movement of parts and cars as they progressed through the works.

splendid occasion with a sumptuous feast laid on in the finest French tradition. It is said the champagne corks could be heard popping as far away as Paris!. Following the luncheon ceremony, Citroën spoke to the large gathering which included the Company workforce, invited guests and the members of the press. Citroën addressed the audience in fluent English but with a heavy accent.

André Citroën thanked everybody for attending the opening of his new factory and he was able to strike the right note of sympathy with the unemployed of Britain; for his part, he said, he would make an effort to employ as many people as possible and it was therefore important to get them working as soon as conditions allowed, the more people that were at work meant greater numbers of cars could be built and after all, the factory was capable of making two hundred cars a day! Citroën thanked all the contractors who had assisted in supplying and building the equipment for the factory in such a short time — merely a few months. In concluding his speech, Citroën lightheartedly remarked that the French Franc had dropped in value and that through the efforts of his employees both in Britain and France help may be given to return his country to a more stable financial basis. There were cheers from the audience and the gathering as a whole sang 'For He's A Jolly Good Fellow'!

The large party were conducted around the works with André Citroën at the head. He pointed to the large span of glass roofing and reminded everybody that his factory had the distinction of having the largest space under one roof in the whole of the country. Making their way to the production lines, the ensemble were shown cars in the course of manufacture. Citroën seemed fascinated, yet, he must have seen a similar operation at his other factories many hundreds of times previously; he stood almost transfixed for several minutes watching the very clever processes aware that at the time his ideas and methods were among the most advanced and the most envied throughout the world. The party stood to watch the all-steel car being made in a most remarkable way. Citroën had wanted to build a factory for his cars in the British Isles for some time and he was proud that his product that had borne his name for the previous six years had been met with so much success. At the end of the conducted tour Citroën addressed the party once more and in faultless English said;

"I hope in the future those present can say 'I can remember the day when it was opened'.

One last word; I am to state there are coming developments as regards the Citroën products that may be watched for with interest."

The press were naturally interested in the views and outlook of Monsieur Citroën with regard to the town of Slough. It was felt that with the opening of the largest factory within the community, Citroën had some level of responsibility not only to Slough but to its residents and, it would appear, to the increase of population into the area. Were it not for Citroën, Slough would carry on with its traditional deep-rooted way of life; it was clear from the outset that Citroën's visions and ideas could only materialise if the conditions were right and those conditions would have to be born and nursed into fruitfulness. The prospective workers would have to be encouraged enough to move house from other areas of Britain, areas which were already experiencing at that time a depression in the job market, to take up the challenge. It was unclear who exactly was going to produce the carrot, Citroën, the Borough of Slough or the Trading Company? Would anyone take the responsibility? Citroën willingly consented to speak to reporters and answered their questions as to how his new venture would affect the town, and in particular, the housing of employees engaged at the factory. Citroën gave the following answer:

"I would employ two thousand people here in the immediate future if only houses could be found for them, that is the greatest factor. At the moment a large number

The Slough Factory was unique when built in that it was constructed utilising the most modern methods known to motor manufacturing. This view, taken about 1928, shows the car finishing chain. André Citroën had instructed the latest ideas he had seen in America be employed at Slough. He sent over from France his inspectors to ensure the equipment, supplied in part by Budd, be installed so utilising to the full the system of conveyors and overhead tracks. On the occasion of the opening of the Factory, André Citroën had led the party of specially invited guests to watch the construction of cars on the main assembly line.

of workers are having to travel from London and spend forty-five minutes on the train each day to and from their work, that is what it means to them. If Slough would build more houses and cottages, the workmen would come here which would mean more life to the undertaking. If Slough would provide the houses it would be a fine thing for us and also it would be a fine thing for Slough. We could make Slough a much bigger town."

Citroën expressed a lot of interest in the town itself and told journalists he had the good of the town at heart — he hoped to see it grow — his message to the local authority was that it was houses that were wanted for their mutual good. Citroën was asked whether, in the event of the council failing to build houses and private contractors also not building them, he would put up the houses himself. He shrugged and smiled, "not for the time being" he said, "but I suppose in the end if houses can be obtained in no other way, I shall be glad to build them, but I cannot say."

With André Citroën at the opening of the new factory was his good friend, Georges Schilling. He was well known in France as a journalist in law but he was also recognised for his good strong feelings upon the relationship between France and England. During the immediate past years the links between the two countries had become healthy and sound, Schilling liked to think the close ties should continue and he assured local business men that Citroën's venture would do much to strengthen the relationship even further. He went on to tell them that in the unlikely event of the special relationship ever being dislocated it would be a sad day for both nations; the car-making business in Slough, he said, would no doubt go a long way to increasing the fellow feelings. However, it would not solve the unemployment situation of Slough entirely, the works were in need of skilled labour but the unemployed on the register were not all skilled so there would be still a problem. Georges Schilling was profoundly hopeful that Slough as a community would build houses in order that workers would be encouraged to come into the area not only to work but to live also, those that only worked in Slough would do little to spread the prosperity of the Town.

At the end of the eventful day when the Citroën works were opened in Britain, when all the dignitaries had returned to their homes, when the bustle and hustle had died down, the factory was allowed to return to some normality and to get on with the business of making motor cars. Together with Brook Green, the Citroën company in Britain represented a highly efficient motor manufacturing organisation in direct competition with even the largest British companies.

Following the official opening of the Slough factory production was put into full swing. There is no doubt British motor manufacturers looked at the Citroën works with some degree of envy; the majority of companies in England had witnessed a rapid development in the design of the motor car and the fight for orders together with costs in producing new models with updated mechanical specifications had resulted in an industry desperately trying to compete in an aggressive market with outdated machinery and lumbering production methods. Yet, here was Citroën, a foreign manufacturer able to set up a purpose-built factory utilising equipment and revolutionary methods far beyond most other car builders could envisage or, for that matter, consider affording. The outcome from André Citroën's far-reaching ideas was a car not only made to the highest standards in spite of mass-production but with a reputation for quality and reliability second to none. Prices of Citroën cars reflected the benefits of modern construction techniques and consequently began to fall putting an even greater strain on British competitors. The motoring press were keen to report on the progress of the works and experience the seemingly astonishing product of the modern age. All this went towards increasing the popularity of the marque.

A correspondent from *Motor* reported a little time following the official opening of the works:

'The British Company (Citroën) have opened a large and up-to-date factory at Slough, Buckinghamshire, fully equipped for producing cars in quantities by the latest methods known to engineering science. With the aid of this factory and the full co-operation of British makers of accessories, a programme of exceptional interest has been formulated for the coming season of which we are now able to give the first full particulars.'

Having vehicle production running at full capacity, the sight of cars leaving the assembly line every ten minutes must have been hard for other manufacturers to swallow, least of all the other French car makers, Peugeot and Renault who no doubt would have liked a much larger share in the sales of the British motor market. In the chassis erection shop a frame would be laid down on a chain driven track; as the frame was conveyed along the shop floor the necessary accessories would be fitted, the

The 'All-Steel' bodies were constructed from pre-formed panels assembled on jigs and were welded and riveted at the same time in accordance with the methods developed by Budd. Once completed, the bodies were taken to the spray plant, as shown in this 1928 view. Spray painting took just one-tenth of the time previously required and gave a far superior finish.

suspension system installed and later along the route, the front and rear axles joined to the assembly so that at the end of the track the chassis rolled off complete.

The body shop was as modern and thorough as the chassis shop. Apart from the two-seater body all other cars were of the 'tout-acier' construction which were all steel. These were assembled on specially designed jigs, the panels were clamped to the steel frame work where they were welded and riveted. On completion of the process, the jig was made to collapse and the finished body removed for further attention. Although the building of the car body constituted a noisy process it was nevertheless highly advantageous as it enabled the body to be light but yet exceedingly strong. From the jigs, the bodies were placed onto steel conveyor tracks and taken along the assembly line where at different stages the supplementary equipment was fitted before the completed unit was offered to the paint shop. The steel bodywork simplified the painting performance considerably; the paint brush was now obsolete, the spray nozzle had taken its place and powered by compressed air as with a number of operations in the factory. It was possible to spray an area in one-tenth of the time it took to hand paint. The finish was perfectly smooth, quite free from blemishes or streaks; in no way was the new method of applying paint inferior to old fashioned ideas, several coats of paint were added to the bodywork and immediate steps were taken to rub down the surfaces with pumice stone and water in order to ensure as superior finish as possible. The painted bodies were moved into huge ovens so that the drying process could be completed as a whole; once out of the ovens the bodies were once again hoisted onto tracks but this time, attached to the assembly line was an accompanying truck containing all the necessary 'furniture'. Housed inside were the roof, seats, plate glass as well as all the trimmings required to complete the coachwork.

It had taken just two hours to construct the chassis in this view, dating from about 1928. It took no more than two people to lower the body, supported at three points, from the overhead track. Once bolted together the car was sent by conveyor to receive the finishing details.

The fitting-out of the body completed, the assembly found its way to the final operations; from the chassis shop arrived the chassis complete with Michelin tyred wheels, engine and gearbox, steering mechanism and brakes, lighting equipment, radiator, driving controls and instruments — in fact a complete car apart from the waiting body. The chassis as it was at that point had taken just a mere two hours to build, such was the advancement of progress. The body, which was now suspended by four points from the overhead track was lowered onto the chassis with the assistance of no more than two mechanics; once in position the car was rolled onto the final conveyor where the body and chassis were bolted together and final attention paid to the remaining finishing details before completion tests were carried out.

The Citroën came off the assembly line, the car now ready for road test. The engine and gearbox had been built and tested in Paris, however, not content with only one test, each unit was bench-tested in the factory before being installed onto the chassis. By the time the customer received the new car the power unit had been fairly well run-in. Returning from the road test each car was taken to the distribution shop where any final adjustments were carried out. The Citroën was by this time ready to be collected by the agent and subsequently delivered to the anxiously waiting owner.

Some of the success of the Citroën Car and the 5CV in particular, can be attributed to the Late F. W.(Freddie) Ridout, who as Representative of Citroën Cars took the model around the country to the agents demonstrating and selling it. Always a popular and jovial figure, Freddie was well known throughout the motor trade, he made many friends and his enthusiasm for the marque sold a great number of cars.

The Light Car and Cyclecar when reviewing the Citroën programme for 1927 wrote -:

'For the coming season two models will be produced — the 11.4 h.p. and an entirely new 12.24 h.p. model — the latter outside the light car class. So far as the 11.4 h.p. models are concerned, truly remarkable value for money is being offered. From the 20th of this month (September 1926), the four-seater will cost £165 and the saloon £210. These new prices represent reductions of £30 and £35 respectively, and these have been made without curtailing the equipment or cheapening the models in any respect.'

The Citroën car production was now well established at Slough, both the car and the works were held in the highest of esteem. By the end of 1926 Citroën's position as a British manufacturer of motor cars was secure with 5299 cars being built and sold. 1927 saw a furthering of popularity of the marque with 5900 cars leaving the factory. It had been clearly shown that André Citroën's principles of revolutionary thinking were quite practical and played a major part in the future design and production of the motor car. Within a few years, as Citroën had intimated when opening the Slough factory, his company would once again astonish the motoring world.

The World's Supreme Motor Car Value!

CITROËN

11.4 h.p. All-Steel Saloon F.W.B. (Four Doors)

£210

These Citroën Cars have as standard—

4 DOORS, 4-WHEEL BRAKES and Fullest Equipment

including—

Electric Lighting and Starting, 5 Wheels and Tyres, Clock, Speedometer, Boyce Motometer, Petrol Filter, Driving Mirror, Licence Holder, Inspection Lamp, Dash Lamp, Oil Gun Chassis Lubrication, Shock Absorbers, Hood with Envelope, Rigid All-Weather Side Curtains, and Rear Windscreen on 4-Seaters. Saloons have Sun Shield, Window Winders, Silk Spring Window Blinds. Interior Lighting, etc., etc. Automatic Windscreen Wiper on all models.

11·4 h.p., All-Steel 4-Seater with F.W.B. **£165**	*Also models without F.W.B.* 11·4 h.p., 4-door Saloon - £190 11·4 h.p., 3-Seater Coupe - £200	12·24 h.p., All-Steel 4-Seater with F.W.B. **£195**
11·4 h.p., All-Steel Saloon with F.W.B. (Four Doors) **£210**		12·24 h.p., All-Steel Saloon with F.W.B. (Four Doors) **£240**

Immediate delivery from British Works, Slough.

Send for the Citroën Book 17, giving full particulars of these and other Models to:—

CITROËN CARS LTD.,
Citroën Building, Brook Green
Hammersmith, LONDON, W.6.

New Showrooms:
DEVONSHIRE HOUSE,
PICCADILLY, W.1.

André Citroën had opened the Slough Factory and production was in full swing by the time this advertisement appeared in November 1926. £210 purchased the 11.4 h.p. All Steel Saloon complete with four-wheel brakes, four doors and a full specification which included a clock, sun shield, winding windows, interior lighting and window blinds. A full tool kit was included in the price of the car which started from as low as £165 for the four-seater, 2-door open car. Whilst Citroën made much of supplying their cars with four-wheel brakes, they did in fact offer 'economy' models based on the 11.4 h.p. but without the added safety of four-wheel braking systems. These cost £190 for the 4-door Saloon and £200 for the 3-seat Coupé.

The steel framework for New Devonshire House nearing completion. Work on the site had begun in 1924 and this photograph was reproduced in the brochure issued by Citroën after its completion, much being made of the parallel between the use of steel in buildings, bridges and ships and its adoption for car bodywork. On taking the lease for the showroom premises, André Citroën set about modifying the structure so as to allow the basement to be reconstructed in the form of a central rotunda. On entering the building from Piccadilly it was to be so arranged that visitors could look down at the cars from a balustraded balcony. Note that, at the far corner of the site, the Rootes concern had also earmarked part of the building for car showroom use — in later years it was to build up the combine producing Hillman, Humber and Talbot cars which was destined ultimately and after a complex history, to form part of the same group as Citroën.

Chapter four:
Comfort far beyond its price

Citroën in England were a long way from the hub of activities in Paris; whatever went on in France was across the Channel and could be looked upon with an indifferent air. The great publicity campaign that continued to emerge from Javel was of little importance to either the British factory or its customers. The triumphant claim to the crossing of the Sahara, the massive exercise of illuminating the Eiffel Tower and the sign-writing in the sky, whilst noted in the small print of the national press, was not shared with the same jubilation as in France. Not merely content at seeing his latest and most modern factory situated in England, Citroën decided he needed

The scene from the balustraded balcony, showing the superb architecture of the building. Cars could be displayed on two levels, the ground floor which gave access from Piccadilly, and the lower floor consisting of the central rotunda. Up to forty cars could be displayed at any one time and visitors could peruse the cars in relaxed but magnificent surroundings.

(Below, right) From the central rotunda of the lower floor, the great vaulted ceiling of the showroom had a 'cathedral effect'. The lighting was quite novel at the time and assisted in producing a calm atmosphere. Cars were taken down to the central rotunda by a special lift cleverly hidden and not showing any signs of framework or mechanism. The interior space of the showrooms amounted to 12,000 square feet and the annual rent was £12,000.

something else that would attract attention to his Company and his cars. Citroën's rivals, Peugeot, and Renault in particular, were vying for leadership in motor sales and had become both frustrated and annoyed at Citroën's antics. Whatever would he do next?

To go with the most modern car producing plant and the largest and best equipped service station, Citroën decided that a splendidly sumptuous London showroom had to be built. It was to be fit for a King! The whole world would marvel at such an impressive and spectacular edifice. The London showroom for Citroën cars had originally been part of the Gaston Company and shared their premises at 212-214 Great Portland Street, later moving to 60 Piccadilly. The site chosen by André Citroën was New Devonshire House in Piccadilly opposite the Ritz Hotel. The showrooms stretched for 100 feet along Piccadilly, the ornamental architecture suiting the aim that the premises were to be the most magnificently placed and luxuriously appointed motor car showrooms in the world. The conception and the design of the showrooms rested entirely with André Citroën himself, as with the rest of his business he always insisted at being at the helm. The premises were to reflect the man's great love of indulgence and naturally there was to be no money spared on what could only be described as the showpiece to the world of his products. London was looked upon as leading society and whilst Citroën could show off his wares in the Champs Élysées and the whole of France beamed with admiration, a demonstration in the most fashionable part of the grandest city brought not only esteem and acclaim, but absolute prestige from the entire civilised world.

The New Devonshire House premises were huge; forty cars could be displayed in the magnificent surroundings at any one time. The design that Citroën eventually decided upon was inspired by the plan of Napoleon's Tomb in

The frontage of Citroën's showroom at New Devonshire House. Stretching for 100 feet along Piccadilly, it overlooked Green Park and was opposite the Ritz Hotel, London's symbol for the best in society. London's Citroën Showroom soon became respected and brought added prestige to the marque. Note how the balustrade of the balcony overlooking the rotunda is visible through the centre windows.

A further view of the interior of New Devonshire House conveying the impression of spaciousness, in this case looking across the full width of the showroom with vaulted ceiling above and rotunda area below.

Paris; in its construction the building resembled in broad lines that famous edifice, with its balustraded balcony and striking central rotunda. On entering the building through any one of three central doorways the visitor was immediately aware of the unique and quite novel lighting scheme using decorative alabaster chandeliers; the result was effective whilst being completely unobtrusive. A great vaulted ceiling was supported upon arches, it was particularly impressive and suspended from it a central chandelier, beautifully designed and complimenting the whole of the interior. Vehicles could be displayed on two floors, which included the central rotunda which was at a lower level than the ground floor and created a most impressive sight. An internal lift to carry the cars between the floors was cleverly hidden and a feature of this was that it was devoid of an external frame which would have detracted from the interior design of the showroom.

To prepare the New Devonshire House premises vast work had to be undertaken to meet Citroën's requirements. Part of the building had to be virtually gutted, the floor, and sections of the girder construction of the framework, had to be removed to enable construction of the new central area and rotunda. This was a great achievement at the time when it is considered that the girders held together the front and rear of the building as well as the seven storeys of offices above the showrooms. All the vertical girders and beams had to be strengthened before the horizontal sections could be removed, the whole process was assisted by oxy-accetalyne equipment and represented one of the first applications of this technique in such building alterations. It was claimed at the time that the building was considerably stronger following the rebuilding than previously. Although it was seven storeys in height the Citroën showrooms took up the space of three floors and it can easily be imagined how the 'cathedral effect' dome must have appeared. With an interior area of 12,000 square feet, Citroën was able to boast of the most magnificently appointed motor vehicle showrooms in the world and considered the enormous expenditure completely justified in opening the show-case premises. Following the opening of New Devonshire House and establishing the most modern factory at Slough, Citroën enjoyed a third extravagant feast, the 1927 London Motor Show. This event at Olympia gave the chance for the public to see, probably for the first time in many instances, examples of the Citroën car built in England. Of course, Citroën had been represented at previous shows in London, but now there was an added prestige, a car built here in the United Kingdom, although of foreign origin, could be classed as British and therefore attracted sales in larger numbers than other makes manufactured entirely abroad.

As in the previous year Citroën exhibited on stand 101 at Olympia, this was the most advantageous position as it was located by the main Addison Road entrance to the hall. It was recognised that the Citroën stand would be one of the main attractions of the show that year. The main theme generated by the company was the benefit that advanced engineering produced in both the efficient and quality manufacturing enabling a reduction in the price of the Citroën car. The 1925 Motor Show had, of course, shown all Citroëns that had, in effect, been built in France, some of the models were fitted with English bodies made by Short Brothers or Weymann; the 1926 show had come at the time of transition from Paris to Slough manufacturing, the factory in England was by no means at full production and therefore again the cars on show had been built in France although serviced at Brook Green before being delivered to Olympia. The story for 1927 could claim a complete turnround, Citroën were pleased, and indeed proud, that vehicles on stand 101 had been built at the Slough works.

The star of the Citroën exhibition at the motor show was the new model known as the 12.24 horse power. Although it had been introduced the year previously and was seen at the 1926 Olympia Exhibition, the year between had been one of much success for the company, a lot had been made in the press of the new factory and this had resulted in a spin-off of interest for the 12.24. In its own right, the car had achieved a deservedly high place in the opinion of the motoring public and its appearance at the exhibition created more attention and received greater popularity than the previous year. On the Citroën stand, examples of the different variations in body styles were demonstrated; both two and four seater cars were to be seen and it was widely considered this car provided just about the best value in motoring that year. It would seem strange today that a motor manufacturer could make claim in advertising their car was fitted with five wheels, driving mirror and low-pressure tyres; the state of the British motor industry was such that some manufacturers supplied only the chassis and it was left to the coachbuilder to provide the extras. The Citroën, therefore, took any chance from buying a new car, also the newest methods of assembly complimented the end-resulting price.

Absent from Olympia was the 7.5 h.p. model. To many critics this was a sad state of affairs; to those looking to the future, whilst the 7.5 h.p. was seen with some nostalgia especially as this had been the first car to have been produced at Slough and indeed had been the mainstay of Citroën production for a period of some six years, it was an indication the company intended to build more sophisticated cars. The earliest Citroëns were a range of fine motor vehicles designed to take the company forward into the next decade. From the original 10 h.p. and from which the 11.4 h.p. was developed, the 7.5. h.p. represented extremely good value for money, with a price tag from just £195 in 1922, it was a favourite amongst those customers looking for a small car but utilising the latest technology with which Citroën had become associated. By 1925 the price of the 7.5 h.p. had been reduced to £145 in three-seater Cloverleaf form and £155 for the Coupé. The

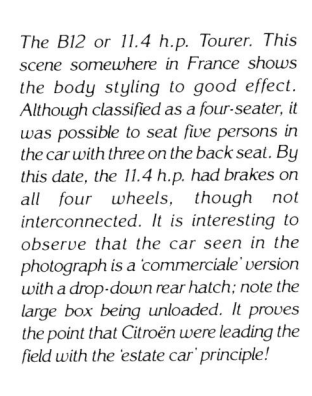

The B12 or 11.4 h.p. Tourer. This scene somewhere in France shows the body styling to good effect. Although classified as a four-seater, it was possible to seat five persons in the car with three on the back seat. By this date, the 11.4 h.p. had brakes on all four wheels, though not interconnected. It is interesting to observe that the car seen in the photograph is a 'commerciale' version with a drop-down rear hatch; note the large box being unloaded. It proves the point that Citroën were leading the field with the 'estate car' principle!

35

The 12.24 h.p. which in France was the B14. The neat design of the 'Doctor's Coupé' is well illustrated here in typical French surroundings. As so often depicted in advertisements, the car was marketed towards lady drivers or professional people and offering the higher levels of trim than normally associated with standard models.

little 7.5h.p. enjoyed acclaim from the world over, indeed it can be ranked against the famous Model T Ford for notoriety and the Austin Seven for bringing motoring within reach of the family man; certainly it was marketed as a ladies' car and in fact Citroën claimed in their 1925 brochure 'an ideal 'first car' for the lady or her daughter'. Sixty-five years on, fine working examples of this car can be found all around the world, in France it was given the name 'Petite Citron' due to its bright yellow paintwork although the car could also be purchased in maroon. By the end of production over 87,000 7.5 h.p. cars had been built in Citroën factories. With the parting of the 7.5 h.p., known in France also as the 5CV or Type C, from the Citroën catalogue, a new generation of cars came of age.

The all-steel saloon was the vogue as it had so many advantages over the wooden body. One motoring journalist expressed pleasure in driving the 11.4 h.p. model in as much as it did away with the 'week-week-weeki' sound whilst driving along. Citroën now had two models being manufactured at Slough, the 11.4 and 12.24 h.p., the latter being available from September 1926. The demise of the 7.5 h.p. had seemed to arise quite suddenly, there were still many orders for the car both in France and England, however, there is no clear reason as to why the production was ceased at that stage. In retrospect, compared, with the advances being made in the motor industry as a whole throughout Europe, it could be said the car had become dated, the saloon bodies of larger cars allowed complete family transport and whilst attempts had been made to transfer a larger and more accommodating body on the chassis, this seems to have been rather unsuccessful. Citroën decided to pull the model out of production in favour of increased sales of the new vehicles. As regards the Slough factory was concerned, the end of the 7.5 h.p. production came almost as some relief; whilst this had been the first car to be produced at Slough it did not share the same assembly line, the machinery had been installed with the 11.4 h.p. in mind, therefore the 7.5 h.p. was built on a separate production basis while the factory was being geared up for its official opening.

The scene at stand 101 at Olympia was that of euphoria, Citroën had the best cars of the day, behind each car was the most advanced assembly procedure ensuring absolute quality of the product; everybody wanted to see these new cars, were they as good as people had claimed? They were. The motoring journalists loved them and reported so. Owners of Citroën cars considered them to be among the finest on the road. Letters were constantly being published in the press, it seems nothing could be said against the cars.

'The Citroën is a wonderful climber, and no car of any make has yet passed me on a hill, although I have passed thousands.'

'I consider the 11.4 h.p. Citroën to be a most satisfactory proposition in the £200 class. During nine months I have covered 5,000 miles and find the car easy and comfortable to drive. My passengers invariably remark on the smooth running and freedom from road shocks, even when the car is travelling over the worst roads.'

'I spent ten days touring in the Lake District, always with four or five up, and sometimes (including one run of 180 miles) with six. I have also climbed Sutton Bank (1 in 3.9) in Yorkshire with four up. Altogether, in a period extending from August 20th to September 12th, I continuously used the car and covered over two thousand miles without an involuntary stop since I bought the car.'

'The Citroën products enjoy an enviable reputation for strength and longevity, and now the All-Steel models bid to uphold these traditions......The makers are prompt and courteous, whilst, in my opinion, the Citroën slogan, 'supreme value', is certainly maintained.'

And so the testimonials continued.

With the introduction of the new model, several changes were seen in the design of the car. While none of these were greatly striking it did, however, amount to some sophistication in the eyes of the motorist at large. The 11.4 h.p. still continued in its existing form but the 12.24 h.p. sported a new radiator cowling in that it was flat-fronted instead of being contoured in shape. The overall appearances of the two cars were similar, the main changes, apart from the radiator, being mechanical. The engine was uprated from 1453cc to 1538cc and the braking system was much improved over the previous model. The four-wheel brakes were now fitted with a Westinghouse licence vacuum servo unit which was operated by means of suction from the engine; with little effort by the driver, the stopping distances were noticeably decreased and it was possible to stop the car within twenty feet at twenty miles per hour. The suspension also received some changes; instead of being equipped with semi-elliptic springs at the front and superposed quarter-elliptic with friction shock absorbers at the rear, the new car was given four semi-elliptic springs aided by friction shock absorbers, a pair for each axle, the rear springs being fitted obliquely to the chassis. A newly-designed dashboard was fitted, this was of oval shape, all the controls were neatly nestled within it and in addition diffused lighting was supplied to it to aid night time driving. The 12.24 was well received by the auto journals, it was seen as a family car and as such was considered very safe. Mention was made of the servo brakes in that it was possible to drive the car on greasy roads in much the same manner as driving on dry surfaces. Citroën had triumphed once again, this time the Slough factory receiving the praise. *The Motor* in the issue of 21st February 1928 summed up its test on the car as such:

'The 12.24 h.p. saloon represents a very practical type of car for the man who wishes to carry four people in comfort under any sort of weather conditions and at reasonable speeds. It is pre-eminently a car which is easy to control and should therefore, we imagine, make a particular appeal to the lady driver.'

On the road, the Citroën 12.24 could be distinguished quite easily, the radiator was fitted with with the unique mascot featuring the famous Double Chevron and the bodywork was painted in a two tone finish with a neat coachline at waist level; three combinations of colours were available. On each running board there was placed a box, the nearside contained the battery whilst the offside housed a comprehensive tool kit.

The introduction of the 12.24 model did not indicate that the demise of the later 11.4 was imminent, in fact, this appeared in the catalogue as a 'standard model'. The 11.4 also received a number of mechanical changes over earlier models in the series, aluminium pistons were fitted to the engine and larger diameter brakes were installed. As against the 12.24, the 11.4 h.p. relied on a braking system that actuated the front wheels only whilst the hand brake operated the rear drums, however, it was not designed that the rear brakes be used as a parking device only, it was intended the driver use the hand brake lever in assisting the car to stop from speed. The suspension system lacked the updated assembly of the 12.24 but still used the semi-elliptic springs at the front with quarter-elliptic on the rear, friction dampers were fitted at the rear as standard. Nevertheless, even without the modifications of the 12.24, the car was still very acceptable and won constant praise. The interior of the 11.4 was very well appointed, seats well sprung and most comfortable, the dashboard lacked the attractive new design but the equipment otherwise was not detrimental and in fact most people found the car to be exceedingly well equipped especially in the face of the competition.

It is no wonder, when looking at the prices of Citroën cars at the 1927 motor show that sales showed Citroën to be one of the more popular cars on the British market; it certainly had the lead over foreign manufactured vehicles even allowing for the fact that the car was being built in Britain. André Citroën made frequent visits to the factory at Slough, to the Citroën building at Brook Green and to New Devonshire House. He was always impeccably dressed with top hat and white gloves and as in France, the Citroën company regarded their Patron's extravagant exhibitions as a way of life. His latest idea was to house around the walls of the New Devonshire House Showrooms, a complete car but in its component form; the idea was to let it be seen that the motor car, although a complicated affair in many respects, was nothing to be afraid of. Customers were able to gaze at will at all the parts—there were some 1200 items—and understand their varying functions.

Even accounting for the popularity of Citroën Cars in the United Kingdom, the company were not without their problems. Whilst the Citroën represented good value and reliability there was a great deal of competition from home and abroad, Austin, Ford, Morris, Renault and Peugeot as well as a host of other manufacturers were all happy to take sales away from Citroën. The Slough Factory was by now producing more cars than it could possibly sell; coupled to this there were clear signs an economic recession was hitting the country and sales of all new cars were being affected. When it was known that Citroën was to visit the Slough works the production lines were re-arranged to make it appear as if cars were coming off the production lines in large quantities. In fact, they were not. Cars were stockpiled so much that fewer and fewer cars could be built.

By 1927, the 11.4 h.p. range was becoming difficult to sell against strong competition. This example of the Caddy model in original French 7CV form looks rakishly attractive today, but contemporary British taste often favoured different styles.

Completed cars of the 11.4 model range were parked around the walls of the factory, the sight of more cars coming off the assembly lines and being stored wherever there was space caused something of an embarrassment. At one time there were over 1400 such cars unsold.

Towards the end of 1927 a further addition had been made to the Citroën model range by the introduction of the 12.24 de Luxe. The car sold for £225 fitted with the saloon type coachwork, for a further £5 the car could be equipped with the Westinghouse braking system. Other refinements to the specification not found on the 12.24 Standard Saloon and the 11.4 model were full instrumentation including fuel gauge, reserve on fuel tank with reserve control switch on the dashboard, carpeting throughout and a rear window blind to further the comfort of the passengers. Upholstery could be supplied either with leather or cloth trim to choice and the seats together with the seat squabs had adjustment. One point of interest was that traditionally Citroëns had always been fitted with Michelin tyres, yet in May 1928 a test car had Dunlop reinforced balloon tyres fitted of size 28ins. x 4.95ins. Differing body styles were available, the two-seater with dickey at £198; either a Drop-head or Fixed coupé at £235; a four door special bodied 'Hoyal' saloon or a six seater saloon both costing £265. Another model was also available, known in France as the 'Commercial' but in Britain as the 'Farmer's Four Seater', the rear seats could be either folded flat or removed in the event of carrying a bulky load. The back of the car had a tail gate door which, when lowered, facilitated loading and unloading of produce; the makers claimed this was the ideal utility vehicle to compliment the country home and at £205 the car was very generously priced. It could be said that the 'Shooting Brake' or 'Estate' Car had been born. Some confusion had arisen in France regarding a certain variant of the B14; known as the B18, 1200 examples of this special vehicle were built and it differed from the B14 by virtue that it was luxuriously equipped, had a wider track and was made in right hand drive form. The cars were intended for the Chinese market, however, as soon as the cars had been built the order was cancelled and the vehicles were sold on the French market. Due to their right-hand steering these particular Citroëns became known as the 'English B14's', this was rather unfortunate as they had nothing to do with the British market, neither were they built or sold at Slough.

Citroën at Slough managed to surmount their earlier problems with regard to the general slump in the economy of the country. Towards 1928 the gloom began to lift and cars once more started to sell in increasing numbers. Since the factory had opened it had witnessed a number of 'firsts' in the automobile industry, one of the lesser appreciated was the fact that from 1928 the Citroën was the first car to have been fitted with an automatic stop light. This gadget, now a legal necessity taken for granted, was positioned adjacent to the rear light and illuminated when the driver depressed the brake pedal. The Citroën exhibit at the 1927 Paris Motor Show demonstrated the B14, known in Britain as the 12.24, with a change to the general body shape; the roof was much more rounded at the rear of the car and the bonnet received redesigned louvres along the side. It was not long after the changes filtered through to the British cars leaving the works at Slough.

Charles Lindbergh, the famous aviator who swept to the forefront of the world's attention with his much acclaimed West to East Transatlantic flight in the aeroplane 'Spirit of St. Louis', received a distinguished approbation from André Citroën who threw a grand party in his honour at the Quai de Javel factory. A beaming André Citroën escorted the hero through his works and naturally the crowds of Parisians were thrilled at the joyous occasion. Later Citroën arranged another celebration, this time in Britain at New Devonshire House. Citroën seized the opportunity to focus attention on his idea to exhibit car components around the showroom, in true style of his exuberant personality he claimed that if all the parts were laid end to end they would stretch from London to Paris, likewise if they were stacked on top of each other they would reach the height of the Eiffel Tower. How true such statements were is a matter of conjecture. At the dinner were many eminent guests including Reginald Rootes, then a dealer, but soon to compete directly with Citroën, expressed his enthusiasm and regard for Citroën Cars. It is ironical that, over fifty years later, the two businesses should be joined under the one umbrella of the Peugeot-Talbot-Citroën group.

Following the success of the 1927 Olympia Motor Show, Citroën triumphed again at Olympia in the same year at the Commercial Vehicle Show where a most impressive array of trade vehicles were put on show. Models converted from private cars to trade vans were of great intrigue, none more so than the 12.24 8-cwt van which sold for £205. The vehicle was supplied with a large box body capable of carrying a considerable load; it had double doors at the rear opening the full width of the body which allowed ease of access to the trader and delivery driver. Alongside the van Citroën showed the chassis separately which proved the durability and utility of the vehicle.

By 1928, the Citroën factory at Slough had been in

*Charles Lindburgh visits Javel. André Citroën (centre front) escorts Lindburgh (on Citroën's left) around Javel when the Patron threw a huge party in his honour. Charles Lindburgh had swept to fame following his highly successful West-East Trans-Atlantic flight in the **Spirit of St. Louis** in May 1927. Always keen to take the opportunity to gain publicity, especially at the expense of his rival motor manufacturers whom he always aimed at impressing, Citroën thrilled thousands of Parisians who gathered at Javel to catch a glimpse of the hero aviator.*

operation for a little over two years, in that time the workforce had increased to over 600. Citroën was a relentless man, he demonstrated this in the way he produced motor cars and it was seen even more clearly in the span of the so far short history of the works. Within the two years cars had rolled off the production lines a whole era had come and gone; the 7.5 h.p. Cloverleaf, probably one of the most famous Citroën's ever produced, and indeed the first car to bear the Double Chevron insignia to be built at the factory, was by now discontinued, so was the 11.4 h.p. Now the enormously popular 12.24 h.p. was the only series of vehicle continuing in production. It is without doubt this last model that brought much fame to the British side of Citroën production for it was this vehicle with its exceedingly competitive price and quite extravagant equipment that won sales and developed Citroën enthusiasm. Citroën's fortunes could not continue to lie indefinitely with this model alone, other manufacturers were bringing out new cars, they were justifiably envious of André Citroën's products, the factory and its output. Anything they could do to curb Citroën's market and put it to their own good was a bonus. Therefore it was seen at the end of 1928, two new models announced: a 2 litre six-cylinder model and a smaller four cylinder car. Both models were intended to see Citroën Cars into the next decade, the era of the 1930's.

Chapter five: The Great Push

For some time before the announcement of the new models for 1929 there had been some anticipation of the appearance of a new and highly interesting Citroën. The rumours had come from France where it was reported the new car was undergoing tests in Switzerland and in France at the Montlhery racing circuit. In fact, when the announcement was finally made, it was not one car but two models that were to be introduced, namely a four-cylinder and a six cylinder. The cars were ready for their debut at the 1928 Paris Salon and the British Motor Show at Olympia. As with previous models, the cars produced at Slough had different model symbols to those manufactured at the Javel factory, as it was always considered the model definitions should reflect the British tradition of referring to models by horse-power rating; the AC4 (later known as the C4) was known as the 13-30 h.p. and AC6 (C6) became the 20 h.p. or 2½ litre. A lot of confusion has always arisen with the differences in model notation of Citroën cars, no less so than when the 7s, 11s, 12s and 15s all represented one basic type of car; more of that later, however. Year after year, Citroën were stealing the show at Olympia, and the 1928 exhibition was no exception.

With the announcement of the new models coming just in time for the event it is no wonder that crowds flocked to see the cars; there was still a great tide of interest in the Citroën factory at Slough and to many it remained the standard by which the progress of the motor industry was measured.

Prices of new cars inevitably increased, however, they still represented the most remarkable value for money. The 20 h.p. was announced with a price tag of £295 for the four-door saloon and just £255 for the smaller-engined 13-30 saloon. Critics of Citroën were happy to claim the company had gone in for 'Americanising' their cars and it was even suggested the cars had been 'Chryslerised'. Of course this was complete nonsense, a move had been made in favour of a somewhat larger car but this mirrored the trend of the market at the time. The cars were as every little bit as French as they could be and the English built cars represented the finest British engineering of the day, the Slough cars were built with virtually all-British components and reflected a true British flavour in car design. However, André Citroën kept closely in touch with the most up-to-date ideas and had always had respect for new technology from the American automobile industry with its ever-lively interest in volume production.

A lot of enthusiasm greeted the cars upon their launch, most of the contemporary motoring magazines considered the models to be of handsome lines and very pleasing to the eye. It was still found worthwhile mentioning in reports that the cars were manufactured with all-steel bodies, many other manufacturers were copying Citroën's ideas but there was a continuing trend to have the body made by separate coach builders and fitted to the chassis and some of the bodies were still being constructed partly in wood. There was quite a deliberation regarding the virtues of the six-cylinder engine, especially that some noticeable popularity had been gained for its use and efficiency, some voices were heard to proclaim that the days of the four-cylinder engine were numbered and that in the future only six-cylinder motors would be engineered and fitted. Citroën certainly did not share this view, whilst it was appreciated the six-cylinder engine fitted particular requirements, Citroën stated that the motor car was essentially a form of transport with four doors, four seats and a power unit of four cylinders. Bearing this statement in mind, André Citroën set off in the direction to produce, within a very short time, increasing numbers of cars adopting the six-cylinder principle.

Like all famous entrepreneurs, Citroën had immense courage and determination often flying in the face of his most severe and harshest critics. For the announcement of the models for 1929 Citroën showed the world he had lost none of the fiery and dramatic personality as well as the splendid organising qualities he had shown when starting

The Chassis Shop at Slough where it was possible to build a complete chassis in just two hours, using the most up-to-date equipment to be found in the motor industry. Note the overhead hoists and conveyor tracks; the equipment allowed the chassis to be constructed at the highest possible production rate and yet ensured that each assembly received individual attention. As the chassis moved along the production line, each mechanic had ample time to carry out the required task using pneumatic tools; necessary components were fitted along the route from minor assembly shops adjacent to the conveyor so that the engine and gearbox were fitted at one point, wheels and tyres at another and so on until the end of the line was reached with the completed chassis ready for the body to be mounted upon it.

his ammunition factory in 1915 or the car manufacturing works in 1919. Once again the great advertising campaigns were thrust upon the French, the Eiffel Tower was floodlit once more and all the daily newspapers of France once a month carried full-page features detailing news of the progress of the company and its cars. Leaflets were printed by the thousands in many languages and distributed throughout Europe. In all, massive sums of money were spent and this no doubt in defiance of all Citroën's financial advisers and creditors. The huge expenditure did not stop there, for the new cars a gigantic re-tooling operation took place, parts of the Javel factory had to be completely transformed and new assembly lines installed. At Slough also, the affects of the new models were felt, the production lines had to be altered to accommodate the building of the new cars, advertising was somewhat less of a problem as this was restricted in the main to newspaper and motoring journal announcements. It is certain that had André Citroën not opened the Slough factory, sales of the Citroën car would not have reached anything like the numbers being produced at the time. The product had gained a very high reputation for soundness of structure, reliability and comfort and the fact that the cars were actually built in the United Kingdom from British parts by British craftsmen was also a major contributory factor for increasing popularity. The factory, together with the service that Brook Green and the agents provided received much praise and comment, especially the stores at Brook Green which, apart from being highly modernised, were a model of efficiency. In his way, André Citroën had developed possibly the best and most appealing advertisement for Citroën Cars by virtue of his own company. The managers of Citroën Cars saw to it that the operations were executed just the way Citroën himself expected; at the helm was a no-nonsense American, Ben King, who had strict ideals and commanded great respect. He expected from his workforce loyalty to the company and had no qualms about dismissing a person on the spot even for a trivial matter.

During the time the factory had been open, the Citroën Company had developed a good relationship with the people of Slough; a social club had been organised which, apart from bringing together staff from all over the factory and ensuring the upkeep of good working relations, it also

The finishing shop where completed cars received minor fittings and adjustments before being taken to the delivery sheds. A batch of 12-24 h.p. Four-Seater Tourers can be seen on the production line. After coming off the assembly line, the cars were taken for a test run from the Factory through to the nearby village of Burnham where it was a common sight to see them undergoing rigorous checking. Almost 6,000 cars were built at Slough during 1927 thereby contributing quite valuably to Britain's motor vehicle output.

re-affirmed the association with the social club at Brook Green and often combined events were held. The club at Slough took an active interest in the affairs of the town and on more than one occasion supplied cars for special functions within the borough. Sports tournaments were held with companies in the area and it was generally felt that the Citroën works were a great asset to the well-being of the area. Needless to say many people living in the vicinity of Slough were persuaded to buy Citroën cars not only because of loyalty to a local company and its associations within the district but because the servicing and supply of parts for the cars was reliable and efficient.

Preparations were complete for the production of the new cars by mid-autumn 1928; the 12.24 h.p. was still in production and it was expected that the model would be continued to be built alongside the new models for some time although it was appreciated demand would eventually diminish in favour of the more modern vehicles. Outwardly, the 13-30 and 20 h.p. had a more of a rounded appearance than the 12.24, the front wings had a pronounced 'flowing' aspect and the bonnet louvres

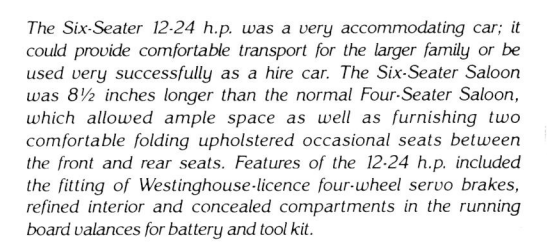

The Six-Seater 12-24 h.p. was a very accommodating car; it could provide comfortable transport for the larger family or be used very successfully as a hire car. The Six-Seater Saloon was 8½ inches longer than the normal Four-Seater Saloon, which allowed ample space as well as furnishing two comfortable folding upholstered occasional seats between the front and rear seats. Features of the 12-24 h.p. included the fitting of Westinghouse-licence four-wheel servo brakes, refined interior and concealed compartments in the running board valances for battery and tool kit.

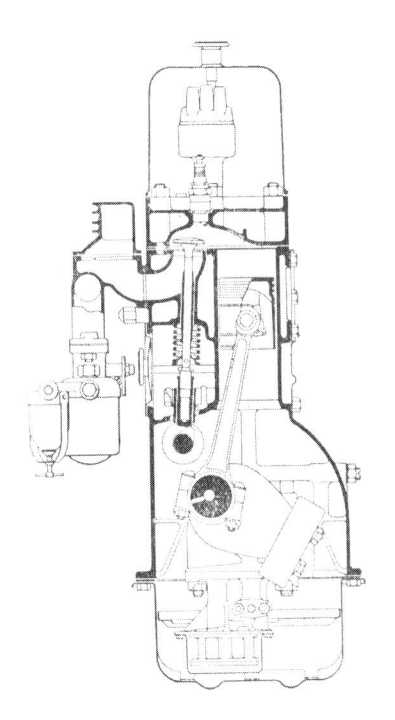

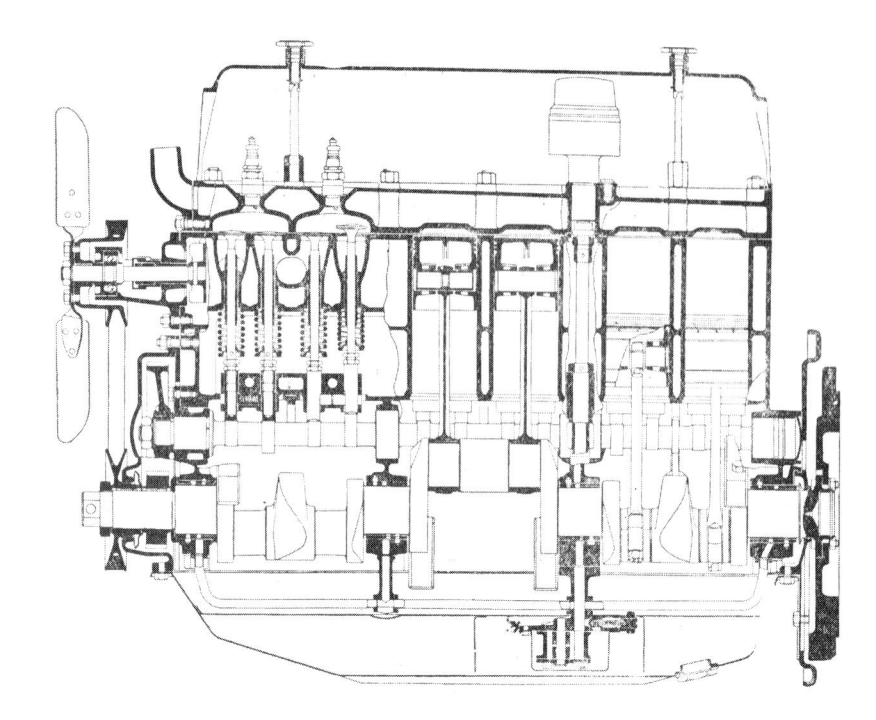

The Michelat-designed 2½-litre six-cylinder engine introduced for 1929. These cross-sectional views reveal the side-valve layout. The catalogue description of this unit refers to the fact that 'the distributor, plugs and high-tension leads are enclosed in a detachable cover which gives an exceptionally clean appearance to the engine', but there can be little doubt that it was also intended to give the external appearance of an overhead-valve engine. The unit had bore and stroke of 72 x 100mm, giving a cubic capacity of 2442cc and an RAC rating of 19.3 h.p. The cast iron cylinder block and crankcase formed one unit extending well below the crankshaft centre line, giving good support for the latter's four main bearings. Four-point suspension using rubberised fabric pads to act as a means of insulating vibration from being transmitted to the car interior was used for the combined assembly of the engine and three-speed gearbox. The four-cylinder 13-30 h.p. engine was of very similar design, with the same cylinder dimensions, but did not have the cover over the distributor and plugs.

extended almost the entire length between the radiator and the scuttle; the radiator itself had a higher line which helped give the car a much bolder appearance, the boxes that were situated on the running boards either side of the car on the 12.24 housing the battery and tools now vanished and were transferred inside the car, the battery was housed under the floor and the provision of a trap-door flap gave easy access for topping up with fluid.

There were a number of features on both the 13-30 four cylinder and 20 h.p. six cylinder cars that heralded a new age and progression. Firstly, the initial step had been taken towards the idea of 'Floating Power', a device which eliminated a great deal of engine vibration. The engine was mounted in the frame of the chassis by four pressed-steel brackets and where the bracket met the frame there was installed a rubber buffer block allowing considerable smoothness in transmission to be achieved. Citroën claimed their six cylinder engine to be of great power and flexibility and that it was possible to accelerate the 'Six' to over 60 m.p.h without the slightest vibration from the engine. The cooling system received attention as well, the thermo-siphoning of previous models was now replaced with a circulating pump, however, provision had been made to enable the water to be cooled by thermo-siphoning on an emergency basis only in the unlikely event any mechanical problems be experienced at any future time. The engine was completely new, it was designed by Michelat who, before working for Citroën, was associated with Delage. Later he was to leave Citroën returning to his old employer, Delage. While new in design, Michelat conformed to conventional standards; for ignition the magneto was replaced by a distributor and a vertical type Solex carburettor was fitted. Not being content with engines capable of two thousand revolutions per minute, Michelat's design was much more energetic and was able to run to three thousand revolutions a minute. For its day, Michelat's engine was quite formidable with its 72mm x 100mm bore and stroke and 2442cc capacity developing 45 b.h.p. leading to a top speed of 65 miles an hour with a fuel consumption of 20 miles per gallon.

The *Autocar* and *Motor* both tested the cars in great detail and both came to the similar conclusion the new models were well worthy of praise. Naturally there were criticisms, never yet has there been anything not to criticise about a vehicle, but in the main the criticisms were restricted to the lesser details of the car such as, in their opinion, the test crews found the cars 'a little lively when empty of passengers or luggage'; the vacuum windscreen wipers were thought to be 'rather more intermittent than those of their type usually are'. The hand brake gave a little food for thought; whilst the foot brake was excellent and could not be faulted in any way, the hand brake failed to hold the car stationary on a 1 in 4 hill. The control layout of the right hand drive cars was very neat and the steering wheel, which was seventeen inches in diameter, was

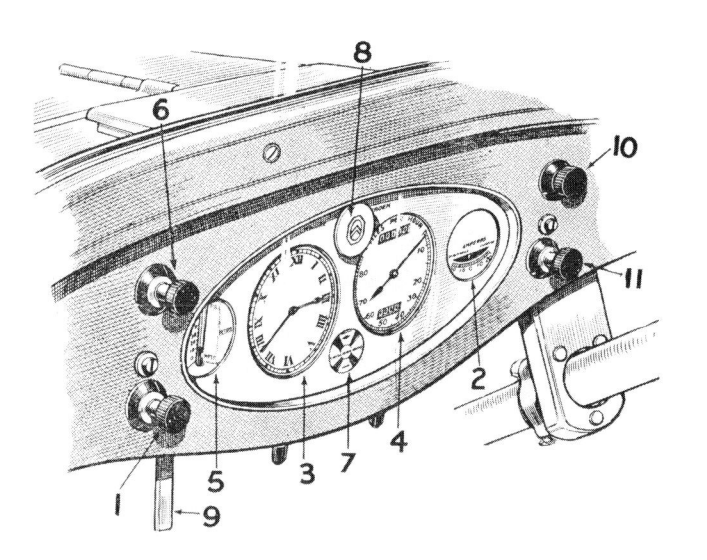

The controls of the 2½-litre and 13-30 h.p. were designed and positioned so as to be easily operated by the driver. The gear lever and handbrake could be easily operated with the left hand whilst the fascia instruments and controls were clear and concise. KEY TO DIAGRAM: 1: Ignition switch; 2: Ammeter; 3: Clock; 4: Speedometer; 5: Petrol Gauge; 6: Electric Starter Switch; 7: Oil Pressure Indicator; 8: Fascia Board and Ignition 'Tell-Tale' Lamp; 9: Scuttle Ventilator Control; 10: Air Strangler Control; 11: Throttle Control.

placed at an angle which all the test drivers found to be exceedingly comfortable. On the top of the steering column, what was considered as a novel idea turned out to be an acceptable feature in that a 'ring switch' had been built-in controlling the lighting system and electric horn, this was obviously the introduction of the equipment stalk now taken for granted. The hand brake and gear change levers were situated side by side to the left of the steering wheel and immediately ahead of the front seat, the gear shift being nearer the driver. The accelerator pedal in

The 13/30 h.p. Six-Seater Saloon differed from the 12-24 h.p. by having a larger engine — 1628cc as against 1539cc, the cylinder bore being increased from 70 to 72mm. The 13/30 could be identified by the extended bonnet louvres and spoked wheels, double windscreen wiper and bumpers front and rear. Two occasional seats provided extra passenger capacity making the car ideal for the hire market. Citroën were able to offer the Six-Seater in choice of colours — Blue, two-tone maroon, or green-and-black. Prices of the 13/30 Saloons started from £255 which represented extremely good value for money especially when considering the high level of trim and equipment.

accordance with design at the time was positioned between the clutch pedal on the left and the foot brake on the right; the instruments were all neatly grouped in an oval console upon the dashboard and in the centre of the car, flanking the console were four switches—ignition, starter, strangler (choke) and throttle control.

The *Motor* were a little more daring with their test, they took the car—a four cylinder version—on a 500 mile expedition from London along the Great North Road (A1) to Stamford and across to the Peak District in Derbyshire. Over the distance of 118 miles from London to Stamford, an average speed of 38 miles per hour was maintained. When appreciating the year this particular test was carried out, 1929, it was by no means an easy task and the result says a great deal of the car. An interesting passage is reprinted from the test report:

'Shortly after taking over the car we commenced a fairly long run up the Great North Road, starting from Finchley on a Saturday afternoon when the traffic conditions were not favourable for quick travel for the first forty miles or so. We soon found that the Citroën, although its best cruising speed from the point of view of quiet running is 40-45 m.p.h., can be kept going at a genuine 50 m.p.h. for mile after mile without tiring, and this speed can be held without taking chances owing to the excellence of the four-wheel braking system. Figures for stopping distances, incidentally, can be read from the graph reproduced and it will be seen that these are particularly good. Furthermore, they can be obtained with but little effort on the part of the driver owing to the powerful assistance rendered by the Westinghouse servo motor, which is operated by engine suction.'

For performance, the six cylinder car was in a different league to the 13-30 h.p., there was talk of the car reaching 70 m.p.h. under reasonable circumstances at the time, however, the cruising speed was more in the region of 35-40 m.p.h. according to *Autocar* (though the latter was perhaps more a reflection of contemporary traffic speeds); *The Motor* were able to suggest a little different theme,

The 2½-litre Six Safety Saloon, as introduced for 1930. This version of the model had chromium-plated bumpers and safety glass all round as well as leather upholstery — a lower-priced version with what was described as 'normal' glass, without bumpers, etc and either repp or leather-cloth upholstery was also offered. Other features included wire wheels, vacuum-servo brakes, Lucas Biflex anti-glare headlamps, a fog lamp, double windscreen wipers, a rug rail with rug, step mats with valence guards and spring blinds for the rear windows. Cellulose finish was available in blue, two-tone maroon, two-tone grey, beige-and-brown.

when they tested the car they found the top speed to be 63 m.p.h. and a cruising speed of between 50-55 m.p.h. without fatigue. This still fell slightly short of the manufacturers claim, of 65 miles per hour. The interior and facilities of the 2½ litre car were very much the same as the 13-30, the real difference being the power unit and the performance. Certainly the price between the two cars was of a very narrow margin, only a mere £40, even at 1928 prices the variation was hardly considerable. The six cylinder Citroën was much more of a relaxing vehicle to drive as against the four cylinder, when placed into second gear the car all but flew away and once on the move it took a steep hill indeed to resort the driver changing from top to second gear. From road tests of the time there is more than a hint that the test drivers were really not quite sure as to what to make of the Westinghouse servo brake mechanism, on one particular test the servo was cut out by disconnecting the engine power and it was agreed that the car's brakes were so good that even with the extra pressure required on the brake pedal the car stopped in adequate distance. The consent was that the servo unit was a helpful device and saved the driver from having to exert too much pressure on the brake pedal; some other makes of cars at the time which boasted a servo type braking unit showed very poor results when put through a similar test, a feather in the Citroën hat!

The 1928 Citroën range of 13-30 and 20 horsepower cars represented a high quality choice of motor car, the varying body styles gave ample consideration for customer needs, both engine configurations allowed for either six-light or four-light bodies, the latter being equipped with a rear trunk. The six-light style was available in both four seat and six seat versions. The Citroën six-cylinder, apart from being a most successful model in its own right also became, in chassis form, a basis for lorries and coaches. The chassis was used throughout a range of commercial vehicles which met with considerable success and received universal acclaim. Although from the outset of vehicle manufacture in 1919 Citroën had marketed utility vehicles based upon versions of the standard car chassis, the 2½ litre six-cylinder saw the beginning of a complete range of commercials under the enterprise 'Transports Citroëns'.

At the end of 1929, the announcement of the 1930 model range was made from both Paris and Slough. The Six-Cylinder continued its completely successful role as a fast comfortable car, very reasonably priced but at the same time complete in every detail at the time of rolling off the assembly line and ready for the road ahead. In accordance with modifications as detailed by the makers, the cars for the 1930 model year differed in alterations in making a good car even better. Immediately obvious was the addition of front bumpers, the inclusion of a fog lamp mounted centrally upon the headlamp support bar and the disappearance of the Boyce Motormeter. What Citroën had done was to break up the range of 20 h.p. cars, where there had been only one model, now for 1930 there were three; at the top of the range, with all the luxury fittings as expected from the marque came the Safety De-Luxe Saloon with a price of £345. Two new cars were also available, the Safety Saloon with almost as many features as the De-Luxe and costing £320 and finally the Standard Saloon at £298. The Standard Saloon had a much lower level of equipment than its two stable mates and was supplied without the Westinghouse servo braking unit, even so the car claimed remarkable value for money. The impressions of the Sixes relating to interior trim and exterior finish were such to evoke a lot of praise and features found in the car were normally only to be discovered on much more expensive makes of car. For the year, there is no doubt the 2½ litre was a most desirable car, its lines were quite handsome, indeed graceful would be nearer the truth, the colour schemes available were varied and showed off its attributes well. Depending upon the body style a large trunk was fitted at the rear of the car, this was reserved for the four light saloons although it was also available for the Weymann bodied Sportsman's Coupé. The term 'boot' had not reached Citroën owners yet, the trunk was solidly made of steel and was equipped with Yale locks so as to be as thief proof as far as practical. Even though of British manufacture, Citroën at Slough made no apologies for referring to the trunk 'of coquille type'. The six light saloons were built on a slightly longer chassis with the six-seat six light saloons mounted on a chassis even longer giving a further 10 inches on the overall length of the car. To compliment the car the interior was equally as grand as the exterior, fine quality leather hide trim covered the seats which were adjustable for forward and rearward motion as well as for rake, carpets fitted closely with the contours of the body which assisted in ensuring a good seal from noise and draughts. The side windows as well as the front and rear screens were fitted with 'Splintex' glass demonstrating yet another safety feature of the car. To retain the condition of the bright parts of the car, chromium plating was utilised, this was, however, standard on all models leaving the Slough works. Of real benefit to the driver and passengers was the installation of the electric windscreen wiper, this was made by Klaxon and at last the driver was saved from suffering the frustration of vacuum operated wipers which had the happy knack of working slowly when they were most needed, ie. driving uphill in pouring rain.

There is no doubt that the six-cylinder concept of motor cars was gaining favour, Citroën was not uncommon in this respect and more and more sales were being made. Citroën believed, however, that ultimately the future lay with four cylinder configurations and not six; this has seen to be true and even a less number of cylinders than four have been in vogue. It must be remembered that even all those years ago, Citroën demonstrated his skill of looking at the future with a sense of realism that few other car builders have possessed. It was no wonder therefore that Citroën allowed the graceful furnishings of the sixes to be allocated to the lower powered fours as well. Sharing the same body as the six but without all the exterior appendages, the four cylinder 13-30 continued to be very popular and made a considerable profit for the company, money that was soon to be so desperately needed. The 13-30 upon its own merits, since being introduced at the 1928 Motor Show, had proved to be a most durable car, it was free from any major mechanical problems and it was considered to be one of the most trouble-free cars on the market at any price and scored high stakes for its economy. Now called 13/30 h.p. it was available in similar body styles as its six cylinder cousin, the range consisted of the Safety Six-Seat Saloon which had the feature of two forward-facing folding chairs neatly positioned between the front and rear seats, the Sportsman's Coupé with body built by Weymann, the

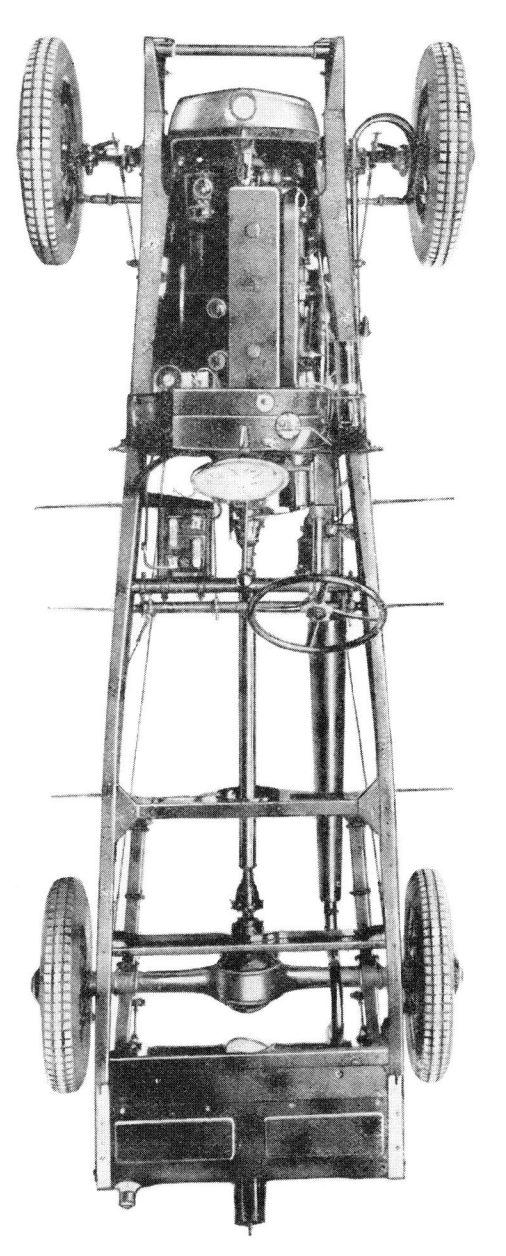

The 2½-litre and the 13.30 h.p. chassis shared many of the same features. This plan view of the former shows the general layout, with tapering frame and a combination of pressed and tubular cross-members. The open propellor shaft had Spicer universal joints and the rear axle was a new design with Gleason spiral level bevel final drive rather than the Citroën chevron type. This six-cylinder car had a 12-gallon petrol tank at the rear — a large capacity at that date — and fuel was drawn by a Weymann vacuum exhauster incorporated in an auxiliary two-gallon tank under the bonnet. The 6-volt battery was mounted in a cradle under the front floor. Note the long exhaust silencer of an unusual tapering form.

Four-Light Saloon with rear trunk, Safety Six-Light four seat saloon and two particularly attractive models, the Coupé with a choice of fixed or folding head and the four door Weymann Saloon with its distinctive body style built by Weymann in their factory at Addlestone with the chassis supplied by Citroën. The Weymann-bodied cars were a most attractive motor car both in four and six cylinder guise, they offered the ultimate in luxury and provided the customer the benefit of the most reliable mechanical engineering whilst at the same time exclusiveness of much more expensive motor cars.

Since *The Motor* had published its 500 mile test on the

The four-cylinder version of the new-generation chassis began to be described as the 13/30 h.p. model in leaflets issued by Citroën Cars Ltd. for 1930, following the fairly common British practice of quoting RAC and b.h.p. ratings separated by oblique stroke. The engine capacity was 1628cc, RAC rating 12.8 h.p., and there were three main bearings. The high-mounted distributor was exposed in this case — it and the coil were by Delco-Remy, another instance of Citroën's regard for American equipment. Evident in this view are the exceptionally deep frame side-members with profile to allow a lower floor than hitherto. In this case the 8-gallon petrol tank was under the bonnet, but the model shared with the six-cylinder the use of what was by then described as Citroën Servo (Westinghouse-licence) four-wheel brakes, 'very powerful in action'. The bracket at the rear was for the spare wheel.

13/30 h.p., the very same car travelled a further nine thousand miles before being returning to the rigorous demands of the same journal. When *The Motor* took the car again it was quick to note that during the 9000 miles since their last encounter no work of any kind had found to have been necessary on the engine or any other chassis component. When considering the treatment the car must have received in the hands of all and sundry it is praise indeed for the engineering and construction of the car. It is interesting to read from the report of this second test:

'A 250 mile test was carried out, followed by acceleration tests, and we found that the performance scarcely differed appreciably in any particular form from that which obtained a year ago. A most noticeable fact was that the engine ran as quietly and smoothly as in the previous trial, so that, as noise is always a measure of wear, it can safely be assumed that the working parts were as a close a fit as ever. The engine was, of course, in need of decarbonising, but even this fact did not make itself very apparent. On this model the ignition advance is carried out automatically, and in no circumstances was it possible to make the engine knock.'

While Citroën in Britain were doing well enough and selling their cars in goodly and profitable numbers, it must be appreciated the same story applied to many other motor manufacturers. André Citroën was a realist as well as being a futurist and consequently there were to be always motorists who, for many reasons, were not prepared to buy his product. A totally British company manufacturing cars for the home market were considered by many to be preferential — even if the cars were outdated and uncomfortable by Citroën's standards — also price, while playing an important part was not always the deciding factor; any copy of a motoring periodical could be found to be brimming over with tests of cars by the dozen, advertisements claimed certain cars to be better than any other company's and to confuse the motorist even further the prices were at war with each other. Competition was fierce; with the change of the decade there seemed to be fresh impetus on design, car makers were looking for something new and in this quest a vacuum began to exist. There was a feeling in the motoring world of a threshold of something new and different, what it needed was a lead. André Citroën was accepted as one of the great car makers and many looked to him to see whether he was the man to herald a new idea. The world would have to wait a little longer, in the meantime the serious task of fulfilling orders for demand was paramount and the cars being produced had to keep pace with developments required of a motoring conscious public.

The sales of Citroën cars in the United Kingdom, whilst healthy, suffered to some extent from a prejudice against foreign vehicles; some underlying currents in road test reports of the time would suggest that the car, although built in Britain by a British workforce and using British components was still very much a foreign car. There is no doubt that in general the car received glowing reports and there was hardly any report condemning the Citroën, all the journalists found it to be quite remarkable and were profound in their views that it was amongst the best cars available. So, what of the opposition at this time? 1931 was looming rapidly, manufacturers were announcing the following season's models; car buying to a degree was by tradition quite seasonal, more cars were sold in the Spring and early Summer than Autumn and Winter. Whilst news of new cars would be released in the Autumn, the demand would not arrive until the early spring, the earlier the car was ordered so the prospective purchaser had better chance of obtaining the exact model, colour and body design required. It was fashionable to purchase a new car from the manufacturer's London showroom and part of the joy of the purchase was the visit to the Capital; there was a campaign, however, to persuade the customer to purchase their new car from a local agent or garage, manufacturers were ensuring their dealers could obtain cars in good time to fulfil the buyer's demands. It was recognised that provincial dealerships might not carry the same stock as a London agent and as a result manufacturers began publishing more comprehensive catalogues and ensuring demonstration cars were always available. Citroën were in the somewhat lucky position that although having a spectacular London showroom and a fine service department nearby at Brook Green, they had an excellent dealer network; this had been set up by the company seeing the state of the motor industry up till Citroën Cars were produced and avoiding some of the pitfalls experienced by other manufacturers.

Nobody could deny Citroën's venture in producing motor cars in Britain had been a success, in hindsight, it must be one of the bravest adventures in the history of car manufacture. The works were a model of industrial efficiency; André Citroën's recipe was par excellence and the proof of the pudding was in the eating. The bias against foreign cars was recognised and plans were put in hand to dispel that idea once and for all. The outcome was a range of cars, based upon the existing successful models but with a far stronger English flavour. The whole operation to follow was, in the words of Works Director at Slough—Mr. McLelland—'a great push' at the British market. The intention was to make huge inroads of the sales of new cars within the United Kingdom market and give the competition something to think about! Some of the ideas that followed could be seen as examples of what André Citroën would have done in the same position. Models were refurbished and horse power ratings for model notation were dropped in favour of 'typically English' names, prices were slashed and production increased. McLelland announced new production lines were to be set up with the appropriate tooling. It was envisaged the new models would be in production by September 1930.

To enable the Company to produce more cars it was necessary to increase the workforce. This could be achieved in two ways, firstly, to enlist staff via the employment exchange, or, secondly, re-enlist staff who had previously left the Citroën Company. Of the second option, Citroën had always adopted a unique scheme in tailoring the numbers of staff employed in relation to the demand for cars; it has already been noted that car-buying in Britain was seasonal and as the demand for cars dropped so workers were laid off only to be re-employed later when the need arose and assuming they had not been re-employed elsewhere. Citroën staff on the whole were of tolerant nature, willing to take on work knowing that within a few months there would be no work. Exactly this happened on this occasion, word had got around that Citroën needed staff urgently and queues began forming at the factory gates almost at once. Preference was given to local labour before staff from further afield were employed. The Works Manager was at times highly critical of some of the local inhabitants, he said they should buy the Citroën car instead of the 'Yankee makes' and in this way much fuller employment could be ensured. He went on to say that he would defy anybody to find a better car than the Citroën for the same money.

The following statement was issued to the press on 12th September 1930:

'The Citroën Factory at Slough, Buckinghamshire, has been organised to produce during the coming season a larger number of cars than it has ever previously undertaken. With the help of British accessory manufactures from whom supplies are drawn, a big programme has been laid out and the prices of the two models are based on large scale production. Between four hundred and five hundred firms supply materials to the Slough works. One of the most reliable and consistent cars on the road last season was the four-cylinder Citroën, known as the 13/30 h.p. and rated at 12.8 h.p. This model has now been immeasurably improved especially as far as its handling and flexibility are concerned and the improvements are of such a nature as to make the older model an out-dated car. There are front and back axles, new clutch, new steering, a new type of gear box and many other engineering improvements.

The 13/30 h.p. sold last year as saloon at £255, the new improved 12.8 h.p. with similar coachwork will sell as a four door all-steel saloon at £185. This popular model will be known as the 'Chiltern'. A de-luxe model known as the 'Clarendon' will also be offered at £215 with sliding roof, best quality furniture hide, safety glass, bumpers all-round and luggage grid. The 'family' six-seater model will also be continued at a very interesting price, chromium plating and servo brakes will be standard on all models. A novel departure in connection with the 12.8 h.p. model is a new and very modern type radiator with a colourful crest design to which the well-known Citroën Chevron badge has been cleverly embodied. Extraordinary values are also offered in the six-cylinder range, the 2½ litre 19.3 h.p. Citroën Six has acquired a fine reputation during the last year for speed, acceleration, power, performance and reliability and only minor improvements have been necessary in the new 19.3 model now offered as a saloon at £235 as compared with the last season's price of £298. The de-luxe model, more finely equipped, will sell at £265. There is also an attractive seven seater model. The £235 model will be known as the 'Buckingham', and the £265 model as the 'Berkeley''.

Citroën's determination to meet the British market head-on seemed to have paid off, the new approach to sales won considerable interest from motorists throughout. All the motoring journals were eager to report on the new cars and likewise on previous occasions they were quick to point out the virtues of the models finding only little constructive criticism of the cars. There was little doubt Citroën had taken quite a major policy change, the company were facing up to a new decade which promised to be turbulent and the storm was already beginning to brew that would break in four years hence. The new cars represented to the British car buyers all that was best in value for money and at once there was a response. There were a number of factors that triggered off the new demand for the latest Citroëns, the style was very 'English', prices were low and attractive and at last drivers had become accustomed to recognising the Double Chevron mascot.

As a guide to the extraordinary value of the cars for 1931,

Citroën's efforts to produce cars associated more clearly with the United Kingdom resulted in a range of four models, the Clarendon as pictured here in this advertisement in 12.8 h.p. De Luxe format, the Chiltern 12.8 h.p. Basic Saloon, the Six-Cylinder Standard Saloon, the Buckingham, and the Berkeley Six-Cylinder De Luxe Saloon. At £185, the Clarendon was £80 cheaper than the model it replaced; in this view the reduced use of chromium-plating and reversion to disc wheels are evident.

the following table is set out to show the 'old' and the 'new' models and prices:

PREVIOUS MODELS   NEW MODELS

13/30 h.p. Saloon	£255	CHILTERN SALOON (12.8h.p.)	£185
13/30 h.p. Sal.d.l.	£295	CLARENDON SALOON (12.8h.p.)	£215
6-Cylinder Saloon	£298	BUCKINGHAM SLN (6 CYL.)	£235
6-Cyl. Saloon d.l.	£345	BERKELEY SALOON (6 CYL.)	£265

French cars, as with most other continental models, were known by symbols such as the Citroën B14, C4 and C6; British cars on the whole were different, drivers were not so keen on symbols, preferring names and hence the models depicted in brochures from Slough had a direct impact with the new model names.

For the year, the British Citroën saloons represented a most handsome machine, everything for driver and passenger convenience was, it seemed, included in the specification. Of the Chiltern, *The Motor* found it to be an 'excellent four-cylinder family car. Roomy coachwork, comfortable springing and a smooth engine are features.' The Clarendon saloon was of course from the same mould as the Chiltern and being the de-luxe version incorporated some extra refinements. The main differences between the two models allowed the Clarendon to have chrome-plated bumpers, a sliding steel sunroof, leather upholstery, safety glass, a luggage grid at the rear of the car and a double windscreen wiper. Of the final extra it seems ludicrous sixty years after the appearance of the car the passenger in the cheaper model was not allowed the privilege of having the windscreen cleared in rain. The safety aspect did not seem to occur to car manufacturers of the day. The dashboard was a vast improvement over the previous Citroën models; all the instruments were grouped together in a central console to the left of the driver with dials provided for speedometer, petrol gauge, oil pressure, ammeter and clock, in addition, switches controlled ignition, slow running, starter motor and choke. On the right of the steering column a switch enabled the driver to turn off the petrol supply from the fuel tank, which was mounted in the scuttle, or to switch-over to the reserve petrol tank in the case of a low fuel situation. The steering of these cars was remarkably light and certainly light enough to allow the steering wheel to be held with one hand and continue driving with ease. Likewise, the gear change was exceptionally smooth and it was suggested that 'lazy' drivers had not the need to declutch when changing down a gear when the speed of the car was under 15 m.p.h.! The cruising speed of the car was higher than earlier models, this was now 45 miles an hour — the days of faster transport having arrived. Having increased general speeds the necessity had arisen to fit more efficient brakes with better stopping power and the Westinghouse servo system proved its worth. On a test where it was required to hold the vehicle on the handbrake only whilst on a steep hill no fault with the system could be found and the braking system was praised in enabling the car to stop without skidding with just the handbrake in use. Tests on comparable cars showed their handbrake systems not nearly so smooth and efficient as the Citroën's. When viewed collectively, the number of innovations and aids installed on these models amounted to a car giving unequalled ease of control to the driver.

If the Chiltern and Clarendon models of the Citroën range represented a high degree of motoring, the six-cylinder Buckingham and Berkeley were the ultimate in engineering and luxury. All the features of the four-cylinder cars could be found in these models but in more elaborate form. *The Autocar* were emphatic about the six-cylinder saloons – 'comfort, roominess and satisfying performance of a car which is remarkable value.' With a car of such modern conception as the two six-cylinder models, it is strange that the old-fashioned layout of the foot pedals were employed. Instead of the accelerator pedal being positioned to the right of the clutch and foot brake it was still centred between the two with the clutch pedal on the left and the brake to the right. The reason for this given by Citroën was that 'clumsy' drivers did not risk depressing two pedals at the same time! It is rather surprising therefore when taking into account the number of futuristic devices found on the cars that this principle was still retained. By the end of 1931, however, Citroën conformed to the practice being adopted by most other European manufacturers and fitted the brake and accelerator pedals the opposite way round. For driver and front passenger comfort the big Citroëns were unsurpassed, the seats were deep and comfortable with the Buckingham being trimmed in cloth whilst the Berkeley had the luxury of finest leather — referred to at that time as 'furniture hide'. The seats were not only adjustable fore and aft but also had reclining backrests, then very unusual. The rear seats were also very well appointed, arm rests were provided and the rear passenger was afforded the utmost leg room and vision from the large window area, even a roller blind which was operated by the driver was provided for extra comfort. The sunroof, it was claimed, was large enough to allow ventilation almost to the same degree to that of an open tourer.

The 2442cc engine gave absolute effortless motoring. The torque was so great that it was unusual, apart from moving off, that the two intermediate gears should be used; the six-cylinder engine could pull the car from walking pace to high cruising speed with very little effort but naturally it was advantageous to use the gears to obtain a good burst of speed when accelerating from slow running or when tackling a steep hill. The control panel of the 6 cylinder was almost a replica to that fitted on the four cylinder cars, the large steering wheel had a ring-switch that when turned operated the headlights, sidelights and beam dipping mechanism. From the driving seat there was a good view over the long tapering bonnet, all the instruments were easy to read and generally the switchgear was set out for ease of use. The Buckingham, as with the Chiltern, had only one windscreen wiper, two wipers being reserved for the de-luxe models. One anomaly appears to be the positioning of the second windscreen wiper switch on de-luxe cars which was placed at the extreme left hand side of the dashboard, to switch the second wiper on, the driver who did not have a passenger to operate the switch had to lean precariously across the car. It could not be helped but think the windscreen wipers were an afterthought and with the British climate these should have been an essential part of the equipment. Night driving by now had become an accepted part of motoring, the Citroën's headlamps were powerful and gave a brilliant beam of light. Such was the design of the car and the thought in general Citroën engineers had given to these models that even with the lights on full beam there was ample surplus of charge from the dynamo. In all respects the Six Cylinder was an ideal touring machine.

During the days of the early 1930's, working at the Citroën factory on Slough's Trading Estate was considered to be a good job, a boy leaving school at the age of fourteen could expect to earn the grand sum of 5d an hour for a forty eight hour week. Although in today's terms 2p an hour, one advantage of working with Citroën meant that the factory operated a five day week whereas most other factories had a 5½ or even a six day week. On a Friday, the young man queued up to collect his wages — £1.00. There was much more involved at working at Citroën than purely assembling cars, machinery employed on the assembly lines had to be maintained to the highest standards otherwise production of cars would have most certainly suffered. Once the vehicles had rolled off the lines a great deal more work was involved before the car was ready to be despatched to the agent or customer and with the advent of more sophisticated models, the procedures for building and testing cars varied from time to time. With the 12.8 h.p. and six-cylinder cars it was found to be advantageous to fit special wooden truck-type bodies to the chassis once it had been completed, this was then driven out of the chassis shop and given a thorough road testing before the steel body was married up to the chassis. These strange half-completed vehicles were taken out of the works on the Trading Estate and driven along country lanes surrounding the area to the nearby village of Burnham via the Dropmore Road and back to the factory. The sight of the Citroëns with their special wooden framework sitting on the chassis platform was a common scene around the area and at least it was a good advertisement for the car. Once back inside the factory, the wooden bodies were removed and fitted to the next car for the same test requirement. On the journey, the test driver was obliged to takes notes of any defect and these were rectified in the faults shop before the chassis was re-entered to the bodyshop for the fitting of the all-steel body. As soon as the cars were completed with full inspections carried out they were driven to large storage sheds to await delivery to the agent; there were times when the period between manufacture and delivery was of longer duration than normal and on these occasions the road wheels of the new cars were removed and wooden disc wheels fitted in their place. This was to ensure that, during storage, the tyres did not become damaged or warping occur. In addition, all the chromium plated parts of the cars were covered in grease to protect the bright parts, batteries were also removed to avoid discharge or leakage affecting the new vehicle. As soon as the car was sold, two mechanics whose job it was to prepare the car for delivery, drove out to the storage sheds which were situated behind the Citroën works, to fit the road wheels and battery, cleaned off the grease and get the car started. It was seldom a car did not start first time even when it had been in store for some considerable time. The storage buildings were quite a landmark, they were no more than huge Nissen-type huts and stood on several acres of ground.

Although much of the car was built from British materials, the cars were based on the general design as directed from Paris. Chassis members were sent to Slough from the Javel factory and these often arrived with large areas heavily tarnished with red surface rust. Not only had the steel panels been stored in the open in France but also they had come across the English Channel as deck cargo

Completed cars being driven out of the final inspection shop on their way to the delivery sheds. The photograph shows the six-light, long wheelbase 13/30 Saloons and emphasises the extensive proportions of the Citroën Factory at Slough. The cars would have already had their road test with any minor adjustments and faults rectified on their return in the finishing shop.

and suffered further exposure at both French and English ports. Before the chassis members could be used in manufacture for cars at Slough, the rust had to be completely cleaned off and treated. Boys having joined the Citroën Company from school always without fail were given this most disliked task; there was, therefore, many a young man looking for alternative employment within a year from starting work at the company.

In Britain in 1931, there was still some novelty in purchasing a quality car complete in every detail ready for the road; there were manufacturers still offering a chassis only onto which could be installed a special hand-built body designed for that particular platform. Of the coach builders there were a number of respected names, one of which was Weymann of Addlestone, in Surrey. There was therefore a section of the car buying market that cared little for having a car ready-built, ready-to-run and mass-produced. In order to capture at least some of the sales in this respect, a number of chassis were built at Slough with this purpose in mind and a contract was signed by Weymann to supply hand made coachbuilt bodies. During 1931 Citroën published a catalogue containing details of Weymann-bodied cars based upon the 12.8 h.p. and 2½ litre six-cylinder chassis. The cars, quite naturally were very distinctive, mechanically the same as standard Slough built cars and sharing in general the same frontal treatment but having traditional wire-spoked wheels instead of the normal disc type. Four models were offered; 12.8 h.p. four-cylinder 2-door Sportsman's Coupé at £230 contrasting with the smaller-engined Rover 10/25 Weymann Sportsman's Coupé at £185 (£5 extra for the facility of a sliding roof); four-cylinder, 4-door 12.8 h.p. saloon at £240; 6-Cylinder 2½ litre Sportsman's Coupé, two door, selling at £275 and the 6-Cylinder four-door saloon costing £280. The Weymann bodied cars were more of a sporting nature and streamlined in appearance than standard production cars, the 12.8 Sportsman's Coupé had a trunk or 'boot' fitted at the rear and to this was attached the spare wheel. The Six Cylinder Coupé did not have a separate trunk at the rear but the body at the tail of the car was contoured to suggest that access to the 'built-in' trunk was available from inside the car. The spare wheel was attached to the tail as in the other models. Both of the four-door saloons were fitted with a trunk but this was of smaller dimensions to that of the 12.8 h.p. coupé. The Weymann bodies were wooden and as such should not be confused with early models of Citroën before the appearance of the all-steel saloon. The body was designed to be flexible in as much that it was built to give and so allowing the main frame to flex without causing damage, this being achieved by the unique construction. The cars were finished in a black pebble-grain fabric finish attributed particularly to Weymann. It is said, however, that André Citroën had a dislike for this particular type of coachwork. The interior of the cars were representative of the de-luxe finish; chromium plating, the use of safety glass, leather upholstery and the provision of an illuminated and comprehensively equipped dashboard was standard throughout. There is no doubt that the design of the bodies were very attractive and graced the Citroën chassis most successfully. For the relatively little extra money it can be seen that these cars were of excellent value and presented a tasteful image for the marque as a whole and as a flagship to the range of cars represented at the prestige New Devonshire House Showroom. Alas there are no records available as to the exact numbers of Weymann bodied cars that were supplied and regretfully very few cars have survived. Owning a 6-cylinder four-door Weymann Saloon was paramount to having one of the finest cars available of the period and there was very little to compare it with.

Complimenting the range of four and six cylinder cars, there was also available the seven seater saloon; this was referred to as the 'Family' model, even years later high passenger capacity cars of the Citroën marque retained the term 'Familiale'. The seven seat cars were available with both engine options, however, the company always seemed rather reticent regarding this model, very little advertising appeared and the literature that did come to light, little enough details were shown, not even the price and it appears the car was built to special order only.

British car manufacturers were keen to offer their vehicles with special bodies similar in principle to the Weymann bodies fitted to the Citroën chassis. At about the same time as the Sportsman's Coupé and Saloons appeared, Austin announced a special-bodied version of

The Weymann-bodied Citroën 20 h.p. Six-Cylinder Saloon. The highly respected coachbuilding firm of Weymann at Addlestone, Surrey, had signed a contract with Citroën to supply a number of hand-built cars on the Citroën chassis. The bodies, constructed in wood (not to be confused with early Citroëns manufactured before the advent of the all-steel saloon), were designed to be flexible so that the chassis frame could flex without causing any damage or squeaks in the body structure. This 1929 example demonstrates the sporting design of the body and the black pebble-grain fabric finish. The price of the car in 1929 was £280.

The Weymann-bodied 2½-Litre Six-Cylinder Sportsman's Coupé. This two-door model was particularly attractive, finished in traditional black pebble-grain fabric material. The interior was finished in the finest quality red leather and, to match it, the car was finished with a red coachline and red wire-spoked wheels. The Weymann Sportsman Coupés were constructed to make the best use of power, eliminating superficial weight and it was claimed that the car could quickly reach over 60 m.p.h. without even a hint of bodywork rattle.

The CITROËN
2½-Litre SIX
The SPORTSMAN'S COUPÉ (Genuine Weymann)

Length approx. - - 13 ft. 7½ ins.
Width   ,,   - - 5 ft. 3½ ins.
Height   ,,   - - 5 ft. 9 ins.

their 16 h.p. saloon. In design there was a strong resemblance to the Citroën, the former having the look of a much more dated machine to the latter. Both cars had luxury trim and the finest driver comforts, however, the price was of considerable difference—the Austin sold at £405 whilst the Weymann bodied Citroën ranged from £230 and £280. Such is proof of the excellent value of the Citroën at very much lower prices than many other cars.

Towards the end of the year an invisible cloak was thrown around the illustrious car manufacturers of the world. The workforce were busy and much hurrying to and fro took place, the reason for all the secrecy and extra work was the nearness of the great shows, the Paris Salon and British Motor Show at Olympia. Always held in the Autumn to stimulate sales when the demand was traditionally at the lowest ebb, this was the motor industry's busiest time. Citroën was no exception. At the end of 1931, the following year's models were being prepared to make their impact on the Citroën stand, new models and designs were on the drawing boards, the press and the car buying public were anxious to see what Citroën were going to do next. Already during the year in other parts of the world, André Citroën had blazoned his name throughout country after country; Citroën was as famous as ever. The great entrepreneur needed this extra boost; he had made bad friends with the gigantic banking group the Banque Lazard, this was not a wise move especially in the light of the recession France was beginning to face,

unemployment was increasing at a steadily alarming rate and the motor industry was always one of the first to suffer the effects of such a crisis.

The 'Rosalie' affair was to put Citroën in a much healthier position, this was a tremendous publicity event which, strangely enough was not of Citroën's doing and at first was quite against the whole business. Naturally, when he saw the situation going his way, Citroën changed his mind somewhat rapidly. The Rosalie affair was a spectacular demonstration of endurance for the Citroën C6; Yacco, the French oil company purchased a standard model from the production line and fitted a racing body to it, the idea was to break the world long-distance endurance record. This had been set up in 1930 by Voisin on the Montlhery race track on the outskirts of Paris, the car had travelled 50,000 kilometres. Since new regulations had come into force, no spare parts other than those considered essential and that could be carried on the car were allowed, also the tools to fit such parts could only be carried aboard the car. On 5th March, 1931, the Citroën car launched into action to take the world record. The test consisted of the car running non-stop except for the re-filling of petrol, oil and water and change of driver. A relay of five drivers took the wheel of the car throughout day and night and to observe the test six officials of the Automobile Club de France acted as timekeepers and a further five officials supervised the whole operation. The Rosalie smashed the world record and by 14th April the car passed the 100,000

To celebrate the success of the Rosalie, Cesar Merchand autographed this photo, following the car's achievement at the Montlhery Race Circuit. Yacco, the French oil company, had put a racing body on a standard Citroën chassis with the idea of breaking the world long-distance endurance record set up by Voisin in 1930 with the car running some 50,000 kilometres. On 5th March 1931, the Rosalie set off; a relay of five drivers ensured the Citroën carried on non-stop apart from changes of driver and refuelling. The event was scrutinised by six officials of the Automobile Club de France. The Rosalie smashed through the world record in mid-April, 100,000 kilometres were passed. The endurance run ended on the 29th April, after 136,083 kilometres in fifty-four days. During 1933, another attempt was made in a different car and the record smashed again, 300,000 kilometres in thirty-one days.

Citroën Kegresse half-track vehicles en route to Peking via the Gobi Desert and Himayla Mountains. The 'Yellow Raid' (Croisiere Jaune) was the third major expedition carried out by Citroën vehicles led by Georges-Marie Haardt and Louis Audouin-Dubreuil. Fourteen Citroën half-tracks and forty men set out to cross some of the most inhospitable country in the world. Between April 1931 and February 1932, the party travelled some 7,500 miles, some of the journey through the Himalayas carried the party up to heights of 13,000 feet on no more than a mule track. On more than one occasion the vehicles had to be dismantled to cross ledges only half the width of the vehicles. The fact that the expedition arrived in Peking is a miracle and a tribute to Citroën engineering.

kilometre limit. Over 60,000 miles had been driven, the Rosalie, however, had not stopped. André Citroën, who at first had been against the idea of his cars entering racing competitions was delighted with the result. The French nation were wild with excitement, the press helped whip up public support and enthusiasm and crowds swarmed to the race track to see the car. So impressed was Citroën that he consented to allow the car to continue its marathon, so on went the car day and night without a stop. Then on 29th April the distributor arm snapped, it was made of a moulded material and the item had worn itself out. Race officials authorised that a replacement part could be fitted under the terms of the test, alas the required part had not been packed into the spares kit. The race was over. Since the start of the endurance test a total of 136,083 kilometres had been driven in fifty-four days. Citroën, the press and the people of France were ecstatic, what better proof of reliability. The affair was not over, Citroën published the retail repair charge for the replacement of the failed part in the distributor assembly, the account came to 168F 40c (old Francs); Yacco had achieved probably the best public relations exercise ever. Later in 1933, a different version of the Rosalie went on again to smash this last record by achieving 300,000 kilometres in thirty one-days.

Also in 1931 André Citroën entered another huge publicity event and again like the Rosalie affair it had a profound impact around the world, not least Britain where the recent Rosalie marathon had been watched with a lot of interest if not with some amusement. There had been a considerable boost in attention to the Citroën car and as a consequence there had been an increase in sales of the car. Between April 1931 and February 1932 fourteen Citroën Kegresse half-track vehicles together with forty men took part in an expedition to re-establish a link between the Mediterranean and the China Sea following Marco Polo's footsteps over the 'Silk Road'. Led by Georges-Maries Haardt and Louis Audouin-Dubreuil of the Trans-Africa Expedition of 1924-25 the famous 'Yellow-Cruise' or 'Croisiere Jaune' had to encounter two huge barriers, the Gobi Desert and the Himalaya Mountains. Split into two parties the expedition covered over 7000 miles, the conditions were nothing but horrific; the vehicles were taken over tracks that crumbled beneath them leaving the Citroëns suspended precariously over ravines and sheer cliff faces, on some occasions the vehicles had to be dismantled, carried piece by piece and re-assembled before the party could continue. Where the path dropped away into abyss the road was rebuilt before the expedition could continue. Temperatures as low as -40C were experienced — yet the exploration party got through. The journey is acclaimed to be one of the greatest expeditions of all time and is a tribute to the vehicles and the men they carried.

The largest four-cylinder engine produced by Citroën to date was fitted in the Big Twelve Saloon De Luxe. The 1767cc engine became renowned for its sturdy but smooth operation and the car offered exceptional comfort and ride with a high level of trim. The Big Twelve and its stablemate, the Twenty, were well received at the 1931 London Motor Show; The Twelve De Luxe sold for £225 (the standard Saloon £30 less) and the Twenty cost £295. The photograph shows a particularly well preserved example which, in De Luxe form, had as standard specification a sliding sun roof, front window louvres, fine quality leather upholstery and full carpeting. The standard saloon did not have the sun roof or the front bumpers and in general the specification was not as comprehensive.

Chapter six: The end of an era

By the time of the 1931 London Motor Show, Citroën had been building cars at the Slough Factory for seven years, during which period they had enhanced their reputation for the manufacture of quality cars. The marketing emphasis was not on the car's French origin but the fact that the vehicles were British built using entirely British labour. Had Citroën decided not to set up a British manufacturing plant the sales story might have been completely different. The Rosalie affair had been well reported and it was this success story that helped give the name of Citroën a further boost to the credibility it had already achieved. There was no wonder, therefore, the 1932 models at Olympia were the concern of much interest and the Company's two newest models, the Big Twelve and the Twenty were the stars of the show.

The Big 12 with its horse power rating of 13.9 was the largest four-cylinder car produced by Citroën to date. The 1767cc engine was a slow revving unit, extremely sturdy and smooth in operation with the maximum engine speed reduced from 3000 r.p.m. from its 12.8 h.p. forerunner to 2700 r.p.m. A number of modifications were made to the body styling over its predecessor and the interior trim benefited from an even more luxurious finish. Until now, the body styling of both four and six cylinder cars closely resembled each other but now the Twenty was easily distinguishable by its new design of bodywork. The latest models did share one common factor in that both cars received a longer wheelbase which allowed greater comfort to driver and passenger alike. The range of models consisted a number of versions and body styles as follows: Big 12, four cylinder saloon £195; de luxe saloon £225; seven seat de luxe saloon £245; fixed-head four-seat coupé and the drop-head two-seat coupé with dickey both at £225 and the Sportsman's saloon with luggage trunk at £265. A chassis only was also available for the fitting of a special body and this could be purchased for £160 and £170 respectively for the short or long wheelbase variant. The 2650cc 20.8 horse power six-cylinder Twenty was available in the following versions: chassis only, £200 for short wheelbase and £210 for the long wheelbase; saloon £295; long wheelbase saloon £315; seven seat saloon £320; limousine £335 with the seven seat version for a further £5; Sportsman's saloon with trunk £345; fixed head four-seat coupé and the drop head coupé with dickey £295; roadster £345 and the town car £450.

There was a good deal of activity within the Citroën company as a whole; whilst the London Motor Show was in progress André Citroën, accompanied by his wife, was on his way to America aboard the German trans-Atlantic liner 'Europa'. Together they were to visit the country Citroën had not seen since 1912. Whilst in America, André Citroën met Henry Ford for whom he had a great respect and took a lot of interest in the manufacturing methods of the company. Citroën, as an admirer of Ford, respected his techniques and was justly impressed with the size of the huge Ford empire. In many ways Citroën was overwhelmed with Ford's ideas; one thing he did not realise was the climate of America at the time, the country was still very young, it was the land of unlimited expansion. Europe was different. The gigantic workshops belonging to the Ford factories stood on ground measured in square miles rather than acres, and thus contrasting

"Big 12" De Luxe Saloon
with Sliding Roof   £225

"Twenty" 7-Seater De Luxe Saloon with Sliding Roof   £320
Limousine 5-Seater De Luxe with Partition   £335
Limousine 7-Seater De Luxe with Partition, and
Folding Seats as above   £340

The Big Twelve and the Twenty for 1931/2. The two cars can be easily identified by the bonnet which, on the six-cylinder Twenty model is longer and has opening ports whilst the four-cylinder has plain louvres. The solid disc wheels of the Twenty give the car a much more sturdy appearance than the spoked wheels of the Big Twelve but note also the deeper bumpers on the cheaper car. Sidelights positioned on the wings of the Twelve appear on the scuttle of the Twenty and note the occasional seats on the 7-seater model. Both types had engines of 75 x 100mm bore and stroke, the Twenty's capacity being 2650cc.

greatly with Javel on the banks of the River Seine which were considered huge in terms of other motor plants within Europe. Citroën returned from America with his head full of ideas and whilst his eyes had seen many visions, his bankers cared little for his futuristic plans. Still intent upon his extravagant advertising and publicity campaigns, Citroën continued his programme of opening luxurious showrooms and sumptuous offices; they were far too grand and out of place for the purpose they were to serve. During 1933, a magnificent banquet was thrown in the Javel works with nearly seven thousand guests in attendance. A terrible blow befell Citroën in 1932; his close friend and loyal ally Georges-Maries Haardt, famous for his direction of the Trans Africa expedition by Citroën vehicles and just recently the Croisiere Jaune, died of double pneumonia caused by a malignant fever whilst in Hong Kong.

Back in Britain, the latest Citroëns were well received, especially the Big Twelve. Motoring journalists were very well impressed with the features of the cars and noted with pleasure the almost exceptional ride and comfort. The Big 12 with its big brother, the Twenty, were without doubt handsome machines; the publicity department at Brook Green had done a good job producing some excellent brochures of the cars which demonstrated their lines admirably. Many of the photographs that appeared in the manufacturer's bulletins depicting the cars quite often showed the vehicles in the care of young women — this may have been to demonstrate that liberated women drove liberated cars! If the cars were handsome when seen from a general and side view, they had the attributes of striking features when viewed from the front.

Although of upright appearance this gave the machine a sturdy look, the large radiator blended in with the lines well and the car's design was enhanced by having the spare wheel positioned neatly on the nearside just aft of the front wing. There were a number of differences between the variants of each of the Big Twelve and the Twenty models; the Big 12 De Luxe saloon was supplied with a full specification including sliding roof and wire spoked wheels whereas the standard saloon was less refined not having front or rear bumpers or the sliding roof; it was fitted with disc wheels instead of the more sporting wire wheels and it had only one windscreen wiper, the passenger's side unit being omitted. The seven-seat de luxe saloon together with the drop head coupé with dickey seat also had the benefit of wire wheels but all other models had the plain disc wheels. The six cylinder Twenty models were even more favoured with good looks, this was achieved by the fitting of five opening ports on the side of the bonnet adding to the longer appearance than the Big Twelve which had plain ventilation louvres. All the Twenty cars had disc wheels except the long wheelbase saloon and the drop head coupé which had wire spoke wheels. The bumper arrangement was also different, with the Twenty having a rather unique vee-shaped structure fitted to flexible mountings while the Twelve's retained the more usual chromed bar forming a cross member of the chassis.

In terms of driver and passenger comfort and convenience, excellent value for money was offered by the Twelve and Twenty. Throughout the British automobile market emphasis upon family cars concentrated on the facilities the bodywork offered. Citroën were of course leaders in providing the car with an all-steel body and pioneered the mass-produced vehicle ready to be sold as a complete package. This new concept in motoring naturally appealed to the ever-growing numbers of people who wanted to experience the joys and pleasures of owning a motor car. The list of features of the 12s and 20s was extensive; wide doors giving ease of access; leather upholstery of the finest quality; fully adjustable seats confirming even greater comfort, arm rests for the passengers and full carpeting. The six side windows of the saloon models gave the interior of the cars a light and pleasant atmosphere and the provision of a sliding roof was a welcome compromise between comfortable enclosed all-weather motoring against the thrill of driving an open car. De Luxe saloons were provided with louvres on the two front windows preventing draughts but allowing at the same time fresh air to enter the car, at the top of the windscreen a blue-tinted visor eliminated glare when driving into the sun. Another aspect that won favour with motorists was the facility of the opening windscreen. The driving position gave the feeling of having complete control over the car, indeed, the driving controls were extremely well placed and Citroën boasted their full specification. Lighting and horn controls were situated in the centre of the steering wheel where they were easy to use, to the left of the steering wheel the handbrake was easily located and adjacent to it the gearchange lever. The three-speed gearbox was smooth enough, first gear needed only to be applied when starting from rest or when negotiating the steepest of hills, normally second gear could be used for all other gradients but in general the top ratio had excellent torque which often avoided the need to change down during normal driving. The accelerator pedal, in Citroën tradition, was still positioned between the clutch and footbrake, Citroën not yet entirely giving way to the American formula of having the accelerator to the right of the footbrake. The bucket seats were very much admired for their ample comfort and deep cushions, this was a feature long admired with Citroën cars and a feature they were to retain and today acknowledged. The design of the instrument panel was changed from that found on the 12.8 h.p. models; the new concept of a rectangular panel set in the centre of the fascia and housing individual dials was very much art-deco, the speedometer, ammeter, clock, fuel and oil pressure gauges were all neatly contained and, below the panel, switches for ignition, starter and choke (referred to at the time as the strangler) were arranged in easy reach of the driving position. On the extreme left of the fascia panel a glove box provided storage for small articles, a rather dubious ashtray was placed just to the right of the passenger and meant a long stretch across the car if the driver smoked; needless to say it would have been better placed for a left hand drive car!

The Big Twelve was no slouch of a car. Whilst it could boast of a maximum speed of 58 miles per hour—60 m.p.h. with a following wind—the car was able to keep up extremely good average speeds over long distances. On a journey from Stamford to North London (this must have been a favourite testing route!), a distance of 82 miles, the trip was undertaken in one hour fifty-five minutes; for 1932 that was not a bad effort. The 1767cc engine had a speed of 2700 r.p.m., a decrease of 300 r.p.m. over the previous four cylinder engine, an unusual move as the trend was for manufacturers to fit higher revving engines; despite the reduction in engine speed more power was obtained from

Citroën continued to use the slightly strange pedal configuration with the accelerator pedal positioned between the clutch on the left and the foot brake on the right. It was not until 1933 that Citroën changed to the standard practice of accelerator on the right.

the unit, this allowed an alteration to the top gear ratio which was now 4.8:1. The engine had undergone quite substantial modification, the objective was to even smoother running and many drivers likened the feel of the motor to a six-cylinder machine. Citroën's claim to the Big 12 De Luxe was 'Better than a small six'. New aluminium pistons were fitted, each with four rings, the cylinder barrels were offset to a slight degree in order to minimise side thrust and wear on the cylinder walls. The crankshaft bearings were made to a greater diameter and also fitted was a vibration damper at the front of the three-bearing crankshaft, it was quite unusual to find this facility on a four cylinder unit especially as it was of the frictional type. The carburettor had been modified and Solex had redesigned the unit to accept a better choke enabling the engine to start easier from cold. A much improved cooling system was fitted, apart from a redesigned water pump, the system received a larger radiator as well as a belt driven cooling fan. Numerous other modifications were made to the car, a more powerful starter motor was substituted and the distributor had an automatic advance and retard of the centrifugal type. The handbrake still operated on the transmission with the brake acting on the propeller shaft just to the rear of the gearbox; front springs were longer than on the previous model and were aimed at giving a more comfortable ride. One of the main changes concerned the chassis, the Big 12 was three inches longer than the 12.8 h.p. model it replaced, the track being 4ft. 8in. and the wheelbase 9ft. 1½in. Due to the longer chassis a larger body was permitted allowing more room inside the car and it was possible to accommodate five people in absolute comfort.

The six-cylinder Citroën Twenty shared most of the modifications of the Big 12 and in all but the exceptional cases the six-cylinder cars were practically identical to their smaller-engined relatives apart from the power unit and resulting performance. In the case of the Twenty, however, a few differences are worthy of note. Tyres were of greater section to suit the extra weight and allowing for higher speeds; thermostatically operated chromium plated shutters were fitted to the radiator and scuttle-dash sidelamps were fitted to compliment the lighting system of the car. To record the importance of passenger comfort it is interesting to note the following passage from *Autocar* -:

'In both front and back compartments there is ample leg room and space for the biggest passenger, and even a tall man can wear a hat without bumping it on the roof over wavy road surfaces, there being comfortable room on the back seat for three people.'

Citroën were always keen to promote the 'family vehicle' and an extensive advertising campaign was undertaken to increase awareness of the seven-seater cars based upon the design of the Big 12 and its six-cylinder stablemate, the Twenty. Built upon the long wheelbase chassis which, at 10ft. 3in. was 6½in. longer than the standard chassis, the seven-seat de-luxe saloons, limousines and town cars were remarkably elegant and well proportioned. In terms of appearance the Twenty was more appealing being due to subtle differences in design; the bonnet had separately opening louvres instead of the fluted grille as found on the Big 12, the heavier looking disc wheels gave the car a solid and dependable look and the auxiliary lights on the scuttle at the base of the windscreen pillar had almost the air of officialdom. The interior of both cars were very well appointed and trimmed in highest quality leather. Auxiliary seats were installed between the front and rear seats, a benefit of the longer chassis allowed them not to interfere with the leg room and comfort of the rear passengers and indeed, passengers who travelled on the auxiliary seats found them to be quite comfortable providing also adequate leg room. When not in use, the occasional seats folded away into specially designed floor wells. The seven-seat cars were a favourite of larger families and were often specified by hire companies. There was on the market at that time no other manufacturer able to offer a similar car at anywhere near the prices Citroën were selling their machines—£245 for the Big 12 version and £320 for the Six-Cylinder Twenty.

"Fashionable yet inexpensive" were the words Citroën used to describe this exquisite motor car. The Twenty Town Car was an admirable Coupé de Ville providing every comfort. It could be supplied in any colour to the customer's choice with upholstery matching the colour scheme of the coachwork. The driver's compartment had a separate canopy for bad weather; the carriage interior was fitted with a dictagraph and ladies companion, two occasional seats folded away against the driver's partition. Thermostatically-controlled chromium-plated radiator shutters were another new feature.

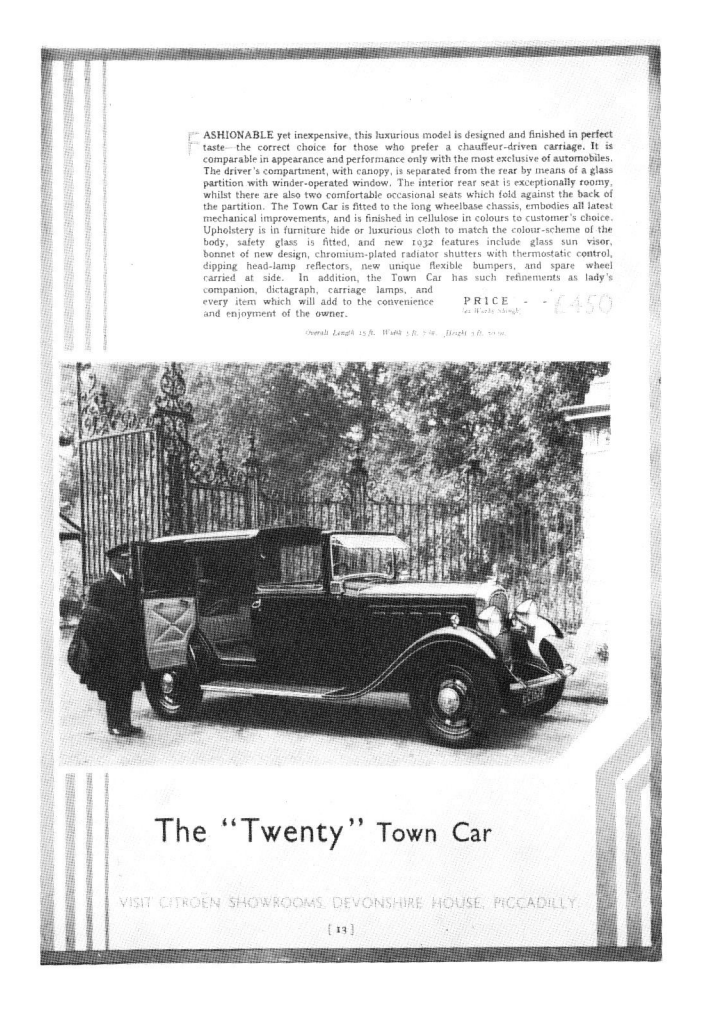

TRAVELLER'S BROUGHAM (Convertible Saloon).

MOUNTED on the long wheelbase (9 ft. 9¼ in.) chassis of the "BIG 12" 4-Cylinder, the Traveller's Brougham is a most ingenious dual-purpose car. All-steel coachwork, Bendix Duo-Servo 4-wheel brakes and rear petrol tank are standard, whilst "De-Luxe" equipment includes safety glass, bumpers, dipping reflectors, spare wheel at side, etc., etc. Cellulose finish and chromium plating for bright external parts. Wire wheels or discs optional, with large hubs.

Citroën based some commercial vehicle models upon the Big Twelve chassis and offered the Travellers Brougham as a 'convertible saloon'. The interior, finished in repp or leathercloth upholstery, was designed for rough usage and the rear seat, being easily removable, allowed a flat floor for loading; side advertising panels bolted on to the car transforming it into a van but removing them gave the appearance of a normal saloon.

As a light van for use by Commercial Travellers, this model is ideal, the entire space behind the driver being available for goods. Detachable advertisement panels can be supplied and are fixed in position by two removable bolts. Double opening doors at the rear provide immediate access to the interior.

When used as a passenger saloon, this vehicle has the normal appearance of a dignified private car. Upholstery is in repp or leather cloth to choice. To enable easy conversion for goods carrying, the rear seat and squab are easily removable, also the side squabs. The interior is panelled with plywood to withstand rough usage. A platform inserted between the front and rear seats gives a level loading line.

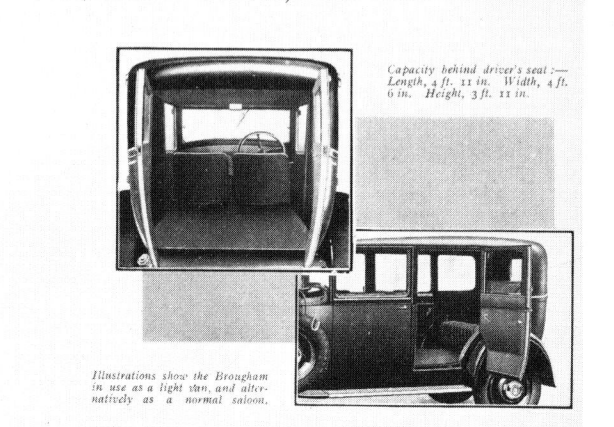

Capacity behind driver's seat:— Length, 4 ft. 11 in. Width, 4 ft. 6 in. Height, 3 ft. 11 in.

Illustrations show the Brougham in use as a light van, and alternatively as a normal saloon.

Citroën offered the cars in two colour schemes, black with the option of either a red or white coachline, or two-tone blue. Possibly the most attractive of all the seven-seat cars was the Twenty Town Car, this was a most graceful and refined automobile; it was fashionable yet inexpensive. Designed for those who preferred a chauffeur-driven carriage, the Town Car compared favourably with the most exclusive of motor cars. The driver's compartment, as with the de-ville style, was covered by a canopy but separated from the rear by means of a winding glass panel and in addition to refinements such as dictagraph and lady's companion, the interior was beautifully trimmed to match the colour scheme of the exterior and benefited from all the features found on the Twenty Saloon De Luxe. Two occasional seats were provided but instead of these folding down into the floor they folded back against the driver's partition. At £450, the Twenty Town Car represented outstanding value and finesse.

Citroën were not purely manufacturing motor cars at the Slough factory, they also had a considerable interest in building commercial vehicles, vans, lorries and coaches. The range of models was impressive and consisted of a Travellers Brougham, 25 cwt, 35 cwt and two-ton lorries, tractor and a six-wheeler as well as a 20-seat coach. The Citroën catalogue carried the following message:

'Citroën Commercial Vehicles are noted above all else for exceptional strength, sturdiness and reliability, and for an amazing capability to stand up to sheer hard work. They are in each case of much more robust construction and greater carrying capacity than the average vehicles of their type, whilst being at the same time very economical in operation. These vehicles are undoubtedly amongst the finest achievements of the Citroën Works at Slough, Buckinghamshire, where none but British labour is employed, and to which famous British suppliers furnish materials.'

The Traveller's Brougham, otherwise known as the Convertible Saloon, was designed as a dual purpose vehicle; based upon the long wheelbase version of the Big Twelve and receiving all the specification of that car in both standard and de luxe form, it could be converted from a most dignified private car to a commercial vehicle with the utmost ease. When used as a private car there was little to distinguish the interior of the Traveller's Brougham from the Big Twelve apart from the upholstery trim and panels, the seats being upholstered in repp, a corded textile fabric, or leathercloth, and the interior panels were overlaid with plywood to sustain the hard wear expected from such a vehicle. For commercial use, the rear seats and side squabs were easily removable and with a platform inserted behind the front seats it was possible to utilise a perfectly flat floor over the entire length of the vehicle behind the driver and passenger. Double doors were provided at the rear of the body and advertising side panels could be fitted over the windows by means of just two fixing bolts. Also based upon the long wheelbase chassis of the Big Twelve, the 25 cwt Delivery Van offered a loading capacity of over 200 cubic feet; twin rear wheels were fitted to the back axle and needless to say, the sturdy chassis complimented the 25 cwt van very well. The 35 cwt commercials offered a far greater range than the smaller 25 cwt's, these were of course much more universal in as much that due to their size and capabilities they had wider appeal. All the models offered in the range were also available in 2-ton versions

PRODUCTS OF CITROËN WORKS

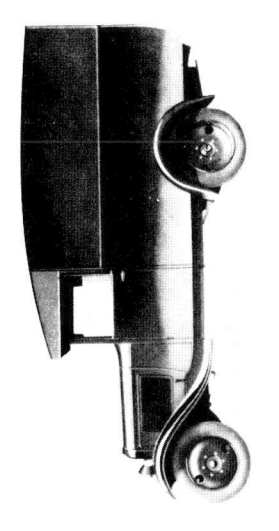

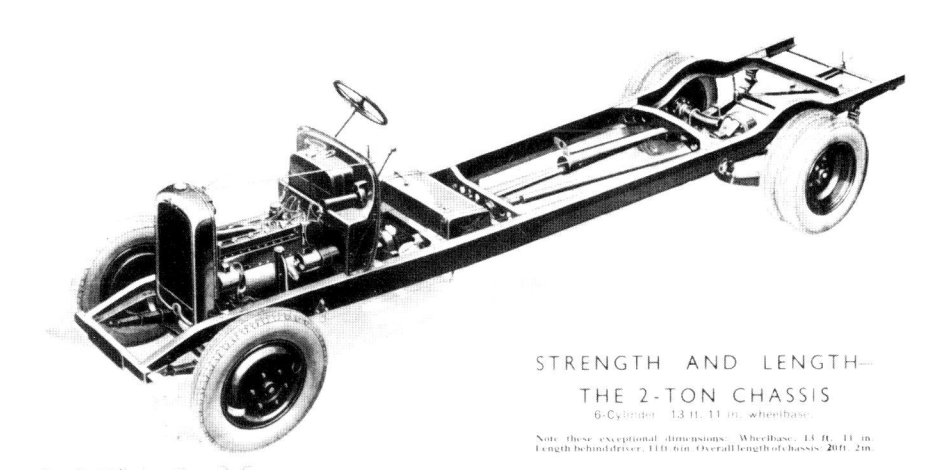

STRENGTH AND LENGTH—
THE 2-TON CHASSIS
6-Cylinder 13 ft. 11 in. wheelbase.

Note these exceptional dimensions: Wheelbase, 13 ft. 11 in.; length behind driver, 11 ft. 6 in.; Overall length of chassis, 20 ft. 2 in.

2-TON & 35-cwt.

USERS' testimonials which can be seen on file prove that the 6-cylinder 35 CWT. Citroën has established for itself a remarkable reputation for dependability and economy, and for ability to withstand the hardest usage day in and day out. For those who require even greater carrying capacity, the 6-cylinder 2-TON model is now provided, and is assured of a wide market amongst discriminating users.

35 CWT.: 19.3 h.p. 6-cylinder engine, 72 mm. bore — 100 mm. stroke. Gear ratios: Top, 6.2 to 1; 3rd, 10.88 to 1; 2nd, 22.13 to 1; 1st, 41.8 to 1; reverse, 49.49 to 1. Wheelbase, 10 ft. 11 in.; track, 4 ft. 8 in. front, 4 ft. 10 in. rear; overall length, 16 ft. 11 in.; length behind driver, 8 ft. 3 in.; five wheels and four tyres 30 × 5 front, 32 × 6 rear; twin wheels and tyres supplied at extra cost.

2-TON: 20.8 h.p. 6-cylinder engine, 75 mm. bore — 100 mm. stroke, heavier frame, specially heavy banjo-type rear axle, new radiator. Gear ratios: Top, 6.83 to 1; 3rd, 12.74 to 1; 2nd, 24.08 to 1; 1st, 44.87 to 1; reverse, 53.84 to 1. Wheelbase, 13 ft. 11 in.; track, 5 ft.; overall length, 20 ft. 2 in.; body space, 15 ft. 3 in.; length behind driver, 11 ft. 6 in.; twin rear wheels; seven wheels and six tyres, 6.50-20, twin wheel equipment.

THE 25-cwt.

EXCEPTIONAL quality, durability and sturdiness distinguish this economical 25 cwt. vehicle, which embodies latest improved type 4-cylinder engine, 4-speed gear-box, Bendix Duo-Servo 4-wheel brakes and twin rear wheels and tyres. The 10 ft. 3 in. wheelbase and long frame ensure ample body space 7 ft. 8 in. behind driver the very attractive Delivery Van as illustrated having the unusually large interior capacity of 200 cubic feet.

LORRY WITH DROP SIDES.

This Lorry is ideal for general transport purposes. The body is well built, having drop sides and hinged tail board to facilitate speedy loading and unloading from either side or at the rear.

The driver's cab is totally enclosed with windows operated by winders fitted to both doors, and has very commodious seating accommodation.

DELIVERY VAN.

This commodious Van is suitable for large businesses or for the individual tradesman. Appearance in addition to utility has received careful study.

The driver's compartment has well-upholstered seats and is completely enclosed. Double doors at the rear open the full width of the body and greatly facilitate loading and unloading.

INTERIOR DIMENSIONS (35-cwt.)		OVERALL DIMENSIONS (35-cwt.)	
Length	8 ft.	Length	17 ft. 6 in.
Width	4 ft. 9 in.	Width	6 ft.
Height	5 ft.	Height	7 ft. 9 in.
Loading Height			2 ft. 9 in.
Weight			46 cwt. 2 qrs.

GENERAL PURPOSE VAN.

This Van is especially suitable for General Transport purposes where goods require protection, e.g. for Carriers, Bakers, Fruiterers, Furnishers, Laundries and Furniture Removers. It is strongly built of ash framing, the main panels being constructed of Plymax finished in weather resisting canvas.

A tailboard suspended on wrought-iron hinges with heavy tail chains and hooks facilitates loading. Canvas curtains above the tailboard extending to the floor provide complete weather protection. The body space is exceptionally large.

3-WAY HYDRAULIC TIPPING LORRY.

The illustration shows an easily operated Tipping Lorry which can be handled by one man. It is available either with three-way tipping gear or with an end-tipping gear only.

The sides and tailboard of both models can be dropped for speedy loading or unloading. The Driver's Cab is totally enclosed, and has winder-operated windows.

For 1932, the Slough Factory were able to offer a range of commercial vehicles from 25 cwt. through to two tons, tractor units and six-wheelers capable of carrying 3-4 ton loads as well as saloon coaches. The 25 cwt. van had a 10ft. 3in. wheelbase supporting a body with an interior capacity of 2000 cubic feet. The four-cylinder engine was the same as used in the Travellers Brougham. The 35cwt. and Two-Ton vehicles were powered by six-cylinder engines, the 35cwt. with the 19.3 h.p. unit and the 20.8 h.p. driving the Two-Tonner. Body styles included a lorry with drop sides, three-way hydraulic tipping lorry, delivery van and general purpose van.

UP to the present, the main difficulty of those who operate passenger-carrying services has been to find a luxury saloon coach of full-sized 20-seater capacity with the following features:—
(a) A really sturdy chassis of adequate capacity (not an adapted chassis).
(b) A body of modern design and construction, built by body-builders of high repute.
(c) A really reasonable price.

The Citroën 20-seater Saloon fulfils all these requirements.

The exceptional resources of the Citroën factories make it possible for this vehicle to be offered at the

LOWEST PRICE OF ANY 20-SEATER ON THE MARKET

An entirely New Standard of Value in Luxury Coaches!

£495

(CHASSIS £250)

POWERFUL 6-CYLINDER ENGINE
FOUR-SPEED GEAR BOX
DUO-SERVO 4-WHEEL BRAKES
HYDRAULIC SHOCK ABSORBERS, FRONT & REAR
ELECTRIC LIGHTING AND STARTING
TWIN REAR WHEELS AND TYRES
WHEELBASE 13 ft. 11 ins.
ROOMY SALOON BODY
REAL LEATHER UPHOLSTERY
PROVED PERFORMANCE

20-SEATER CITROËN SALOON COACH

A splendid proposition for City, Suburban, Country or Seaside Services.
A Luxury Coach embodying the latest road coach features at an amazing price.

The Citroën 20-seat bus (its description as a coach is a bit of a euphamism) offered in Britain as part of the 1932 range was based on the Slough-built 2-ton 13ft. 11ins. wheelbase chassis with modification to make it suitable for passenger-carrying work — the petrol tank was repositioned from the goods version position under the driver's seat, for example. The ash-framed body was of similar design to those being offered on competitive chassis and its style makes it seem probable that it was built for Citroën by one of the British firms specialising in such work.

Although vehicles of similar general pattern were favoured by numerous small operators especially in the more rural areas and the Citroën offered exceptional value at its £495 price complete, only a few were sold. The market leader was the Bedford WLB model introduced by the Vauxhall concern a year earlier, of which the chassis price was £265, or £15 more than the Citroën, not dissimilar in character but aided by a well-developed sales network and a sense of continuity from the very successful Chevrolet, assembled in Britain by Vauxhall from 1929.

although a different engine was used. The power units were both of six cylinders, the 35 cwt being fitted with the 2442cc 19.3 h.p. engine as used in the Berkeley and Buckingham Saloons which had appeared in 1930/31 whilst the 2-ton versions received the later 2650cc six-cylinder 20.8 h.p. engine. The cars and the Traveller's Brougham were all fitted with three-speed gearboxes but the commercials of 25 cwt and over had four speeds. Twin rear wheels were fitted as standard to all commercials above 25 cwt. but strange as it may appear a spare wheel was supplied with the vehicle but without a tyre on it!

The 2-ton vehicles differed from the 35 cwt's in the design of the chassis, they benefited from a stronger and heavier frame with a heavy duty banjo-type rear axle which was able to cope with the larger and heavier loads it would be required to carry. The range of 2-ton commercials consisted of a delivery van, general purpose van, lorry with drop sides and a three-way hydraulic tipping lorry. At the other end of the scale were the heavier vehicles, the Saloon Coach, Six-Wheeler and the Tractor unit, the two latter models being available in chassis form only. The heavier commercials, whilst based upon the two-ton chassis, were designed for three to four ton loads, again the 20.8 h.p. 2650cc engine was used with the gearbox and ratios the same as the two-ton version. The chassis of the six-wheeler was lengthened to accommodate the extra rear axle to which double cantilever rear springs were added. Increased engine cooling was necessary in order to deal with sustained engine use and lower road speeds resulting from heavier loads being carried. To effect the increased cooling requirements a four-bladed fan provided additional air flow over the large surface-area radiator. Citroën went to great lengths to emphasise the capabilities of the six-wheeler, the sales brochure of the time commented:

'After exhaustive tests by the Research Department of the Factory, this chassis has been produced and perfected to exclusive Citroën designs. It is a properly designed six-wheeler, not an adaptation or extension, and has, therefore, definite advantages over the ordinary vehicles of its type on the market.' The wheelbase of the six-wheeler measured 15ft. 5in. and the length behind the driver to the end of the frame an impressive 14ft. 9in.; to assist the heavier loads the double rear axle was fitted with a reduction gear device. The Tractor was also fitted with the same 2650cc engine and shared many of the features of the six-wheeler, the main difference was the chassis with a much shorter wheelbase at 9ft. 4½in. while the rear axle had twin wheels and reduction gear but also had the facility of an automatic trailer attachment mechanism. The track at the front was 4ft. 11in. and 5ft. 1in. at the rear, a three-seat cab model was available but at extra cost. The load capacity of the tractor unit was calculated to be five tons so was capable of most road haulage activities of the era.

One of the most interesting vehicles in the Citroën range had to be the Passenger Coach. This could be provided in chassis form only allowing the operator to fit bodywork of their choice, alternatively, Citroën could supply the coach ready for service in standard body form. The loading capacity of twenty seats was quite adequate in size and in terms of passenger comfort which was excellent. The seating provided was trimmed in leather; four windows of large glass area were fitted each side, three of which were adjustable for ventilation by winding mechanism, and on these louvres allowed the glass to be lowered without causing draughts. At the rear of the coach a single emergency door was provided whilst a folding door at the front on the nearside opposite the driver gave normal access. It is interesting to note that a 'one-man operation' device, similar in principle to that found on today's buses, was fitted. There were several features on the vehicle that were attractive to the coach and bus operator alike — interior lighting, passenger buzzer, centre gangway, roof ventilation, destination indicator, fire extinguisher, first-aid kit and life guards. The fact that the Citroën coach was the cheapest of its type on the market did little to promote its sales to large operators. Citroën had hoped to sell the vehicle to major bus companies; instead they had to be content with the smaller business which often operated as little as one vehicle. At £495 the Citroën was certainly very competitive and it could be obtained in chassis form only for just £250. The mechanical specification was just as impressive as the body; either the 19.3 h.p. 2442cc engine or the 20.8 h.p. 2650cc unit could be specified, both chassis were fitted with the Delco-Remy battery and coil ignition with automatic advance and retard. The engine was constructed with aluminium pistons, four-bearing balanced crankshaft with integral countershaft weights and vibration damper, light steel connecting rods were lined with anti-friction metal. There was a four-bearing camshaft, forced fed lubrication and the cylinder head was detachable to facilitate decarbonisation. Cooling was enhanced by the four-blade fan in addition to the centrifugal water pump and large surface area radiator. Solex provided the carburetion, a single dry plate clutch was fitted and the gearbox had four forward speeds and reverse. Open type, Spicer pattern universal joints front and rear completed the transmission. The chassis frame was constructed as a channel section with very deep side members, these were well braced with seven pressed steel cross members; very strong semi-elliptic springs were installed throughout and hydraulic shock absorbers were fitted front and rear. The front axle was made up as an 'H' section from special steel, Timken roller-bearings were fitted to the front hubs. A banjo type rear axle with final drive by Gleason spiral bevel gears and Timken roller-bearings completed the specification. The brakes were of the mechanical duo-serve type operating on all four wheels with the transmission brake being hand operated. The electrical equipment consisted of headlamps, sidelamps, interior lighting, starter and horn as well as the passenger buzzer.

The Citroën commercials were never as popular in Britain as they were in France and other European countries. The opposition was fierce from British companies and it was considered that a French manufacturer, although British-based, specialising in motor cars would find it difficult to meet the requirements of British transport and bus service industries. Whilst a high proportion of medium-weight commercial vehicles were built by car manufacturers, some effort was put into giving them a separate identity by the use of different names, such as Bedford, Commer and Fordson for the products of Vauxhall, Rootes and Ford respectively. Sales campaigns could emphasize their rugged quality without risking the respective firms' cars being damaged by the 'trademan's vehicle' image, a significant factor in those days.

Floating Power

The motor industry in France and Britain were undergoing some growing pains; by 1932 petrol was costing between 2s.2d. (12p) and 2s.10d. (14p) per gallon and there was a general trend for cars to be designed with a lower consumption of fuel, as a consequence there was also a move towards a new ideology known as aerodynamism; upright bodies with square styling were being outmoded by softer, more rounded lines, longer flowing front wings and wheelarches were the vogue. Citroën had little heed for this, in fact there was evidence his cars were beginning to date. As a result to the approach to lower fuel consumption a new car was launched to coincide with the 1932 Paris Salon which opened on 6th October for ten days and ending on 16th. The car made its debut at the London Motor Show the same Autumn, on this occasion the car had been built at Slough. The new Citroën became known as the Ten. For 1933, the Big 12 and the Twenty models were to continue in production, the Ten, referred to as the Big Ten, filled a much wanted gap in the vehicle range with its 1452cc four cylinder engine. This engine is not to be confused with the unit fitted to the 11.4 h.p. model which had a cubic capacity of 1453cc, the new power unit with 68mm bore and 100mm stroke was mounted on completely flexible pads and followed the true 'Floating

The famous 'Floating Swan' symbol which appeared on Citroën cars employing the 'Floating Power' engine mounting. The concept of 'Floating Power' had been derived from the Chrysler Corporation and was fitted to Citroën cars under licence. Floating Power was a device which greatly reduced the transmission of vibration from the engine unit by utilising specially designed rubber blocks at the two mounting points of the power unit with the chassis. The radiator badge on cars fitted with the Floating Power engine also showed the elegant swan as well as the double chevrons, the wheel hubs proudly announcing the car's technical feature — note the French wording 'moteur flottant' on this example. The symbol was used as a marketing aide where, in France, wooden motifs depicting the swan on water were hung over Floating Power models and the motif was used to great emphasis in contemporary catalogues.

Power' engine design. So there would be no doubt about the new car's engine, a revised Citroën emblem was designed for this model. Whilst it incorporated the famous Double Chevron, the radiator badge depicted an elegant floating swan, the effect was without doubt immensely striking. The Floating Power symbol was maintained as a sales and marketing feature, special wooden motifs the same as the radiator emblem but very much larger were suspended over the cars in the larger Citroën agents' showrooms in France; in Britain the campaign took on a lower profile but the same technical message was portrayed through visual point of use advertising, the round symbol appeared in catalogues, Citroën driver's handbooks as well as on all magazine and newspaper advertisements. French models of cars received very attractive wheel hubs with the floating swan embossed upon them. The Citroën Ten appeared in the catalogue as three versions, the saloon selling at £198; drop head coupé at £195 and a fixed head coupé at £205. The saloon was a compact car utilising every amount of usable space. The front of the car received considerable attention, a new radiator with a plated grille sweeping down in shape to an obtuse vee was fitted, redesigned bumpers with the Citroën emblem in the centre gave protection to the front wings whilst side lamps appeared on the wings for the first time. The wide opening doors allowed easy access to the interior, four-light body design found favour in place of the six-light styling as previously but at the rear a substantial boot permitted a large amount of luggage to be stowed under dry conditions. The boot had two opening panels, one at the top which gave access to the tool kit and the lower panel which dropped down leaving room to pack suit cases and the like. The spare wheel was relocated from the nearside wing as on the Big 12 and Twenty models to be mounted on the drop down boot lid. Half bumpers were fitted at the rear so as not to be in the way of the spare wheel and tyre assembly. The opening port type of louvres of the Twenty were fitted to the Ten which enhanced its appearance considerably giving the car a sturdy and solid appearance.

The 'Floating Power' system created a great amount of comment within the motor industry; it will be recalled that this idea was first used in America by Chrysler and Citroën considered the principle to be of fine concept and so fitted the system under license from the Chrysler Corporation. The engine and gearbox were mounted to the chassis by two points only, at the front of the engine where an inverted 'V' shaped bracket was positioned between the water pump and the fan belt pulley, where between the bracket and the chassis there was fitted a thick rubber supporting block, the other mounting point was provided at the rear of the gearbox unit where it was attached by means of the same principle. With the engine and gearbox attached to the chassis in this way any tendency for the power unit to convey vibration and noise to the car interior was much reduced. To check any undue movement however, a leaf spring and damper were also fitted; precautions were made also to check for undue movements being transferred to the gear lever and clutch pedal. The gear change of the Big Ten was a joy to use, the second and top ratios were synchronized and for the first time double de-clutching was quite unnecessary.

To ensure the new Citroën followed the trend towards more rounded lines, the body on the Ten had taken quite a jump forward in design and manufacture. The assembly lines at Slough were still the most modern in the country, every device was available for all the work to be carried out for production as required. When the new car was announced and the production lines re-tooled accordingly it was a relatively easy task to adapt the existing manufacturing processes. The new body was built on the 'monopiece' principle — not to be confused with the monocoque style of construction — where the body is made up from four sections only, ie. the two sides, rear and front section. Each section consisted of a steel pressing

This picture of the Ten in idyllic surroundings, possibly by the River Thames at Henley, aimed at marketing the car to women. The Ten had a 1452cc side-valve engine with three main bearings developing 32 b.h.p. with 'Floating Power' mounting system and the new Monopiece body. The example shown is a 1934 model, with the wire wheel option then introduced, together with 12-volt electrics in place of the previous 6-volt system and a four-speed sychromesh gearbox in place of the earlier three-speed.

made in the factory using the most advanced equipment for the day, the jigs being able to produce highly substantial steel pressings. The welding was done electrically, the two sections being joined acted as the negative and positive poles which allowed the two surfaces to fuse together with the electricity current passing between them. In this way it was possible to produce almost invisible joints which had immense strength. The doors were constructed in rather a similar fashion but steel strips were added to the inner and outer panel only. The floor of the interior of the car was quite flat, this meant that while extra passenger comfort was available the propeller shaft was open and slung below the vehicle. The usual refinements were found within the vehicle's interior, a sliding roof was fitted on the saloon and the seating fully lived up to Citroën tradition and expectations. On the fixed head and drop head coupé models, the boot, or trunk as it was still referred, was replaced by a luggage grid.

The motoring magazines of 1932 and 1933 noted the Citroën Ten to be not only of larger dimensions than most other ten horse-power cars but also to be very quiet whilst running, this was put down to the Monopiece body and the fitting of Floating Power engine suspension. The engine in performance represented many of the features usually found on six-cylinder cars, it was possible to take the speed of the vehicle down to a mere walking pace in top gear and still be able to pull away, the whole operation being undertaken without any snatching of the transmission. In second gear the car could accelerate from 10 m.p.h. to 30 m.p.h. in 8½ seconds. The springs of the car were said to give a superior ride that few people had experienced before. Although still of conventional form with semi-elliptic springs it was said to be possible to travel over roads at speeds it would be virtually impossible to attempt in the majority of other cars. The Ten had a cruising speed of between 50 m.p.h. and 55 m.p.h. and the petrol consumption averaged at 28 miles per gallon. *The Light Car and Cyclecar* said of the Citroën Ten:

'Anyone who prides themselves on a catholic knowledge of modern light cars should certainly drive a Citroën Ten—which is another way of saying it is a car distinctly out of the normal run.'

For 1933 the Big 12 and the Twenty were retained but

CITROËN

- FLOATING POWER. ● SYNCHRONISED GEAR CHANGE. ● FREE WHEEL. ●
SUPER COMFORT TYRES. ● "MONOPIECE" ALL-STEEL SAFETY COACHWORK.
● ENTIRELY NEW TYPE RIGID BOX FRAME. ●
● HYDRAULIC SHOCK ABSORBERS. THERMOSTATICALLY CONTROLLED. ●

THE CITROËN "BIG TWELVE," FOUR-CYLINDER SALOON DE LUXE

£230

THE CITROËN "TWENTY," SIX-CYLINDER SALOON DE LUXE

£295

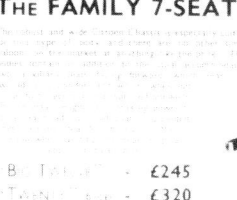

The FAMILY 7-SEATER SALOONS

B... — £245
...... — £320

This advertisement for the 'Big Twelve' four-cylinder 1767cc and 'Twenty' six-cylinder 2650cc cars conveys their character as introduced for 1933, both those illustrated having London registration numbers issued in late 1932. The new-generation design features were accompanied by standardisation on hinged ports for the bonnet sides and wing-mounted sidelamps among both ranges. Disc wheels were standard that year. The Family Seven-seater saloon shown at the foot of the page had a longer body extending further to the rear and eliminating the external trunk to allow space for the folding occasional seats; the spare wheel moving to the front wing and a folding luggage grid being provided at the rear. In France these models were known as the 10CV and 15CV.

with certain modifications. Floating Power was adopted on both models in the same way as the Ten, in addition a free wheel device was fitted to the gearbox. The gearboxes of the larger models were given synchromesh facilities also as found on the Ten and in addition the 'silent second gear' was fitted. Both model ranges of cars were modified with the improvements as outlined but with little change in the prices. The Big 12 saloons were, for 1933, given the bonnet ports, as fitted to the Twenty, side lamps were installed on both front wings of the two models and it is interesting to note that for the first time the famous Double Chevrons appeared on the radiator grille.

Car production at the Slough factory showed a marked increase, the Big Ten was selling well, its features being received as very favourable to the British car buying public. Austin had introduced their Twelve Four and Light Twelve Six, the latter being priced at £218 whilst Ford's model BF cost £225. Rover, yet to move upmarket, had announced their Family Ten at £195 and for a further £5 four-speed transmission was provided, the Rover Ten Special Saloon appeared at £228. In the Summer of 1933 Citroën announced a further two models to their range, the Light Twelve and the Light Twenty. These two additions to the marque were produced in conjunction with the existing models, the Big Ten, Big Twelve and the Twenty. The Light Twelve was produced by placing the engine from the Big Twelve into the chassis and body of the Ten, the result was car of sporting qualities with the ability to maintain high cruising speeds. The Light Twenty was a sports edition of the Twenty saloon, it was based upon the 114ins. wheelbase of the Big Twelve and, like its stablemate the Light Twelve, afforded a great range of speeds in top gear while also maintaining a high cruising speed. Floating Power featured on all models which assured smooth running and once more, as so many times in the past, Citroën were in front with new ideas, this time with low pressure tyres; at 20 lbs. per square inch Citroën were edging into a field his competitors had not yet dared to investigate as such low pressures were considered not to allow sufficiently good roadholding. What would Louis Renault have to say about this? Sharing the same body as the Ten, the Light Twelve was immediately blessed with all the Ten's features mentioned previously. A few changes were made however, the interior received minor modifications while twin electric horns were fitted just below the headlamps. With a top gear ratio of 4.7 to 1 the Light Twelve was an attractive car, so was the price tag of £225. The Light Twenty cost just £50 more at £275.

The 1767cc engine as fitted to the Light Twelve enabled the car to maintain a speed of 50 miles per hour quite easily, on a one hundred mile test journey on the Great North Road the time taken 2 hours 28 minutes, no mean achievement in the days before motorways effectively reduced travel time. On a test at Brooklands motor racing circuit, a top speed of 63.5 miles per hour was reached. The new low pressure tyres gave the feeling of extra soft

The exotic interior of New Devonshire House is aptly conveyed by this photograph dating from approximately 1933. Pictures of the London Showrooms are rare but fortunately this photograph is of particular interest. The surroundings are in keeping with André Citroën's desire for these premises to be the most prestigious showrooms anywhere. In the foreground is the Light 12 Sports four-seater; only very few of these cars were built and even fewer have survived. Other cars in the picture are models from the Ten, Twelve and Twenty ranges.

Another of the very rare Light 12 Sports, this superb example might be the only survivor. It is in splendid condition and a credit to its owner, Graham Brice. Originally registered in Ipswich in 1935, its Ranalah bodywork differs slightly from the earlier car shown overleaf in having rear-hinged doors and more conventional bonnet louvres. Sporting versions of volume-produced models with simple side-valve engines were made by several manufacturers at that time, including Austin, Ford and Morris (this quite distinct from the related one more genuinely sporting MG). Citroën had the advantage of the Rosalie record-breaker, and Ranalah, a small specialist body-building firm based in Kew, may well have been inspired by that car with its sloping tail, but produced a more English-looking version constructed in traditional style with wood framing and a combination of steel and aluminium panels.

suspension and a side effect was the tendency to roll slightly on sharp corners, otherwise the drivers testing the car found the tyres to be ideal. The interior with its comfortable seating was all as expected, the dashboard and fascia was the same as on the earlier models of the Big 12 and Twenty, all the required instruments were fitted, fuel gauge, speedometer, clock, ammeter and oil pressure gauge. The Light Twenty saloons mirrored the general features of the smaller car, a brisk performance was gained from the 20.8 h.p. six-cylinder engine. Whilst providing rapid speeds through the gears a high speed could be sustained in the top ratio, it seemed to be almost possible to stay in the same gear for an entire journey, the only time it was really found necessary to change down was either on a steep hill or when propelling the car from a walking pace to a higher speed than merely allowing the torque of the engine to replace the loss of momentum.

Within a few months of the announcement of the new models revisions were revealed in time for the 1933 Motor Show. The range of cars were supplemented with additional sporting models as well as a de-luxe version of the Ten. An impressive display of cars was therefore exhibited.

The full range of models and prices were as follows:

Perhaps the most significant addition to the range was the de luxe version of the Ten. The announcement of the car certainly filled a gap in the models and it was considered the car would have a marked effect upon the sales of Citroën cars in general. Improvements were also made to the basic 10 saloon and naturally those features were incorporated in the de luxe version. The six volt electrical system was discontinued, a changeover to 12 volts being executed. A Solex carburettor was fitted in place of the existing vertical unit and wire wheels took the place of the disc type. Another feature of consequence was considered to be the ventilation system; yet again Citroën had scored a first, such an idea being exclusive to the Citroën marque. The system which used a 'double dash' was designed to keep the interior of the car cool in Summer but in Winter to maintain a warmer temperature than could normally be expected. On the scuttle a hinged plate could be opened or closed from within the vehicle by means of a knurled knob on an arm connected directly to the mechanism. Once opened allowing the air to penetrate through the gap, it would pass between the two 'dashboards'; any warm air or fumes from the engine would be taken with the airflow and deposited through a channel below the floorboards and effectively away from the

TEN	LIGHT TWELVE	TWENTY	LIGHT TWENTY
Saloon............£198	Saloon de luxe..............£235	Saloon de luxe..............£310	Saloon de luxe..............£285
Saloon de luxe.......£218	Open Sports 4 seat........£275	7 seat saloon de luxe.....£325	Open sports 4 seat........£305
	Sports coupé.................£305		Sports coupé.................£340

BIG TWELVE

Saloon de luxe.......£245
7 seat saloon de luxe..£255

passenger area. During the Winter when it was expected that the scuttle flap would be kept closed, some amounts of warmth from the engine would be able to permeate into the car body interior. Car heaters were then extremely rare. In time, all 1934 models received this feature.

The De-Luxe Ten, whilst incorporating the features added to the range of cars as a whole, remains to be viewed as a model being highly desirable and well worth the extra investment of £20. The foremost feature of the De-Luxe Ten was the provision of a four-speed gearbox together with the free-wheel device. Other additions were Lucas trafficators which were neatly concealed within the door pillars, windscreen wipers fitted in tandem, ignition lock and electric fuel gauge. Long range headlamps gave good night vision and Triplex toughened glass was utilised for the windscreen. Adjustable sun visors, pockets on all doors and three ashtrays were included within the specification whilst a somewhat greater degree of comfort was afforded from the leather upholstery. The four-speed gearbox and free-wheel mechanism added considerable boost to the car's sales appeal, the free-wheel could be locked into position by the pull of a fascia-mounted knob and as soon as reverse gear was selected the device was automatically cancelled. The following was said of the free-wheel contrivance in a Citroën advertisement that appeared circa 1933:

'By this device, running costs are reduced and gear changing is further simplified.

The difficulties of gear changing are completely eliminated, an absolute silent change up or down being possible without de-clutching. Considerable economies are effected in petrol, oil, wear and tear.

A simple and positive locking device conveniently operated from the driver's seat puts the free wheel in or out as desired.'

The gearbox had synchromesh on third and top ratios, the third gear was of the silent type as fitted to the middle ratio of three-speed gearboxes. Confusion had arisen over the supplier of tyres, when low pressure tyres were first introduced and fitted to the Citroën range of cars, only Michelin were specified to be used. *The Motor* in October 1933 reported, however, the tyres fitted to their test vehicle were found to be the Goodyear Airwheel super low-pressure type. It can be assumed that Citroën in Britain experienced some difficulty in obtaining the specified tyres but in order to fulfil demand settled for what they considered to be a suitable alternative subject to availability. On French-built cars no other manufacturers tyres other than Michelin were fitted; this policy was to have an important significance within the foreseeable future.

The performance and reliability of the De-Luxe Ten was found to be practically beyond reproach. The numbers of faults reported by owners of this car were minimal but there was, however, some criticism to the heavy steering especially at low speeds; it took four complete turns of the large steering wheel to direct the front wheels from lock to lock and this coupled with steering the car through narrow streets at a speed of walking pace or less was found to be exhausting work particularly for lady drivers. Steering the car under normal conditions did not constitute a problem and the steering in this case was noted as being light and positive. The free-wheel device enabled the driver to change gear very easily with the mechanism locked into position, all that was needed was to allow a slight pause after releasing the accelerator pedal and then the lever could be moved without any difficulty to the gear required. Even with the free-wheel disengaged synchromesh allowed gear changing to be carried out quite simply; the handbook of the Ten De-Luxe advised the driver to take full advantage of gear changing to enable brisk get-away and to handle hills quickly! It did point out that most hills of undue gradient could be taken in top gear if the driver so wished. The revision to the carburettor and manifold ensured trouble-free starting of the engine, the *Light Car*

*The 1934 version of the 'Big Twelve' reintroduced wire wheels and a four-speed synchromesh gearbox with free wheel was also among the new features. The text in this advertisement of July 1934 in **The Motor** refers to 'virtually preselective gear-changing', an interesting allusion to the Wilson-type preselective epicyclic gearbox then in favour on quite a number of the more 'high-class' British makes of medium-sized saloon, such as Armstrong-Siddeley, Daimler, Lanchester, Riley and Talbot. The Riley 12/4 introduced a couple of months later was among the less expensive of these and cost £335 in saloon form. Citroën's price of £245 was pitched nearer to the level of models such as the Austin, Morris or Standard 12 h.p., all with equally simple side-valve four-cylinder engines though less roomy than the justly-named Citroën Big Twelve.*

July 24, 1934. The Motor

SPACIOUS LUXURY
at low cost....

Spaciousness—room to stretch your legs—room to give free play to elbows—room to sit as much at ease as in your favourite armchair, with the same feeling of comfortable luxuriousness.
That's the sort of accommodation provided by the Citroën "Big Twelve" for *five full grown* passengers.
The flat floor—another comfort point—need not be cumbered with luggage; in the unusually commodious luggage trunk there is room for *all* passengers' luggage.
In the summer heat the refinement of the Ventilated Double Dashboard, Sunshine Roof and 6 large, winding windows, which give wide uninterrupted views, will be readily appreciated.
Added to these features there are the Citroën undisputed reliability, Super Comfort tyres and long flat springs, synchronised 4 speed Gear box with Free wheel, giving virtually preselective gear changing; box section frame and "Monopiece" all steel body—the safest form of construction—and many other features. The Citroën "Big Twelve" is by far the best car value for the family man.

"BIG TWELVE" CITROËN £245

"The Motor" says :—"Extreme roominess a feature."

PRODUCED AT CITROËN WORKS · SLOUGH · BUCKS

CITROËN CARS LTD. (Dept. 17), Brook Green, Hammersmith, W.6. West End Showrooms: Devonshire House, Piccadilly, W.

The Index to Advertisers will be found on page 51

could not find a car that started any easier and in fact said of the vehicle:

'We can say without exaggeration that we have never tested any car which gives easier starting than the Citroën, for the simple reason that easier starting is impossible to imagine. On one occasion the car was left in the open air for over six hours with the radiator uncovered, and although the temperature was below freezing point during the last two hours or so, the engine appeared to fire simultaneously with pulling the starter knob; the usual preliminary 'whir-whir-whir' was entirely absent.'

The Light Twenty models created a lot of interest as they were considered to be sporting machines. Citroën had never gained very much of a reputation for producing a true sports car, even the Light Twelve had the appearance of a certain 'stodginess' whilst in fact it could give more powerful cars quite a run for their money. The Light Twenty had the image of a sporting machine; they were graceful cars with a lower bonnet line and raked louvres producing a rather dashing effect. The instrument panels were given a facelift, the redesigned speedometer combined a revolution counter and in general the interior resembled the dignified plushness of an illustrious grand sporting tourer. The engines did not receive any special tuning but much greater response was felt through the accelerator pedal due to the greater power to weight ratio and higher gear ratios. The top gear ratio of 4.3 to 1 allowed a somewhat higher top speed and enabled to reach it within a quicker time than the ordinary Twenty models.

During 1934 the entire catalogue of Citroën cars received minor modifications but in general continued in production based upon the specifications of 1933 and in fact the cars with only further minor revisions were announced for the 1935 model year. The Ten and Ten De-Luxe gained a slightly more powerful engine at 1496cc; spare wheels were relocated from the trunk to the front near side, fitting neatly between the wing and the scuttle. Fashion dictating a full circle of design, the accelerator pedal in all cases was uniformly positioned to the right of the brake pedal, so ending Citroën's stance at being at odds with other manufacturers. The rear windows of the Big Twelve received winding mechanism. Most significant, perhaps, was the appearance in 1934 of slightly raked radiator grilles; had aerodynamism really been accepted by Citroën? Another development at this time was the decision to construct a diesel engine suitable for cars and small vans - this dated from July 1933, when so small a unit was considered by many to be beyond practical limits. It took some years to develop, but once again André Citorën was determined to keep ahead of his competitors.

Whilst in England the Citroën factory churned out cars by the hundreds, seemingly unaware and possibly almost uninterested of what was happening in France, André Citroën had become a worried man. In 1931 he had upset the Merchant Bankers Banque Lazard, he could now do with their assistance but they were not quick to rush to the car manufacturer's aid. More eccentric publicity events had been arranged, this time two more expeditions, the Blue Cruise and the White Cruise, the former to the North Pole and the latter across the USSR. To organise these feats Citroën badly needed the expertise of his compatriot and friend Georges-Maries Haardt. But Haardt was dead. The expeditions never took place. To aggravate his dilemma even further, Citroën was losing sales of his cars to old rivals Renault and Peugeot; these companies and others were eating into the market Citroën had retained since his early manufacturing days to such an extent it was enough to push Citroën into desperate action. With his usual flurry of publicity André Citroën announced that the Javel works were to be completely reconstructed. His fellow directors, politicians, his closest friends, rivals, his workforce and even the French people as a whole were horrified.

Citroën was determined to see the reconstruction programme be completed in as short time as possible; 30,000 square metres of buildings were pulled down and in their place 50,000 square metres manifested. It is quoted from 'Histoire Mondiale de l'Automobile':

'Begun in April 1933, work proceeded in feverish manner, Citroën himself always present, planning and urging maximum speed. For more than four months, the site was like an anthill, lorries, lifting machinery, cement mixers, and men everywhere, it was hard to believe that the pre-planned schedule would be kept to.'

1933 was a grave year for France, it was also a grave year for Citroën; the international scene was no better and a feeling of depression hung over Europe, unemployment was high and the average French income had dropped by about 30%. André Citroën's own confidence had also been shattered, a strike at Javel had severely crippled both him and the company. The strike had been called in retaliation to Citroën's efforts in complying with the Government's instructions to effect a reduction in the earnings of the workforce by 10%. The morale of the employees and the relationship between them and the management received a severe setback and sustained substantial damage.

The circumstances that led to Citroën making the decision to reconstruct Javel followed an invitation to visit Louis Renault's Billancourt factory. No doubt Renault, 'The Bear of Billancourt', delighted in escorting 'The Little Jew of Javel' around the factory proving his production methods to be a match for the Javel works on the opposite bank of the Seine. The invitation coincided with the completion of major refurbishment work at Billancourt; Renault had made extensive alterations in the interests of increased car production and efficiency. Citroën was furious at what he had seen, as soon as he returned to Javel the order was given for the rebuilding to commence immediately—Citroën was not to be outdone. The entire alterations at Javel were carried out without production of a single car being lost, such was the extent of the organisation and skilful planning. From April to September 1933 over 600 machine tools were moved, none of them were out of use for more than half a day at most.

During the eight years the factory had been manufacturing vehicles at Slough the overall image of the car had changed relatively little. The body shape was still quite upright and followed in principle the tradition of the coach, a great deal had been achieved in the respect of

CITROËN

Dans une usine moderne où chaque opération est réglée avec précision, règnent l'ordre et le silence. Chaque ouvrier, au bord de la chaîne, est à sa place. Il y accomplit posément sa besogne, sans hâte, soigneusement, mais aussi sans perte de temps. En défilant devant lui, le cadre auquel chaque main ajoute une pièce devient châssis, et le châssis, voiture. A tous les stades du montage s'exerce un rigoureux contrôle. C'EST AINSI, AVEC DES DIZAINES DE MILLIERS D'AUTRES, QU'A ÉTÉ CONSTRUITE LA 8 CV "PETITE ROSALIE" QUI, EN COUVRANT 300.000 KM. A 93 DE MOYENNE, A PROUVÉ L'INCOMPARABLE QUALITÉ DES FABRICATIONS CITROËN.

This impressive photograph of the reconstructed Javel factory was published in an advertisement dated 4th November 1933, two months after the work had been completed. The wording refers to 'each operation being regulated with precision' and a reign of 'order and silence'. Each operator carries out his work without haste, carefully but without waste of time. The vehicles on the line include a few delivery vans as well as saloons, and the text makes reference to the construction, among thousands of others, of the 8CV 'Petite Rosalie' record-breaking car. The spaciousness suggests that there was scope for further production lines or other activities to be added later.

driver and passenger comfort and in the question of safety Citroën were way ahead of the field. Within the group of motor manufacturers in Britain an outstanding lead had been shown by Citroën in the art of designing and building motor cars. In those eight years considerable development had taken place, firstly the advent of the car entirely ready to be driven away from the factory production line; the all-steel body; servo brakes that saw to it the car stopped quickly and efficiently; the use of flexible engine and gearbox mountings; the monopiece body structure and the widespread use of low pressure tyres — all this combined with the very effective suspension springing allowed some of the finest and smoothest rides of any car on the market. The Citroën car had an enviable reputation, it was noted for its reliability and capability of hard work under the most arduous conditions, the fact that the cars were built in Britain and using British components and British labour did much to enhance its appeal.

There appeared in 1934 a new dawn and an interest in getting away from the old-fashioned upright concept and shape of the motor car, certainly the Morris Minor and its big sister the Ten-Four retained their boxy image as did the Hillman Minx as well as the majority of Austin models. The Riley Nine Kestrel sported a 'fastback' and the Singer Eleven Airstream featured faired-in headlamps within a wind-cheating bodystyle, the Railton had all the looks of a sporting saloon while the Crossley Streamline with its rear engine was positively out of this world. The Bentley Saloon cost £1460 as against the Ford Model Y two door saloon at just £120.

On that Thursday afternoon on the 18th February 1926, André Citroën had told the gathering at the newly opened factory:

'I am able to state there are coming developments as regards the Citroën products that may be watched for with interest'.

The end of an era had been reached. A new era was to begin.

The final series of Ten models built at Slough had their appearance modernised by revised front mudguards with valances in the style which had become fashionable and a new radiator design which showed slight resemblence to that on the Traction Avant cars by then in production. In France, similarly restyled cars were described as NH (nouvel habillement) and also had independent front suspension, but Slough-built cars retained a conventional front axle with semi-elliptic springs. This view, again posed by the Thames, dates from 1935, this generation of cars still being available at that date; output of the Ten continued into 1936. The Traction Avant cars appealed to a different market, and there was a large part of the British car market which tended to regard so radically new a design with suspicion.

THE "TWELVE"
The Super Modern Car

The 'Traction Avant' stunned the motoring world when it was first announced in May 1934. This cover of the brochure issued in August of that year for the launch of Slough-built cars seems to have been prepared before any British-specification cars were available — careful examination shows that the 'Superconfort' lettering on the Michelin tyres is reversed, while the sidelamps, not fitted on French cars, had been added by an artist. Even so, this was a strikingly modern-looking car, yet its appearance no more than hinted at its revolutionary technical features — in particular the front-wheel-drive which, in the more elegant French phrase, gave this series of models its best-known name, unitary construction body and independent front suspension.

Chapter seven: Pulling power

During the fifteen years up to 1934, André Citroën had shown remarkable progress and technological development in the production of the motor car. He had set new standards in the motor industry, not only in France but around the world. It was Citroën who had helped cultivate the 'peoples's car', bringing the motor vehicle within reach of the many instead of a luxury plaything for the privileged few. The Patron had always been fascinated by new ideas; he appreciated the principle of driving the motor car through the front wheels instead of the rear wheels and although this idea was far from new it had never been successfully applied in volumes of mass production. Alvis, DKW, Rosengart and Cord had all tried transmitting power from the engine through the leading wheels, none of these succeeded to any extent. Whilst on his visit to America, in 1931, Citroën was invited to the Budd Company and it was there that his thoughts suddenly became more productive to the ideals of front wheel drive; Citroën was shown a model of an experimental car which had a chassisless body and transmission via the front wheels. The model had been built by Joseph Ledwinka, Budd's leading engineer. Since the mid-1920s, Budd had been a close ally to Citroën and it was they who had originally supplied some of the tooling for Citroën's factory at Slough. Realising the proposed idea's potential and the fact that the engineering design was so much akin to his own, Citroën set about immediately to plan a new model that he knew could revolutionise the motor car.

There were those within the Citroën Company who were less excited about front wheel drive than the Patron; one of his closest advisers, Charles Mauheimer, was against the project on both financial and technical grounds, fearing that Citroën would not have the resources to be financially stable to research and develop such a venture. For some time Citroën had been teetering on the brink of disaster but in his usual flamboyant manner he waved all the protestations out of the way and became all the more determined to proceed with the new car. André Citroën had a passion for the gaming tables at Deauville and Monte Carlo and it is said that he made many of the financial decisions of his Company in the same bizarre way as he played the cards and roulette. Certainly many of the extraordinary publicity events staged by him would not have been tolerated by other business people. In 1931 Citroën met André Lefebvre, a talented engineer having some experience in the design of front wheel drive vehicles with the Paris motor car manufacturer Gabriel Voisin. Lefebvre shared his enthusiasm of front wheel drive with André Citroën who was impressed by both Lefebvre's ideas and personality, so much so that The Patron recruited him to the Company and at once placed him in charge of the design team to produce Citroën's new car. Citroën laid down strict guidance for the design of the car; it should have a speed of 60 miles per hour, carry four passengers in great comfort and safety, have a fuel consumption of 30 miles per gallon and above all be of completely new image. Ironically, Lefebvre had earlier been to see Louis Renault and discussed his ideas with him at Billancourt. Renault had sent him away telling him he had no thought for such a project and disregarded the principles of front wheel drive.

On the 7th May 1934 the motoring world was stunned. Motor manufacturers, their agents and car owners alike gasped at the news that came from Javel. In Citroën agents' showrooms throughout France there appeared a new car, not just a revised model released upon existing designs, but a completely new car representing a totally novel concept and construction, the like of which had never been seen before. It adopted the principle of front wheel drive, making obsolete the requirement to drive the motor car through the rear wheels. Gone also were the upright lines, the side valve engine, running boards, ponderous performance and mechanical brakes. Gone was everything evident of previous models with the exception of one major factor, the Citroën logic and the quest for something ingeniously new. In a single stroke the new design outdated every other motor car on the market.The new car became known simply as the 'Traction Avant'.

Citroën's Traction Avant was a model of elegance, the new car had clean sporting lines emphasised by its lower centre of gravity, raked radiator and sweeping wings. All this was made possible by the unique monocoque body construction, doing away with the need to build the car upon a separate chassis, and permitting a flat floor with absence of propeller shaft or transmission tunnel. No longer did one have to climb up into a motor car but rather step down into it. The interior of the car was also revolutionary in that passengers no longer sat upon a chassis frame but instead were protected inside the specially braced body hull. The Traction Avant was a masterpiece of engineering as well; the gearbox was situated in front of a new overhead-valve engine with the drive being taken via the gearbox by means of helical gears, drive shafts and universal joints. The car's performance was outstanding and a Lockheed hydraulic braking system was another up-to-date feature.

France loved the new car; the French took to it instantly although many Citroën agents declared that the car would never catch on. Rivals of Citroën at once set about to discredit his new car together with the era facing them; Peugeot went as far as stating in their publicity brochure a car was completely unstable unless it was driven through the rear wheels. Louis Renault, angered at Citroën's success and not wishing to be outdone by his rival, announced within a few weeks following the appearance of the Traction, his new car, the Celtaquatre. Renault's car was hardly a new model; it relied upon existing designs and retained its rather dubious three-point suspension of semi-elliptic springs at the front and transverse springs at the rear. It also kept its rear drive transmission. All that really had been achieved was the streamlining of the body to make it a little less bulbous. The rigid front axle, side valve engine and mechanical brakes did not add to the car's selling features; a year later Renault even went as far as to produce the Celtaquatre without running boards and giving the car a slightly wider body.

In producing the Traction Avant, Citroën had played the biggest gamble of his life, but it was not enough. Success had come too late. In 1933, when Citroën had given the order to rebuild Javel it was in anticipation of producing the Traction Avant. After fourteen years of continuously intensive mass production of cars the assembly lines had become dated. Seeing Louis Renault's newly laid out Billancourt, Citroën knew that if he was to survive then he had to act quickly, sales of existing cars were falling and reduced cash flow presented a serious problem. Already the Patron was concerned at the financial state of his company; he was borrowing heavily, the money had to be repaid and the creditors would not wait forever. He considered the only way to come through the crisis was to knock out the competition even for a relatively short period in which time he could produce a car that everybody would want to buy. Convinced that the future lay with driving the wheels through the front axle, it was whilst in America that he received the final impetus to proceed with the project; the prototype front wheel drive car shown to him at the Budd Company also favoured a monocoque body which confirmed Citroën's own designs

Typical Paris street scene of the late 1930s; the Traction Avant cars appear sleek and streamlined against the upright designs of other vehicles. Note the Double Chevrons on the radiator of the Traction; on British-built cars the Double Chevrons were fitted on the inside of the grille. During April 1934, an invited audience had been gathered at the Citroën Exhibition Hall to see the unveiling of the new car. When the wraps were taken off the two cars on show the gathering were not only dumbfounded at the design but even alarmed, certainly sceptical at whether it would ever sell. History proved them wrong and Citroën right.

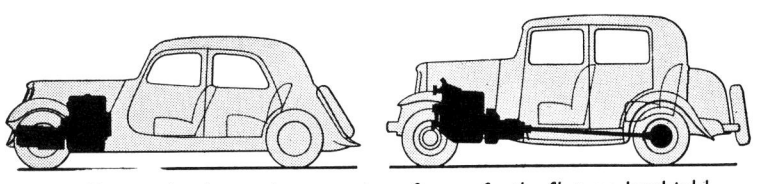

These diagrams appeared in publicity material for 'The Super Modern Citroën Twelve', as early British examples of the Traction Avant cars were called. The side elevations, as well as illustrating the change in transmission layout, graphically convey the altered proportions from the previous range — the bonnet top of the old model was at driver's eye level on the new one. The cornering and suspension drawings somewhat over-simplified the complex combination of forces acting on the wheels and structure of a car but conveyed an unfamiliar concept, for the Traction Avant did form a landmark in design. Perhaps as telling was the statement that the maximum angle of tilt when concerning at the limit of road holding was 7½ degrees compared to 16 degrees for 'an ordinary car', presumably one of the previous range.

1. Front wheel traction permits of a perfectly flat undershield

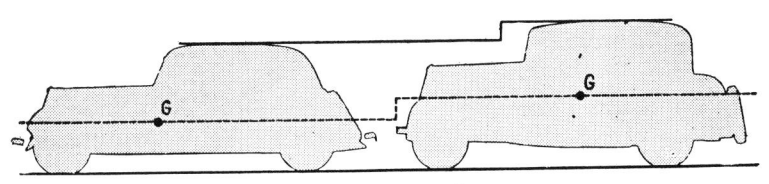

...a very low centre of gravity

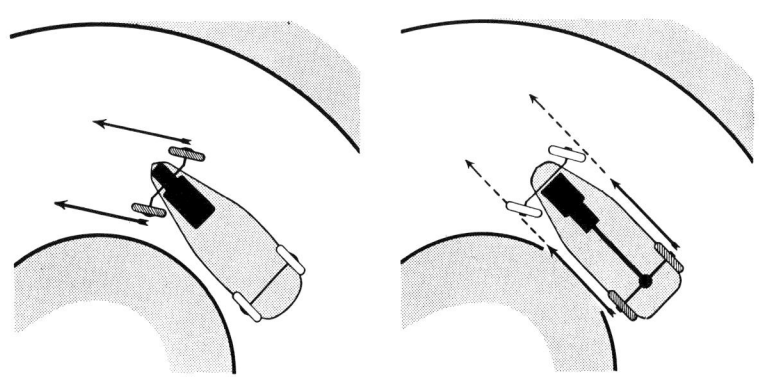

...absolute safety when cornering.

Independent front wheels ensures perfect stability under all conditions.

as to the construction of the car. On returning to Javel, Citroën called a meeting of his trusted design staff, he told them "I want a miracle—a light car of entirely fresh conception to succeed the 8s, 10s and 15s (in Britain the Slough models were the Ten, Twelve and Twenty) we are just starting to make". The consequence of Louis Renault's inviting Citroën to Billancourt in 1933 had far reaching effects.

From the time Citroën had conceived the principle of his new car through to its birth there was a long saga of dramatic dilemmas. Life was not easy for the team of designers led by Lefebvre, they were the best team any motor car manufacturer could wish to have yet day in, month out, they suffered the frenzied demands and raging tempers of the Patron. Troubles beset the Citroën team in perfecting the transmission systems; the Patron had specified that an automatically operated gearbox be designed for the Traction Avant for, as he had once stated, a streamlined aerodynamic car should have a transmission to match. It also seems that Citroën had a dislike for gear levers and even stranger, the Patron was a reluctant driver—he hated driving motor cars—even his own. Sometime earlier, André Citroën had met the inventor Robert Dimitri Sensaud de Lavaud who had developed an automatic transmission of unusual design. Though knicknamed 'The Turbine', it was based on a system of rocking levers and one-way clutches, giving an infinitely variable effect, but reliability over a reasonable operating life was a problem. A number of tests were successfully carried out at Montlhery with the gearbox fitted into a number of Rosalie cars. Even Citroën himself tested the car and found the transmission to be perfectly smooth. At once Citroën's enthusiasm for Sensaud de Lavaud's gearbox got the better of him and ordered it to be designed for the Traction. Once the prototype cars were tried under normal conditions away from the test circuit problems were experienced with the gear oil overheating and boiling. The Patron would not hear of the difficulties.

Lefebvre, foreseeing that the problems experienced with the automatic gearbox were not going to be easily resolved, took the situation into his own hands. Secretly the design team developed a conventional gearbox that fitted into the same housing as the Sensaud de Lavaud box but due to the short space of time available it suffered from a lack of perfection and therefore sustained a number of faults. Still Citroën insisted the automatic gearbox be made to work but to no avail. Problems were also experienced with the drive shafts and stub axles, they snapped as if they were made of china; torsion bars were found to be too weak and the brake drums overheated.

The Traction Avant, which had been designated as the '7', was tested under the most extraordinary secrecy. Even many of the workers at Javel were unaware of the details of the model although they knew some great plan was afoot, such was the independence of the various departments.

Using the Montlhery circuit, tests on the early prototypes were exhaustive, drivers worked in eight hour shifts all the time being spent behind the wheel of the car. The only time they stopped was for refuelling or carrying out repairs. Citroën pressed hard for the car to be finished, the design team often declared they would never get it ready in time. The Patron constantly arrived at the Javel works early in the morning demanding to see how the project was progressing. He seemed frenzied with panic. Creditors were clamouring for their money and the entire Company was at great risk of going bankrupt. Another factor aggravated the situation; Citroën was a sick man. In February 1934 the crisis broke, loans taken out by Citroën amounted to 150 million Francs and the sum of 15 million Francs to cover the interest was due. The money was sought by various devious means but only just in time. The repayment was made on the 29th February, much of the money being raised following a direct approach by the Patron to the Company's agents. Citroën had desperately hoped the new car would have been ready, trusting that its appearance would have restored some of the faith of his creditors and therefore allowed him to play for time. But there was no car.

Citroën was committed to launch the car by May 1934 which meant that production should have commenced during April; the designers fought to extend the launch date to perfect the car but Citroën would hear none of this. Eventually Lefebvre convinced the Patron the problems with Sensaud de Lavaud's automatic transmission were not going to be resolved in time and in desperation as well as acknowledging their predicament he agreed to have the Traction Avant fitted with the conventional gearbox. It was all the more frustrating by having some of the automatic systems seemingly operating perfectly well in the Rosalie cars, especially as the Rosalie was a much heavier car than the new 7. W. F. Bradley, a British Journalist, revealed that he had driven over 10,000 kilometres in a Rosalie fitted with Sensaud de Lavaud's gearbox and had experienced no difficulty at all. Once fitted, however, the conventional gearbox transformed the performance of the Traction; test drivers enthusiastically pushed the car to its limits treating it as if it were a sports car; it was the most stable vehicle they had known. Roadholding was unbelievable; Lefebvre's team had also worked hard on producing a highly effective four-wheel hydraulic braking system, it was among the first times that such a system had been used on a car in Europe and later the Government insisted that all cars manufactured in France be fitted with this braking system. Another advance for Citroën but it is often overlooked that this was an important feature in the development of the car.

By the end of March, Citroën could wait no longer; he announced to the design team the car was to be put into immediate production. Lefebvre was horrified, the car was far from ready and pleaded for the order to be postponed for a few weeks in which time it was hoped to resolve the teething problems. It was sheer folly but there was no point in furthering opposition as the Patron was by then fanatical in getting production under way. By early April the Traction Avant was leaving the assembly lines which had been reconstructed to facilitate Citroën's dream.

On Wednesday 18th April 1934, Citroën Agents from all over France gathered at the Citroën exhibition hall in Paris. Punctually at 9.45 in the morning André Citroën addressed the meeting. There was a peculiar uneasiness amongst many of the delegates, they were aware of Citroën's financial instability and wondered just how much longer he could survive. The meeting had been called to introduce the new model to the dealer network yet Citroën, it appeared, was a little reluctant to show off the new car. He kept them waiting, they were told of forthcoming campaigns and were shown a film of the successful Central Asia expedition. Then at 12.30 Citroën unveiled his new car, the wraps were removed from two cars, one of which was at ground level and the other suspended above the floor in order the underside could be inspected.

The audience were dumbfounded, sceptical, even alarmed. The low slung body, lack of running boards, revolutionary interior and above all, front wheel drive were, they lamented, a recipe for disaster. The agents were convinced nobody would buy the car. Here were two sleek aerodynamic cars which one had to stoop to get into, the advanced technology together with front wheel drive created a tremendous leap forward in motor car design, in a single step the new Citroën had taken the lead by ten years. They need not have worried for, on the 7th May a stunned motoring population fell in love with Citroën's 7. The Traction Avant had arrived.

There was no doubt the 7 had been launched prematurely, the initial customers found themselves beset with frustrating teething troubles; failure after failure

Traction Avant models under construction at Javel. André Citroën's desire to produce the Traction Avant emanated from a visit to America during 1931 after he had discussed the idea of a chassisless car driving the front wheels with Joseph Ledwinka, Chief Engineer at Budd Motors. Citroën had already met André Lefebvre who shared his own enthusiasm for front-wheel drive, he put him in charge of the design team and later became acknowledged as the 'Father Of The Traction'. Lefebure had been to see Citroën's old rival, Louis Renault, only a short time before but he had not been persuaded of the advantages of front-wheel drive.

occurred with the drive shafts and gearboxes, even failure of the bodywork was reported. Within a few months of the launch of the 7 the 7B was announced, a much better car, this was the car that should have launched the Traction. To prove the durability of the Traction Citroën performed extravagant feats of endurance; a new car was filmed being pushed over the precipice of a cliff letting it bounce and roll to its destiny. Whereas a traditionally built car would probably have broken up with complete

André Citroën's old friend Francois Lecot standing with his beloved Traction Avant. On the launch of the Traction, Citroën had wanted to stage another of his publicity exploits to demonstrate the excellence of the car, in which Lecot had agreed to participate. In the event, Citroën, due to finance problems, pulled out. Lecot, however, decided to carry on and achieved one of the greatest trials in the history of the motor car.

Lecot, a restaurant owner lived near Lyon, halfway between Paris and Monte Carlo. Each day for a year, Lecot arose from bed at daybreak, one day he would drive to Paris and back, the next to Monte Carlo and back; after a year, taking in time to join the Monte Carlo Rally, he drove a staggering 250,000 miles. The event was scrutinised by the Automobile Club de France and did much to boost sales of the car.

devastation, the monocoque-bodied Traction, when it finally came to rest was still in one piece suffering little damage. The bonnet had slipped its catches but once placed back upon the car the engine was started and driven away by the test crew. Then Francois Lecot proved the car beyond all doubt with his marathon 250,000 mile test over 400 days. Lecot, in a standard production car drove his car each day from his home near Lyon to Paris and Monte Carlo and in the duration managed to enter the Monte Carlo Rally as well as making a diversion to Moscow.

Citroën's biggest gamble had paid off but it also failed him. Successful as the Traction Avant was, it came too late to save him from his worst fears. The interest on the 150 million Franc loan had been gathered just in time, the Patron's friends had rallied round him but it was the last time his allies would bail him out. Soon the creditors were demanding their money again, but there was none. Although the 7 had started to sell well it was not bringing in enough capital to start repaying the huge amounts that had been borrowed for the production of the new model. Michelin were Citroën's foremost creditor and it was only a matter of time before they broke their silence and asked for their money. In the event it was not Michelin who broke the camel's back, Citroën already owed them in excess of 60 million Francs, but it was the Societe Franco-Americaine de Jante des Bois who led the charge of other creditors with their demand for a mere 10 million Francs. To Citroën and his Company the sum was relatively small, alas, no money was available and there was no one Citroën could turn to for help. The Patron was at his lowest ebb, he was ill with a stomach tumour, not only was he tired but had also lost the will to fight. The Company shares tumbled, a run of selling took place and the Citroën empire crumbled. Industrialist, entrepreneur and founder of the Double Chevron, the force behind some of the most incredible advancements in motor engineering throughout the world, humbly submitted himself to a commercial tribunal where judicial liquidation was pronounced.

Sitting alone in the court room, André Citroën heard with anguish he was to concede the company he had built up since 1919 to his largest creditors, the Michelin Brothers. This was the final straw for the Patron, he was a broken man in spirit, in health and in wealth. Sometimes he returned to the great factory at Javel, then, one day he was told not to go anymore, no longer was it his factory, he was not wanted. This was the last crushing blow.

On the 3rd July 1935 André Citroën died. He had been in hospital for six months, much of the time in solitude. Very few of his friends had visited him. His funeral was attended by thousands, many of the workforce at the factory walked silently behind his coffin, many of them in tears. There is one epitaph to the man in Paris; the blue enamel sign 'Quai de Javel' has been removed. In its place another blue enamel sign 'Quai André Citroën'.

....

With the news breaking of the announcement of the Traction Avant in France, immediate arrangements were made to begin alterations to the assembly lines at the

In death as in life, André Citroën attracted publicity. He died on 3rd July, 1935, and although a stomach tumour had made him ill, the pressures of creditors demanding payment at a time when sales had been falling and of battling to get the Traction Avant into production must have played their part in aggrevating matters. Mourners filed past his coffin to pay their respects to the great man, yet ironically his company had been sold to the Michelin Brothers as the largest creditors.

In addition to the saloon, roadster and fixed-head coupé models were included in the range offered in Britain as the Twelve from September 1934. The attractive looking roadster had a wide front seat for three passengers and a dickey seat for two. This view from the initial brochure again shows evidence of retouching of a photograph of a French-specification 7CV car in regard to lamps, etc. The text of the brochure refers to the windscreen folding flat, but this seems to have been a misunderstanding, as the screen frame can be seen to be part of the Monoshell body structure.

Slough Factory. Considerable changes had to be made to enable the building of the cars in England, so it was not until September 1934 that production commenced. The car caused almost as much sensation in Britain when it was launched as in its native France; the motoring press were ecstatic, never had they quite seen anything like it before. *The Motor* ran a headline....'A car we could not overturn'. *The Autocar* said of the vehicle 'the car can be allowed to be driven at amazing speeds over a pot-holed surface that you would not take at more than a cautious 20 m.p.h. in the average car'. As on past occasions the British models built at Slough were given different names and models from their French counterparts. The specification of the vehicles also altered in some respects to suit the British market. It was still intended to utilise as much British material in the manufacture of the front wheel drive cars as there had been on the rear-drive models. Of course, with a completely new car of entirely revolutionary ideas it was appreciated it might be a little time before sales of the car were to be realised; in France, where Citroën's rear drive models had seen declining sales the situation was opposite in Britain; a conservative car with such classic principles was quite acceptable and therefore production of the Ten, Twelve and Twenty models was anticipated to continue at a reasonable level for some time to come. Manufacture of rear drive cars carried on at Slough until 1939 with a number of very interesting cars being produced.

On announcing the Traction Avant to the British market, Citroën Cars designated the car 'Super Modern Twelve' and priced it at £250. A Fixed Head Coupé and roadster were announced at the same time and were priced at £275 and £270 respectively. The Super Modern was noted as being outstanding for four reasons; the introduction of front-wheel drive as a mass production venture together with its amazing road holding qualities; the suspension in the form of torsion bars which afforded hitherto unknown comfort; the streamlined and ultra-modern bodyshape which, as soon as it was introduced, set new standards to which other motor manufacturers would eventually be compelled to follow, and finally, the use of the monocoque body shell which did away with the need of placing the body upon a separate chassis. The torsion bar suspension was like that on no other car at the time though widely copied later; any doubts the critics had of the system were soon demolished by the way the car made light work of rough road surfaces taken at high speeds.

The body design was no less than a delight. The cars built at Slough varied slightly with those at Javel but more of this later. The entire concept of the car was almost beyond belief, the rakish lines and the decidedly sporting appearance at once put the vehicle into the category of motor car the more adventurous person wanted to own. Although many in Britain knew of the Super Modern Citroën and respected its forward approach to technology they were nevertheless wary of it and even frightened by it. Conservatism prevented leaving behind the principles of rear-wheel drive and all it stood for. It is difficult to believe that almost sixty years after the announcement of the Citroën Traction Avant there still remains to a certain degree a feeling towards this principle in Britain. Viewed from both front and rear, the car had a low, wide profile, the centre of gravity being lowered gave the look of being completely sure-footed and master of its own destiny. From the side view, the design was very satisfying, the low bonnet with its raked radiator and sweeping wings, the absence of a bulky boot and the neat rear styling gave the whole car a well balanced attitude. There could be no doubt the car was a winner, yet its appearance looked strange to people used to more upright lines.

The technicalities of the car are of some interest. As has already been mentioned, the power unit adopted for the Super Modern was a four cylinder overhead valve engine, the first time a motor of this type had been used in a Citroën car. Placed ahead of the engine sat the gearbox, the drive shafts replaced the propeller shaft and were connected to the front wheels. The Floating Power system of engine suspension was used and the whole of the power unit was

The engine, gearbox and differential formed one unit, arranged in the car so that the gearbox was in front, the whole being flexibly mounted using the Floating Power principle. The first Super Modern cars had 1303cc engines of 72 x 80mm bore and stroke, developing 32 b.h.p. Although overhead valves were used for the first time on a Citroën, it was soon realised that this engine size was inadequate, even though the new cars were remarkably light, 18 cwt being quoted for the saloon. It also had a particular disadvantage in Britain, where the system of taxation for the annual licence was based on cylinder bore only and the model was rated at 12.8 h.p. by the RAC rating used. Increasing the stroke to the 100mm familiar on earlier Citroën engines, and widely used for other comparably-sized cars of the period, brought the capacity up to 1628cc and this came into effect from February 1935, being designated 7C in France but still Twelve in Britain, with no change in taxation class. A larger bore version introduced at the same time became the 11 in France and the Fifteen in Britain, with 78 x 100mm dimensions and 1911cc capacity (although briefly this 1911cc engine was used in a model called the 7 Sport in France and the Twelve Sport in Britain before logic led to the adoption of 11 Legere or Light Fifteen). A noteworthy feature of these engines was the wet cylinder barrel construction, these being made in a special quality cast iron to give minimum wear.

fitted into a cradle which formed the front of the car. It was possible, therefore, to remove the entire transmission, engine and associated equipment which were housed within the cradle from the main hull of the car. In crude terms it was like the horse and cart—the engine, gearbox and transmission were the horse and the trailing body the cart! The 1303cc engine propelled the Traction Avant up to a maximum speed of over 60 miles per hour through a three speed gearbox having synchromesh on second and top ratios. The gear lever sprouted through the fascia panel but in fact the gear change pattern was as used with a floor change. The position of the gear lever on the dashboard appeared to be somewhat strange however; it had been designed with left hand drive cars in mind therefore the lever was in a perfect position for the right hand to alter the ratios. On right hand drive cars the lever had been left in its original position, the result was that the driver was forced to change gear with the left arm virtually outstretched. Funnily enough none of the critics commented upon this fact, no doubt they found the gearchange comfortable enough and disregarded it without further question. The clutch was of the single dry plate type and was operated by a sheathed cable connected to the foot pedal. Also worthy of note were the control pedals which were hung from the bulkhead in similar pattern to those found on modern cars, though then novel.

Returning to the torsion bar suspension fitted to the front and rear of the car, this represented a great step forward in engineering methods. It was not without its problems though and caused many a headache for the engineers before and after the Traction Avant was launched. There were problems also with the drive shafts; on early models a number of modifications had to be carried out before a permanent solution could be effected. The drive shafts had a habit of breaking; however, following much time spent on solving the various teething troubles the Traction earned for itself an enviable reputation for reliability.

Owners of Slough built cars were made more comfortable than their fellow Frenchmen, this was due solely to the requirements of the British market. In place of cloth trimmed seats there was full leather upholstery of the finest quality, a sliding sun-roof designed for single-handed operation provided extra ventilation and comprehensive instrumentation adorned the dashboard for the British, who had a preference for multifarious dials. Visibility from the driving position was excellent, over the tapering bonnet it was possible to see both front wings and headlamps. The large steering wheel assisted the reassurance of the fine roadholding and extra space was afforded to the car's interior by the absence of a transmission tunnel and floor-mounted gear shift lever. It goes without saying the introduction of the front wheel drive Citroën in Britain certainly appealed to the sporting driver and it was possible to purchase a car with definite sports capabilities whilst at the same time retaining all the advantages of a luxury saloon car with the comforts it provided. In retrospect, the engine fitted to the Super Modern although considered adequate at the launch of the Traction was underpowered. Within the year an uprated power unit of 1628cc was installed, being more appropriate to the Super Modern Twelve.

Towards the end of February 1935 Citroën Agents and representatives of the motor trade gathered at the Trading Estate to receive news of additions to the range of vehicles. A further new four cylinder engine, rated at 15 horse power, was announced for the front drive cars and at 1911cc constituted a major increase in power for the model range. The new engine was to be fitted to the Super Modern Twelve as an option but in addition was to power a longer wheelbase version of the same car. In essence, this move formed the start of the world famous Citroën Light 15 with its long wheelbase relative, the Big 15.

The 1.9 litre engine was received with great acclaim, the front wheel drive range of the cars now presented the

The All-Steel Monoshell did away completely with the chassis and in effect was much stronger than a car built upon a platform. Tests were carried out in France where two cars were rolled over a cliff; the first, a traditionally built car suffered major damage with the car breaking up, the second, a Traction Avant had purely superficial damage and could be driven away once the bonnet had been refastened. The monocoque body was built up from light steel box-section members of girder construction which offered, when the body was completed, better resistance to stresses than a normal body built upon a chassis. Torsion bar suspension played its part in distributing these stresses and at the same time provided the car with a very stable and comfortable ride.

prospective purchaser with a considerable choice. The Big 15 came in two options — a five-seater saloon of four-light construction with a wheelbase of 10ft. 1½in. and a six-light 'family' seven-seater saloon on a 10ft. 9in. wheelbase. This latter machine had two occasional seats fitted between the front and rear seats, and when not in use, could be folded away into purpose-built floor wells. Access into the luggage compartment was via the rear seats, as on all the Traction Avant models, and it was to be a year before the cars were fitted with an opening boot hatch at the rear. In appearance, the Big 15, apart from having larger dimensions, was almost identical to the Twelve and Light 15, it shared the same methods of construction i.e. monocoque body, torsion bar suspension and front wheel drive.

The 1911cc engine, whilst somewhat larger than the earlier units, conformed to the same principles of four cylinders, push-rod operated overhead valves and mounted flexibly in accordance with the Floating Power system. The new engine developed 48 b.h.p. as against 38 b.h.p. of the 1628cc engines; it was not specially tuned but able to produce some fine performances. Journalists who were becoming acquainted with the front wheel drive Citroën were finding the road-holding so exceptional they were able to push the cars to extreme limits and still with absolute safety. On no other car could such road-holding

The driving position of the Super Modern Twelve gave a clear view of the road ahead. As the contemporary brochure put it, 'The large screen and windows, combined with the low seating position, give exceptional visibility.' The driver sat close to the wheel and windscreen, the front wings were not hidden from sight, enabling easy parking.

The Traction Avant drove through bends as if the car were on rails. Motoring journalists soon acquainted themselves with the front-wheel drive Citroën's handling techniques and found they could push the cars to extreme limits. The Traction's qualities were soon realised by the French Police who used the car to great extent. Naturally, the gangsters also used the Traction. One motoring magazine when reviewing the car stated it was the only car it could not overturn.

be achieved. One journalist described driving a Light 15 round a bend as if it had rails under its wheels. The Traction was put through the severest of tests; in every case the cars came through with flying colours. Test drivers and critics could not find any malice about the car's stability. The cars were taken up grassy banks, along unmade roads and over surfaces that could only be termed as appalling; each time the Citroën took the grade, it leapt ahead of all its competitors.

The standard-length Traction Avant saloons had very generous leg-room by modern standards, but this view of a French-built 11 Limousine shows the remarkable spaciousness of this long-wheelbase model. The French version was available as an ultra-roomy five-seater or a 'familiale' model seating eight or nine. The Slough-built equivalent was the Big Fifteen seven-seater saloon, with two folding seats behind the front ones.

The Michelin Brothers, having taken over the Citroën Company, were at once faced with huge debts. The reconstruction of Javel and the development of the Traction Avant had to be paid for and it was necessary, therefore, to iron out the teething troubles with the front drive cars as quickly as possible. It was essential the new car attracted high volumes of sales in order to restore cash flow into the Company. The Michelin Brothers appointed Pierre Boulanger to take over the Citroën Empire and it soon materialised that he was as forward thinking as André Citroën himself, in fact Boulanger shared many of the Patron's beliefs and enthusiasm for the advancement of technology and logical engineering. He retained the design team responsible for producing the Traction and instructed them to continue their research and development.

The events at Javel after Citroën had been forced into judicial liquidation had only been lightly covered in the British press. There were rumours, however, the Citroën Company would fold and production of cars cease. *The Autoocar* carried a statement of reassurance that following the take-over by Michelin, car production would be continued at Javel and other Citroën factories in France and that the Slough works were in no danger of being affected by the crisis within the company. Although the statement that appeared in *The Autocar* gave some relief to the Citroën workforce, agents and owners alike as well as manufacturers of component parts, there was looming a very serious period involving the British Citroën network. The affairs of the Company were closely examined with the result that the prestigious London Showrooms at New Devonshire House and the Citroën Building at Brook Green would close. Devonshire House was an expensive edifice, even when André Citroën had taken over the lease on his premises the rent amounted to £12,000 per annum.

Three pre-war Slough-built Traction Avant. Pre-war cars can be identified by the bonnet ventilation flaps which are replaced by louvres on post-war cars. Note the Pilote wheels on all the cars. The two cars on the left are rare as relatively few Roadsters in right hand drive form exist today.

The closures were a terrible blow to the Company's morale but gradually arrangements were made to transfer the huge stores to the Factory site and the Devonshire House showroom was put up for sale. By 1936 the changes had taken place and the Company and workforce settled down to face the future. At least there was the Traction Avant, nobody could take that away.

If the Super Modern Twelve and Light 15 were handsome cars then the long wheelbase models did the marque even greater credit. Their longer bodies and generally more sweeping features took full advantage of the streamlined design. With a 'wheel in each corner', a term later used by the British Motor Corporation with reference to the Mini, the Traction Avant gave the appearance of a car of a new age. By the time the Motor Show was held in 1935 the Traction Avant had been in production for over a year. Those who doubted the car's capabilities at the outset of its production could be forgiven for wondering just why it attracted so much acclaim and publicity. If there was one car everybody wanted to see at that motor show it was on the Citroën stand. For those people who went to the Citroën stand at the show there was little disappointment. All the front wheel drive models were displayed. For the 7-seat family model this was its first show appearance, its striking looks must have made other car manufacturers envious; Citroën's own advertising stated that their front drive cars were two years ahead of their time—this was an understatement as it was at least ten years ahead in body design and even more mechanically. It would be almost twenty five years before front wheel drive would be seriously considered by a British motor manufacturer.

Included in the Citroën catalogue were the front drive Roadster and Coupé versions, these cars were built only small numbers, especially the Coupé of which only four were constructed in right hand drive at Slough. It is a sheer miracle that over fifty years later all four models have been accounted for. As confirmation just how advanced the new range of Citroën's were, the rear drive models, which were displayed alongside looked comparatively dated with their upright features. Sales of rear drive cars were relatively strong, in 1933 2,037 cars had been delivered, this figure dropping to 1,928 cars the following year. Production for 1935 slipped down to 1,253 cars but in part this was due to the uncertainties within the Company and prospective buyers waited until the front drive models had established themselves. Now that the Traction Avant had become firmly recognised both in France and as an important challenger for the British markets, serious questions were being asked of the car's handling characteristics. So keen were rival companies to undermine the Citroën's qualities it left many showing caution to the manufacturer's claims. The *Autocar* of February 1936 went a long way to dispel any fears that prospective owners might have had; it reassured its readers that anyone with driving experience could get into the Traction Avant and at once feel completely at ease with it. What the normal motorist would notice as being different though was the suspension and the quality of ride which allowed the car to be taken over really rough roads with potholes at a safe speed of 25-30 miles per hour. The ease at which corners could be taken at speed was also noted together with details of trials undertaken in the West Country on hill starts and braking tests.

It is ironical that after André Citroën's death his dream had come true. The Traction Avant had arrived and made its presence felt. Even if Citroën were dead, his ideas were alive and well within the boundaries of Javel and whatever happened there would sure to follow in some form at a later date at Slough. All the time the front drive car was notching up success after success and sceptics of the car were beginning to look at it with admiration. On the British market the cars from the Trading Estate were finding homes with a new wave of motorist, happy with their independence to adventure with their vehicles enjoying the experience and sure-footedness of front wheel drive.

By 1937, the difficulties with the drive shafts and universal joints had been completely ironed out. It had been necessary to modify a great number of cars at tremendous expense to the Company. With the teething troubles finally behind them the Citroën Engineers were able to concentrate on the future programme of cars. In 1938 the last of the rear drive models were introduced, this was the six-light 7-seater Diesel based upon the Family Fifteen 15 h.p. saloon. The aim of the car was to capture the hire market and the family motorists driving higher than average mileages for whom a diesel-engined car

The Citroën 1766cc four-cylinder diesel engine was introduced in 1937 and this led to the appearance of the Diesel 7-seater Saloon, derived from the Big Twelve 7-seater model of 1933-34. The engine was among the smallest road transport diesels in production at that time, with 75 x 100mm bore and stroke and an output of 40 b.h.p. at 3500 r.p.m., a figure not far short of the 45 b.h.p. developed by a Mercedes-Benze 2545cc diesel introduced in 1936 for the 260D model said to be the world's first production diesel car. The Citroën engine used the Ricardo Comet indirect injection cylinder head developed in England, originally for AEC buses, but still very widely favoured today for small diesels. The construction of the engine followed Citroën practice of the time with the detachable wet cylinder barrels. It had an unusually slow idling speed of 350 r.p.m. and was mounted flexibly in Citroën's manner. In France it was largely intended for light commercial vehicles.

The Diesel 7-seater saloon had a 9ft. 10ins. wheelbase, 14ft. 8½ins overall length and weighed 29½ cwt. The chassis retained semi-elliptic springs, wire wheels and Bendix brakes while the Monopiece body had leather upholstery and sliding roof. The appearance was made slightly more up-to-date by the adoption of a radiator rather like that of the Traction Avant models, but the external luggage grid was a dated feature by 1938.

would pay dividends. The diesel cars consumed fuel at only two-thirds of the rate of their petrol counterparts and with the cost of diesel oil at a third of the price of petrol, the idea of running such a car was naturally appealing. The cost of the diesel was £90 more than the petrol version therefore it was only after some 32,000 miles the car would effect savings on running costs. At £375 the 7-seat diesel was an attractive proposition. There is little to suggest the Citroën Diesel sold in any great numbers, there existed some wariness as to the reliability and performance of the oil burning engine for private car use.

Output of cars from Slough dropped to an almost all-time low in 1936. Just 679 cars were delivered. The Factory was preoccupied with modifying production techniques on the front wheel drive cars and prospective buyers were anxious to receive more information on this totally new concept of car. Many would-be buyers of existing rear drive cars delayed their purchase in order to watch the Citroën's intentions concerning the future model ranges. During 1937 production of cars returned to some normality and 1,026 cars were delivered.

As increasing numbers of Twelves and Light 15s were seen on the roads of Britain so the the car began, in general, to receive greater acknowledgement than on its introduction. The principles of front wheel drive in mass-production methods of construction were by now becoming accepted and understood and those lucky enough to have driven the new Citroën were emphatic about its qualities. Both *The Motor* and *The Autocar* admitted being won over by the Light 15, but the former expressed its views to suit the more cautious reader when it said 'to drive the Citroën one could, in the main, fully imagine that it is based on conventional layout, in so normal a way does it handle.'

Before the Motor Show of 1938, Citroën announced an extension to the model range. Although no major alterations were made to the existing models, the Company were able to demonstrate that the British Citroën network were aware it was time to make the car more attractive to greater numbers of customers with the aim of selling more cars. With that policy, the 'Popular' models were introduced in the Twelve and Light 15

1934
CITROËN CARS
fit
TORSION BAR SPRINGING
•
INTEGRAL ALL-STEEL BODY & CHASSIS
•
FRONT WHEEL DRIVE
•
INDEPENDENT FRONT WHEEL SUSPENSION
•
FACIA-BOARD GEAR CHANGE

What did Citroën say in 1934?

"TWO YEARS AHEAD"... but they were FOUR!

Four years ago CITROËN anticipated the trend of car practice by introducing, amongst other things, TORSION BAR SPRINGING — INTEGRAL ALL-STEEL BODY AND CHASSIS — CLEAR FLOORS FREE OF CONTROLS, FOOTWELLS AND TUNNELS — FRONT WHEEL DRIVE — AND INDEPENDENT FRONT WHEEL SUSPENSION! This remarkable union of the best in progressive automobile design resulted in motoring that was safer, smoother and more comfortable than ever before. Skidding on any surface was made well-nigh impossible, cornering risks were eliminated, and the inequalities of any road ... or no road at all ... were magically smoothed out. Today, these features are being hailed and introduced as notable innovations, but wise motorists know that only on CITROËN cars are they *all* available, and ONLY ON CITROËN CARS ARE THE FULL BENEFITS OF FOUR YEARS CONTINUOUS PRACTICE OBTAINABLE. Be safe and buy safe...and you can buy a CITROËN for as little as £198.

1939 MODELS & PRICES:

"Twelve" Saloon - - - £238	"Twelve" Roadster - - £265	"Light Fifteen" Roadster £275
"Twelve" Popular Saloon £198	"Light Fifteen" Saloon - £248	"Big Fifteen" Saloon - £278
	"Light Fifteen" Popular Saloon £208	"Big Fifteen" 7-seater Saloon £298

STAND **141**
MOTOR SHOW
EARLS COURT
OCT. 13—22

CITROËN THE CAR WITH THE PULL

CITROËN CARS LTD., SLOUGH, BUCKS.

*This advertisement in **The Autocar** of 7th October 1938 for the Twelve and Fifteen models proclaim the car four years ahead of its time; this was an increase of two years against the claim on introduction and still a huge understatement. However, in retrospect, the car was twenty years ahead when launched in 1934. Note that the range included the low-priced Popular version of the Twelve and Light Fifteen.*

Saloon form. The Popular models were equipped to a lower specification and were marketed at correspondingly lower prices. In both versions, the Popular was £40 cheaper than the De Luxe model. The lowering of the price was at the expense of the level of trim; cloth seats replaced leather, bumpers were made from light steel and there was no sliding sun roof. The instruments were clustered within a single unit which resembled that fitted to the Paris built models and the exterior of the car was finished in black cellulose with chrome fittings. The famous Chevrons were fitted to the radiator grille but on the De Luxe models these were replaced by the Citroën insignia.

Further changes were made to the De Luxe cars; the gear change received modification to make it lighter and in addition the gear lever was connected to the clutch assembly with a locking device preventing movement of the lever until the clutch pedal had been depressed. A new type of Michelin wheel had been introduced, it was lighter in weight and provided for better performance. The wheels, known as 'Pilotes' became almost as famous as the cars themselves, they were built up of steel pressings with wide steel spokes. The tyre section and configuration of the rims were exceptionally wide to accommodate the 'Superconfort' tyres introduced by Michelin, the pressures of which were a mere 18-20 lbs. per square inch. Despite such low running pressure the deformation at cornering speeds was so slight that roadholding was nothing but incredible. Slightly wider wings were given to the models, apart from a finer appearance they allowed greater protection from mud and water. Improved shock absorbers of the double-acting hydraulic type were fitted which gave a better ride. Under the bonnet, an improved air filter was specified whilst on the dashboard the oil-pressure gauge was eliminated in preference for a warning light.

Aluminium protectors were fitted to the front and rear wings; the rear 'spats' prevented loose stones from chipping the paintwork and the front protectors, having their origins in France, not only prevented damage from loose chippings but acted as a shoe and boot cleaner. Built into the front wing guard was a split edge in order the driver and front passenger could scrape mud from their feet before getting into the car.

The 1911cc engine gave the Light 15 a very positive performance. Whilst the top speed was, perhaps, not exceptional, speeds through the gears and the rate of acceleration were no less than lively. Being a flexible power unit, the car was able to pick up speed from a low pace in top gear but, used with deliberation, the gear ratios created a definite sporting feel. Drivers of the Traction Avant soon learned they could quite easily take corners at speeds not found possible on other cars and at the same time feel perfectly secure.

The Motor, in their road test of 16th May, 1938, found the Light 15 almost overwhelming. Their report opened as follows:

'Seldom do we drive cars which give such an outstanding sense of safety and security as that which is enjoyed when handling the Citroën. It is an unconventional car which one might describe as unconventional stability. Drive hard over any sort of surface in the wet, even over the despised wood blocks, or any other known slippery surface which you may encounter in the course of your everyday motoring, and it will be found that the Citroën goes just where it is steered—truly as if on rails. Corner a bit faster than usual, and round the car goes, with all the certainty that one can desire. No front wheel dither and no tail slide-stability such as is available with very few cars indeed.'

A Royal Visit to Paris by Their Majesties King Geoge V1, Queen Elizabeth and the Royal Princesses, Elizabeth and Margaret in June 1938 included a visit to the Citroën headquarters at Javel. On the outside of the building was hung a huge Union Jack. It was on this occasion that the Princesses were each presented with a scale model of the Roadster complete with a doll at the driving wheel. Naturally the cars were right hand drive. Included in the cars were a full wardrobe for the dolls. It is ironical that the cars, which are the ultimate in Jouets Citroën, were built at the Slough Factory.

During September 1938, there came from Paris the announcement of a six cylinder version of the Traction Avant. Citroën Cars at Slough made it clear the car would not be put into production at the British Factory until the Autumn of 1939 when the programme for 1940 was available. The announcement of the six cylinder model created some excitement when news of it was released from Slough. It was a handsome machine with a specification to match its looks. Under the bonnet lay a power house of 2866cc putting the big Citroën within reach of the three-litre league of cars. Never before had so much power been driven through the front axle. The Six was designed around the already successful Big 15 and used the same body shell. The bonnet was slightly different and signalled a change in design that was eventually to adopted by the whole range of Traction Avant cars. The hinged ventilators on the bonnet sides were replaced by fluted louvres that ran almost the entire length between the radiator cowling and the scuttle. The Six had larger headlamps and fitted below them were twin air horns. At the lower part of the front wings auxilary driving lamps offered capacious illumination. For the first time on Traction models windscreen wipers were attached to the scuttle instead of immediately above the windscreen.

The engine and gearbox of the Six followed the general design of the Four by being suspended within the front cradle customary to the Floating Power system on the Traction. With the engine being of greater size than the four, the gearbox was modified in order the whole assembly fitted into the same space. The specification was also similar to the Fifteen with the bore and stroke 78 x 100mm and with detachable cylinder liners. The locking device for the gear lever re-appeared, so did the Pilote wheels. Coming onto the market some five years after the introduction of the Traction Avant, the Six Cylinder benefited greatly from the lessons that had been learned in the intermediate years. It at once became a sound car achieving high standards of ride and comfort. The Six fell into the luxury class; the interior was trimmed with quality leather and the usual equipment of opening windscreen,

This view of a 1939 Big Fifteen Saloon was taken inside the Slough Factory and demonstrates the distinctive profile of the Traction Avant. By that date, Pilote wheels were standard on British-built cars. Completed Light and Big Fifteens await delivery nearby — note the white sheet held up to eliminate any distractive background. It seems probable that this photograph might have been intended as a basis for a cut-out illustration for advertisement purposes.

sunroof, arm rests on front and rear seats and map pockets in the doors were all provided.

The Six was not to see its production launch in 1939; War was declared and, like other motor manufacturing plants, the Citroën Factory was requisitioned for the war effort. All car production ceased at the factory, the end of another era had dawned and car production in Britain was on the verge of change.

During hostilities the Citroën works were engaged in producing armaments for the forces. The assembly lines were at work twenty-four hours a day; existing personnel not called upon to enter the armed services joined women and enlisted staff in the manufacture of arms in the form of guns, cannons, tanks and other war machines. In the place of Citroën cars, military vehicles and Bedford lorries rolled off the assembly lines; parts for Churchill tanks as well as aircraft were manufactured and throughout the period the factory was a major supplier of products for the Canadian forces. The production of Citroën cars were not resumed until 1946.

This page from a booklet issued by Citroën in March 1939 shows the recently-introduced six-cylinder version of the Traction Avant range, designated the 15 in France — it was to be simply the Six in Britain. The longer engine was accommodated in a bonnet extended forward but it was not found necessary to extend the overall length of the car as compared to the 11 (British Big Fifteen) as the radiator grille was positioned closer to the front bumper. Note the louvred bonnet and Pilote wheels. Unfortunately the planned British launch in the Autumn of 1939 did not happen due to the outbreak of war.

BERLINES
15
6 CYLINDRES

5 places - 2 sièges séparés et réglables à l'avant - Banquette à 3 places à l'arrière avec accoudoir central escamotable - Indicateurs de direction et feux de position - Cotes intérieures : Longueur 2 m. 18. Largeur 1 m. 35. Hauteur 1 m. 23.

After the diversion of the Citroën factory at Slough to military production during the Second World War, production of cars was resumed with the Light Fifteen, announced in October 1945 and with deliveries beginning in 1946. Post-war cars differed from those built before 1940, notably in the use of louvred bonnet sides in place of the type with hinged ventilation ports and in the repositioning of the windscreen wipers below rather than above the screen. The particular car in the photograph, registered in Lancashire at the end of 1946, is a superb example of the post-war Light Fifteen - note the Pilote wheels and 'straight' door handles, contrasting with those on Paris-built cars which were of a 'curly' shape.

Chapter eight:
Peace and the road ahead

With the ending of the War, Britain's motor industry began to get back onto its feet again. The road ahead was not smooth, not even the Traction Avant could make easy work of all the bumps. The Government had given the industry an ultimatum - export or bust! And so the challenge was accepted. Enormous efforts were made to sell the British car abroad; there was no choice, the Government told manufacturers steel would be supplied only to those companies selling 75% of their production overseas. Almost all the car makers, whether small or large, offered left and right hand drive, imperial and metric instruments. The orders for cars rushed in, waiting lists for home sales grew longer by the day. The majority of cars produced were exported immediately and in many cases an entire production left the Country. Austin's 1947 A40 production were destined, as a whole, to go abroad, out of the first 50,000 cars built only 3000 found their way to British customers. In addition to the problems this created for satisfying sales to the British market there was a general ban on the importation of cars until 1953.

Citroën recommenced car production at Slough in 1946 and in that year produced 1050 cars, 408 cars were exported leaving just over half of the total production for the home market. In 1947, the situation changed, 1,940 cars were built with 1,373 cars going abroad; this pattern was to continue all the way through to 1955.

Many of the cars produced in British factories following the cessation of hostilities were seen to be old-fashioned; production had been hastily resumed using pre-war designs and presses, so great was the effort put into building for export little time or money existed for the development of new models. So great was the demand for cars abroad that neither the purchaser or manufacturer cared as to the design of cars available. The luxury touches of sliding roofs and leather trim were often forfeited in the rush to sell vehicles and it is no wonder that Britain became the largest exporter of cars in the world for a time.

Citroën were in the fortunate position of having a highly advanced design of car; in 1946 the Traction Avant had been introduced twelve years before, yet, if the car had

A partly completed car arriving by overhead conveyor in the Slough works, ready for engine, gearbox and transmission system to be installed. Note how the car was built, in as much that the power unit was installed within a cradle and then bolted to the hull.

been launched immediately after the War it would have created almost as great an impression for being ultra-modern as it did when first announced. The features of the Light 15 were profound; it had front wheel drive, torsion bar suspension, monocoque body and its methods of mass-production had been perfected. Little had needed to be changed at the Slough Factory, assembly lines were re-tooled to facilitate new models as required but as the original conception of the plant was so thorough, it was an easy task to keep the machinery updated to allow for efficient production.

On reopening the Citroën Factory after the War, one aspect had changed. There had been a shift in policy that would eventually alter the entire operation of producing motor cars. From the 1920s when Citroën's strategy was to build the whole car from virtually all-British materials, there appeared a shift in attitude. The factory was to become purely an assembly plant of ready-made materials constructed in France or Britain so that no longer would there be any real manufacturing at Slough.

Most of the materials arrived at the factory by rail via the Trading Estate link from the main Great Western Railway or by road transport. The body parts, the main 'coque' which served as floor and chassis, roof, wings bonnet and body furniture, were unloaded and placed into especially designed racks for eventual use. Major heavy components such as engines and gearboxes were unloaded by gantry crane which carried up to five units at a time, still on their pallets, and were then stored within the factory. Engines and gearboxes were manufactured in France.

At the start of the process of building the front drive Citroën, the coque, which was identical to the type used in French production, had first to be adapted to British specification. This included the alteration to the battery mounting to accept 12 volt electrics, repositioning of body mounting points for steering, clutch and braking controls. The blue protective coatings that had been placed upon the body panels in France, were removed, and the pressings placed into jigs to create a complete body side, scuttle and back. When trimmed and cleaned all the sections were fitted together and welded. Once carried out, the body was placed into a special jig that allowed this to be welded to the coque; the jig for this operation was unusual in as much it could be rotated so that the underside of the floor could be welded in a particular position in order that the base of the car could be welded underside uppermost. All the work up to this point had been carried out on the moving assembly lines for which the factory was so famous when it very first opened. With the main assembly of the body being made, the unit was removed from the automated conveyor and placed upon a tracked trolley on rails, so that the interior fittings could be installed such as seat mounting brackets. The roof was placed into position (many of the cars had openings for sliding steel sunroofs) and welded to the frame to make a complete body assembly. Next, door hinges were fitted and the doors hung; slots were cut out for the trafficator arms in the door pillars and the necessary mechanism fitted.

With all motor vehicle manufacturing, requirement exists for some re-finishing work. According to an article in the magazine *Motor Industry* very little remedial finishing was necessary on the Traction Avant due to the extremely

Special rotating jig allowing welding to be carried out on the underside of the car. Note the ease in which the jig could be turned. The floor pressing, which also formed the 'chassis' was called the coque, a word more familiar in the form relating to the complete shell — 'monocoque'.

high standard of workmanship and quality of assembly maintained on the production line. Much has, of course, to be said of the mass-production methods at the Slough Factory which proved to be very effective. There was the need for some panel beating and the filling in of any depression with body solder, but little time had to be spent in this respect. Assembly line supervisors were careful to watch the progress of the vehicles coming off the production conveyor systems and checked for any defaults or irregularities. Their eyes were keen and any offending work was chalked so that remedial work could be carried out.

From this point the body underwent a series of treatments to make it suitable from weathering and climatic agents. Firstly, Deoxidine cleaning and then into an oven for a 15-minute bake after which, the powdery residue was removed by a special vacuum cleaning process. Bitumastic paint was brushed on to the underside of the wings followed by the interior and exterior of the bodyshell being sprayed with a zinc-chromate primer. Back into the oven for an hour's bake at a high temperature; two more coats of primer followed and yet again into an oven, but this time for a longer period of 1 hour 50 minutes. Further inspections were carried out once the shell had returned from the oven to ensure that all the surfaces were perfect. Any surfaces that required stopping or treatment at this stage were dealt with and the shell returned to the oven for a final bake. The initial colour coats of paint were applied and checked before the final coats were sprayed on; after a rough hand polish the body was ready for the trim shop.

The Factory had an exclusive trim shop that provided all the materials required for completing the interior finish to the cars produced at the works. Leathers and fabric trim were marked and cut out in bulk. At the time of fitting the trim all interior fittings and furniture were installed before the completed body assembly was ready for the conveyor system again when the power unit was fitted together with the front and rear axles. It was then the whole article looked like a finished car ready to be driven away. Before that though, it was directed to the finishing hall where final adjustments were made and the car given a deep polish before the road test and final approval.

The resumption of production at Citroën after the War gave the sales of the car a new impetus. Whereas buyers of 'British' cars had to be content with little choice and uncertain availability as well as often old-fashioned design, Citroën tempted the purchaser to decide upon a well-tried but highly modern machine at a competitive price. Whilst it was the intention to use as much British material as possible by way of accessories, there were occasions when it was not possible for these to be obtained. Alternative supplies often had to be found at very short notice to prevent the production lines grinding to a halt. There were times, therefore, when cars left the Factory with differing specification to that given in the catalogue or the owner's handbook. In general, Lucas supplied the majority of electrical equipment including the lighting; Pyrene, the bumpers; Fairey Aviation, the radiator shells while Newton and Bennett manufactured and supplied the shock absorbers. Triplex supplied the glass, leather hides and trim from Connolly and Ruben-Owen supplied the wheels.

The 1628cc engine was deleted from the catalogue as was the Twelve on resuming delivery of cars, leaving the 1911cc Light 15 to represent the range of cars. The Six Cylinder, whilst announced before the War did not appear for a further two years. Neither were the 'Popular' models reinstated; there was no need to market a model with down-graded specification as Citroën were in the position of selling as many cars as they could possibly build. Minor changes in design included the anchoring of the windscreen wipers to the scuttle and changing the opening ports on the bonnet to fluted louvres although the latter change did not take place until the Autumn of 1946, ready for the 1947 production year of vehicles.

The cost of the Light Fifteen increased by over £200 on its re-launch in 1946 to £573-3s-11d. This was in contrast to £640 (plus purchase tax) for the Jowett Javelin, £672 for the MG 1¼ litre YA Saloon and £735 for the Sunbeam Talbot Ten. *The Motor*, when reviewing the Light Fifteen in March 1946, wrote of the car:

'It is true to say that if the Citroën Light Fifteen had been making its first appearance today instead of continuing where it left off at the out-break of war, it would have created a buzz of sensation as the latest in advanced automobile engineering thought.'

The Light Fifteen was, at 21¼ cwt, the lightest car per foot of wheelbase on the British market. It was also one of the strongest cars, resulting from its unique construction. The torsion bar suspension helped eliminate any tendency to run wide on cornering, an inherent hazard with some front-wheel drive design cars. It ensured a safe and smooth ride for which the car received justifiable fame. It was possible to obtain high average speeds with the car without the necessity of attaining maximum speeds. The Motor, even referred to the Light Fifteen as having a 'racing car stability'. With its proven record of roadholding and its capacity for speed over rough surfaces, it is no wonder that the Traction Avant soon found its way to practically every corner of the world, especially where good road surfaces were limited. Many of the cars built for export went to Australia, New Zealand, South Africa, the Middle and Far East and the colonies of Central and North Africa.

In the hands of motoring journalists and test drivers, the Traction Avant was virtually a plaything. Against many other cars of the period immediately after the War, the Light 15 offered a great number of features alternative cars were unable to match. The British car industry was in a process of successive amalgamations. The Morris combine had become known as the Nuffield group, with Riley added in 1938 to its MG and Wolsley subsidiaries, but a far bigger upheaval was to come in 1952 when Nuffield merged with Austin to form the British Motor Corporation with a growing trend to 'badge' engineering.The Rootes Brothers, who at one time had shown immense interest in the Citroën Company and, no doubt, regretted never gaining control of some of Citroën's United Kingdom outlets, had taken over Hillman, Humber, Sunbeam and Talbot. Standard made a bid for Triumph in 1944 and won

A Big Fifteen somewhere in France.... Not a Slough-built car but a Paris-built 11CV in its home surroundings. The photograph emphasizes the painted radiator and the external chevrons which give the car the impression of a lower profile compared to the chromed radiator of Slough cars. This late model car has not been made to look more beautiful with the rectangular fog lamps!

the day, leaving the market with large combines and a number of very much smaller companies that owed their existence to their providing a specialist type of vehicle such as luxury and sporting cars. Citroën competed ably with both and held a somewhat unique position in the league of manufacturers in Britain.

Most products of the large combines were no match for Citroën in specification or performance, yet cars such as Rover and other exclusive marques of the period aimed at different attributes not pursued by Citroën. After testing what could be termed 'normal' cars, the difference was very much perceived to be in the handling of the Traction; it would go into bends and come out of them at much higher than average speeds with far greater stability. The Light Fifteen was able to demonstrate excellent fuel consumption figures even when the car was driven to its full potential – a fact that has remained true of the Citroën marque ever since. This was important since the good handling, and the type of driver to which the car appealed, was likely to make use of the performance available. *The Motor* reported that only two cars overtook during the 500-mile fuel consumption run with a Light Fifteen in 1951 the figure obtained being 25.2 m.p.g.

It was not until 1948 that any significant change in car assembly at Slough took place. The introduction of the Michelin X radial tyre transformed the front wheel drive performance even further, though not available here until 1954. The Six-Cylinder front drive, announced before the War but shelved, was at last put into production. With the reputation of the four cylinder model there was little doubt the Six would be anything less than a success.

The Six-Cylinder Traction Avant was well received on the British market. The Six, of course, had a very special character of its own; whilst its pedigree was instantly recognizable it soon created a highly respected niche in the large, luxury and grand-touring class of motor car. The engine and power output allowed for long distances to be covered comfortably and quickly, outpacing the Light Fifteen and indeed many other production cars of the time. All was not quite perfect though, with the engine and gearbox weighing 9½ cwt in the front cradle, the car was able to cruise very easily with absolute smoothness, but town driving did present some minor irksome tendencies.

A little roughness could be experienced when changing down through the gears especially at lower speeds. There was one saving factor, as the torque of the engine was so pronounced it was possible to leave the car in top gear at much lower speeds, and experience a smooth take-up of power, than it would normally have been thought possible. By alteration of the ignition timing control on the dashboard to the retard position, it was possible to save on some gear changing as the top ratio could be retained over longer periods. Some drivers criticised the controls as being too heavy; when the Six Cylinder was driven as intended, that is utilising it to its full potential, any suggestion of undue heaviness in normal driving could be dismissed. *The Motor* allowed itself to be the subject of some male chauvinism - a report of the Six Cylinder Traction ended as follows:

'Essentially masculine in its character, the Citroën Six is undoubtedly a car which will appeal most strongly to those drivers who especially value a car displaying willingness to be driven hard on main roads. The reputation of its manufacturers suggests that it should be extremely durable, as well as effortless in feel in the hands of fast drivers.'

The family resemblance between the Light Fifteen and the Six was quite evident; the Six was longer and wider, the bonnet and radiator sported a lower, sleeker profile which accentuated the look of extra power and speed. The headlamps on the Light Fifteen were smaller in design but were well suited to the overall dimensions of the car when viewed against the larger car. Interior specifications, while similarly equipped, enabled both cars to enjoy absolute comfort and the trim could only be described as superb. The main difference amounted to the space available for driver and passengers; the seats on the Six were wider with the front bench seat having provision of a central armrest, there was more shoulder room and rear passengers had the advantage of extra leg room. The Light Fifteen was equipped with separately adjustable front bucket seats.

Instrumentation was almost identical between the two models, all the necessary information required for the driver was available within a neat array of dials. Over the years of producing the Traction Avant differing forms of fascia style had been tried. Firstly, the design had been

The Familiale, or Family Saloon, was one of the most elegant of Traction Avant. Identified by the long wheelbase and six-light body, it afforded supreme comfort and accommodation having occasional seats, positioned behind the front seats, which could be folded down into the floor well when not in use. The extended boot facilitated the carrying of extra luggage and housed the spare wheel. The car depicted is a French-built 11CV having the four-cylinder 1911cc engine. Note the curly door handles, indicators on the rear flank above the wings, painted radiator and headlamp shells.

similar to that found on Paris built cars, then, a change in favour to round instrument dials and after the break in production a further change was instigated with an emphasis on more of the 'British style' using separate visual indicators for each major function whereas French drivers were content to have all the relevant information condensed neatly into one nacelle. On both the Slough cars, instruments were designed to be easily read through the spokes of the steering wheel; the speedometer was placed centrally with the fuel gauge to its right and ammeter to the left. A clock was positioned to the extreme left, which enabled it to be seen by the front passenger, and on the extreme right, housed in a small binnacle, were the starter button, choke control, ignition key and oil pressure warning light. The handbrake lever could be found underneath the dashboard and was simply a 'pull and twist' lever that actuated drum brakes on the rear wheels.

With such a technically advanced car as the Traction Avant it seemed almost archaic that Citroën deemed to install a manual back-up to the windscreen wipers in case of failure of the electric mechanism. On the dashboard two knurled wheels, corresponding to the windscreen wiper arms, allowed manual operation of the wipers. Imagine the problems of trying to be a contortionist in clearing the windscreen whilst steering and changing gear! Between the steering wheel and the protruding gear lever there were two further controls, the ignition advance and retard, and the direction indicators. In the case of Slough-built cars the indicator switch operated semaphore trafficators. In time, the trafficator assembly was found to be the cause of rusting on some cars; water had a habit of entering the

Three post-war Citroen Traction Avant. The car in the foreground is a Slough Light Fifteen, note the Pilote wheels, and also note that the door handles are from a French-built model! The centre car is a Big Fifteen, denoted by the smoother radiator cowling and again a Slough-built car. Furthest away from the camera is is Paris Big Fifteen, identified by the headlamps which are painted, the painted radiator cowling and Double Chevron on the outside of the grille.

A beautifully prerserved Slough-built Six, UEH 735 was first registered in Stoke-on-Trent in 1954. It is noteworthy that the radiator badge reads '15, 6 cyl' as on the Paris-built cars even though the designation Fifteen referred to the four-cylinder 1911cc range of Traction Avant cars in Britain. The 10ft. 1½in. wheelbase and 5ft. 10ins. width were common to the Six and Big Fifteen but the style of bumper made the Six slightly longer at 15ft. 1ins. overall at that date. As well as the distinctive radiator grille, the Six had a different pattern of headlamp. Just visible in the pillar between the doors is the trafficator — this concours-winning car has draught deflectors on the front windows.

semaphore orifice, dripping down to the floor pan and after a time rotted the sill area. The horn and headlamp dipping switch were attached to a long fixed arm that protruded from the right hand side of the steering column which enabled the driver to operate these controls without having the need to take hands off the steering wheel. A vision of things to come. Apart from the winding windows, extra ventilation was attainable by the forward opening of the windscreen by means of a wheel attached to the top of the dashboard. In addition, a scuttle vent could be opened via an almost inaccessible wing nut under the fascia but again this was an area, if not checked, rain water could enter and apart from rotting the metal played havoc with the electrical wiring. Most Slough cars built at this period were equipped with a sliding steel sunroof providing even greater comfort.

By 1949, the light switch, which before had been located in the small nacelle as the starter button and ignition key, had been moved to a redesigned arm on the steering column. Still on the right hand side of the wheel, the control now consisted of a twist-and-push lever action rod which incorporated the horn-push and headlamp dip control.

The heater device was a somewhat Heath-Robinson-style affair. Merely a hollow tube that fastened behind the radiator, it delivered warm air into the front footwell of the car. This was relatively successful whilst the car was moving at speed as the forced-air intake over the engine permitted a ramming effect. As soon as the car slowed down or stopped so the heat was lost. The cost of this optional extra - just £1. Later a valve was fitted via a switch on the fascia panel which went some way in providing a regulated heat output.

The Citroën front wheel drive was an enthusiast's car. It certainly held an enviable reputation for performance, reliability and safety. On the Continent, Traction Avant were used as taxis as well as being widely chosen by police forces. It was also used by gangsters alike. No more famous a policeman than Georges Simenon's Maigret drove a Traction Avant in the famous detective stories. The car became instantly recognisable in the long-running British television series during the 1950s and '60s. Rupert Davies, the Actor who portrayed Maigret, owned the car used in the filming of the series. Even after a total of fifteen years following production of the first Citroën Traction Avant, the car was not in the least outdated; the Citroën was reinstated following the break in manufacture. It was found to perform with distinct freshness. André Citroën would have been proud.

In London at the 1952 Motor Show, models for 1953 were displayed. The Citroën stand was of particular interest, certainly to those favouring the marque. Existing models

The 'London Rally', 19th September 1952, organised by the London Motor Club. A 1946 Light Fifteen (11BL) with hubcaps removed checks in at a control point. Production of cars did not recommence after the war until early 1946. Upon resumption of car manufacturing, Slough were only able to offer one model, the 1911cc Light Fifteen Saloon which sold for £573 including purchase tax. The car was offered in just two colour schemes, black with beige interior or beige with beige trim. It is noteworthy that quite a high-ranking US Army officer appears to be doing the paperwork as an RAF officer looks on. A lady in Women's Institute-style attire and a man in a 'syren suit' add to an oddly wartime-like atmosphere.

underwent some alteration and an addition to the range appeared in the form of the Big Fifteen. It will be remembered that the Big Fifteen had been available before the War but this was the first time the model had been marketed since car production ceased in wartime. To many, therefore, its reintroduction was seen as an alternative car. The outline of the Light Fifteen underwent considerable change by the inclusion of an enlarged boot. On previous models the size of the boot was never the car's strongest point but now an effort had been made to remedy the situation. The spare wheel, and its cover, were moved from the boot lid to inside the trunk and still managed to allow a very generous 11½ cubic feet of luggage space on the Light Fifteen and even more space on the Big Fifteen and the Six. Other improvements concerned the fitting of a new type of Lucas distributor; that while retaining manual control of ignition advance and retard from the dashboard, it was operated by speed and throttle opening. A filter was installed in the fuel system and metallic paintwork became available for cars in colours other than black.

The Big Fifteen was welcomed back onto the market. There was a demand by motorists who wanted the space and facilities of the six-cylinder model without necessarily the extra performance or, indeed, the higher fuel consumption. The Big Fifteen with the 1911cc engine from the Light Fifteen was, therefore, a popular choice. In 1953, *The Motor* referred to the Traction Avant in the following terms when reviewing the Big Fifteen:

'When the front wheel drive Citroën was first introduced, it was a boldly unconventional design. That, however, was eighteen years ago, and although owners of other types of cars still tend to look on the design as 'unorthodox', it must in fact now be regarded as one of the most thoroughly proven layouts existing anywhere in the world.'

In the majority of cases, by 1953 the design of British cars had changed. A more rounded concept had arrived with bulbous bonnets, boots and wings. Radiator cowlings and headlamps were incorporated into neat new frontal images. Headlights were either nestled neatly each side of the radiator grille or faired daintily into the wings. Not so the Citroën. Headlamps remained in the same position as

Paris built Big Fifteen (foreground) meets Slough-built Light Fifteen on wedding duty. The larger headlamps of the Paris car are evident whilst the Slough car has the chromed radiator. The Big Fifteen also has a large boot whereas the Light Fifteen of 1947 vintage has a small boot.

they had in 1934 and the general overall styling was retained. Yet overall the car still seemed streamlined and sleek. It is difficult to believe that a car could be visually dated some ten years but have such advanced features compared to the new designs in automobile engineering. Some of these new models had quite atrocious performance and road-holding tendencies dating way back beyond the introduction of the Traction Avant.

There were a number of examples of Citroën front drive cars that were never destined to be built at Slough. These included special-bodied cars, some of which were designated for French Presidential duties. A number of coachbuilders fabricated cars with modified front wings or radiator cowlings but in reality relatively few cars were supplied and even fewer have survived. One version of the Traction, alas, never destined to be sold in the United Kingdom was the Commerciale. Designed on the Big Fifteen and using the 'Familiale' six-light bodywork, the rear panel opened to roof level, a forerunner of the modern hatchback. This elegant car was ideally suited to the businessman or farmer and an advertising poster of the day showed a vigneron loading two barrels of wine into the boot hatch.

Probably the most famous non-survivor was the ill-fated '22', a car that is still revered to this day, well over fifty years after the first prototype had been built. Based on the long wheelbase car, the 22 was to have had an engine of Vee-Eight configuration, 3822cc, which would in effect have been two four-cylinder 1911cc engines on a common block. In 1935, it would surely have been a 'supercar'. Continuing problems with the power unit led, it is rumoured, to the testing being undertaken with a Ford vee-eight engine under the bonnet. Finally the project was abandoned. Funds were short at Javel and the decision was taken not to spend any further money on it.

Instead of the vee-eight 22, Citroën settled for a large car with an engine just under three litres and it was this that founded the six-cylinder range of models. If the 22 was planned to be the ultimate Traction Avant then Citroën managed to produce another vehicle that equalled the claim. It appeared twenty-one years after the 22 was

The famed 22. This was to have been Citroën's supercar, for in 1935 it was hoped to launch this vee-eight version of the Traction Avant. It is rumoured that the car was demonstrated at the Salon and Motor Show with a Ford V8 3622cc engine instead of Citroën's own unit under the locked bonnet. The 22 was an impressive looking car with its headlamps faired into the front wings. These views show the red-painted roadster displayed at the 1934 Paris Salon and a saloon version. Sadly, all prototypes were thought to be destroyed although a rumour exists there is one prototype 22 hidden away.

conceived and apart from the detail of the headlamps and a few minor points, had practically the same body in design. The six cylinder engine was employed, the front torsion bars were extended and an anti-roll bar fitted. On the rear suspension, however, torsion bars gave way to a hydropneumatic system. The result was considerably

Long before the hatchback, as now understood, came on the scene, Citroën's Paris factory was building the Commerciale version which used the same body shell as the Familiale, but with the rear end opening up to roof level. The weight of the spare wheel made it necessary to retain the bottom-hinged lower section. Note how the side passenger door opened wide enough to lie almost flat alongside the driver's door. This illustration came from a brochure issued in March 1939.

5 places - 2 sièges séparés et réglables à l'avant - Banquette à 3 places à l'arrière pouvant occuper 2 positions - Garnitures amovibles en moleskine grise - Cotes intérieures : Longueur 2 m. 35. Largeur 1 m. 37. Hauteur 1 m. 22.

COMMERCIALE
11
VOITURE DE TOURISME

Demander la

Another supercar, but this time a success story, was the 15 Six H, as it was known in France, and also produced at Slough where it was described simply as the Six (Hydro-pneumatic suspension). The new suspension was confined to the rear axle for this initial application, though the torsion bars of the front suspension were lengthened. The car's kerb weight went up from 26½ cwt to 27¼ cwt. Put into production for the 1954 season in France, over 3,000, including the car shown, were produced by the Paris factory in the period up to 1956. The Slough output was much smaller, two cars being built in 1954 and 74 in 1935. In Britain the basic price was £1,040, rising to £1,474 with purchase tax. **The Motor** *road test of March 1955 quoted a timed maximum speed of 84 m.p.h. and an overall fuel consumption over 665 miles of 18 m.p.g.*

enhanced road-holding and a marked increase in passenger comfort. The car was known as the 6H, 'H' standing for hydropneumatic. It was identified by its luxurious specification of interior trim and the unique stance of the car when at rest, with a noticeably lower profile at the rear. When the engine was started, a pump sent hydraulic fluid to spheres on the back wheels which quickly lifted the car to the correct driving position irrespective of the load carried.

The 6H was ideal in France where roads were at the time noted for their roughness. In Britain, with good surfaces, the qualities of the car were not always at first appreciated. The 6H was marketed only in saloon version, other body styles were never quoted in the Citroën catalogue. It was available from Slough from the end of 1954, having been announced earlier during the year. Just two 6H models were built at Slough in 1954 and a further 74 were produced

The under-bonnet space of the 15 Six H was well filled, with the top of the engine only just clearing the bonnet top.

in 1955. In France, during the two years only 3,062 examples were manufactured. The colours available for the car were black, red, grey and green, the latter being a metallic colour. Best quality leather was used for the upholstery and optional extras to the car's specification included a sliding steel sunroof, de-icers and fog lamps. At its launch the 6H cost £1,474 9s 2d including purchase tax.

When reviewing the ride and performance of the car, *The Motor* stated:

'When the car is driven away on an ordinary southern English road the benefits of this apparently complicated arrangement are not immediately apparent. The driver certainly and the passengers probably are more immediately impressed with the high standard of stability which arises from some of the other novel features of the design. Having by modern standards an exceptionally long wheelbase, a track of 4ft. 10½ ins., and an unusually low centre of gravity, the car is almost wholly free from roll. This in conjunction with the remarkable cornering power inherent in the Michelin X tyres gives a feeling of safety when sweeping through quite severe bends at between 60 and 70 miles per hour, which must be experienced to be believed.'

The Traction, and especially the Six Cylinder (even more so the 6H) were truly remarkable cars. There was no doubt, even *The Motor* admitted taking the 6H through 'quite severe bends at speeds between 60 and 70 m.p.h., the roadholding was way and above that of any average car on the market and it most certainly had the feeling that the wheels were attached to rails.

'Let us continue, reported *The Motor*, 'on to even worse surfaces. When the driver chooses to demonstrate by taking the car on to unmade roads he instinctively braces himself for the shock which will attend the striking of 4 inch or even 5 inch obstacles at speeds of between 60 and 70 miles per hour. But if the passengers can be persuaded to read a book or newspaper they will find that they will continue to do so and have little or no knowledge of the road surface, appalling as it is, over which the car is being driven'.

The idea of an air suspension was not new but Citroën though did lead the way in which it was applied to a motor vehicle. General Motors had experimented and shown a similar system a year before the 6H appeared but chose not to proceed with it, shelving the whole conception. The basic drawback to an air suspension was of how to store the air without it leaking. Citroën pioneered the project like so many other features now found on the modern motor car. The principle of the 6H suspension was that a seven piston pump was driven by the engine which took fluid from a reservoir and fed it under pressure to a hydraulic accumulator. A sphere was positioned by each of the rear wheels and in each of these a volume of gas was retained by a diaphragm and, according to the wheel movement, an amount of gas was then compressed by the action of the circulating fluid having an affect upon the diaphragm. The constant height of the suspension was attained by means of a lever connected to an attitude compensator which measured the amount of fluid entering the sphere on each wheel.

The author's 1947 Slough-built Light Fifteen. The headlamps are not standard equipment but appear to have been original. Painted instead of chromed, the shells and lenses are slightly smaller than the type normally fitted. As the car was built soon after production recommenced in Britain, it can only be assumed that the standard equipment was in short supply and to save a wait the car was despatched with alternative lamp units.

An excellent example of a Slough-built Light Fifteen. Well loaded with camping equipment, the car arrives at a Citroën enthusiasts meeting. The bonnet louvres and large section bumpers date the car as post 1951, and the registration number indicates that it was first licensed early in 1952. Note the rear wing guards, these were made by Robri and sold as an add-on item.

The Citroën 6H had signalled a new thought in automobile design. The development in suspension had been hugely successful even if the car was not built in great numbers at Slough. Had André Citroën lived he would have been immensely proud of the cars he had conceived. Even with Pierre Boulanger at the helm, the Company had followed a great many of the principles the Patron had lived and struggled for. The last of the Traction Avant rolled off the assembly lines at Slough in 1955; in that year a total of 1,400 examples were produced - 716 Light Fifteens, 500 Sixes, 74 6Hs and 110 Big Fifteens. When the announcement was made that Traction production had ceased there was general dismay throughout the entire works. Order books were still full with 400 orders outstanding. These cars were never built. As the last Traction Avant left the Factory there was, without doubt, a tear in the eyes of many who had lovingly worked on the cars over the twenty-two year span of manufacture. The car that had caused so much to be said of it when it was first introduced both in France and Britain was still as famous. After twenty-two years it was still ahead of its time and in 1955 front wheel drive was still not fully appreciated in Britain.

Although the demise of the Traction Avant was significant in that it represented the end of an era, it was also the end of an entire epoch. Car production without the Citroën Traction Avant was to consider Paris without the Eiffel Tower or London without Big Ben. If then, this was the end of an epoch, an entirely new age was about to begin.

End of an era. The rear view of one of the final version of the French-built 15 Six H cars, with tail lamps in both rear wings and the model badge moved to the centre of the boot door, as introduced from September 1954. Production of these cars continued in Paris until July 1956 though only small numbers were built in that final year.

It is difficult to imagine a car more utilitarian than the prototype 2CV, as built in 1939. In 1936, Pierre Boulanger, the Director of Citroën, had asked for a car that was simply 'an umbrella on four wheels' carrying four passengers and 50 kg of luggage at 50 k.p.h (30 m.p.h.) in comfort. The suspension had to be soft enough to allow a basket of eggs to be carried over a ploughed field without one being broken. Thus the Citroën design team produced this car, code-named Toutes Petite Voiture — TPV in short. Boulanger wanted a small, economical car (the 'minimum automobile francais') that would put the whole of France onto the road; it had to be simple to drive and even easier to repair. Despite its name, and its 375cc engine, it was not as small as, say, the Austin 7 or the original Fiat 500. The single headlamp added to the general look of austerity, yet complied with contemporary legal requirements.

Chapter nine:
Two horses and a jewel

Two years after the introduction of the Traction Avant, Pierre Boulanger called a meeting of the design teams. It has already been demonstrated that Boulanger was sympathetic to Citroën's principles and philosophy; the Patron had pioneered the mass production of 'The People's Car' with his determination to enter into motor car manufacturing in 1919 and he had seen the far-reaching potential of building the front-wheel drive car as a large volume product. Boulanger had sufficient foresight to understand that before too long, France and Europe would have the need of a low-priced, go-anywhere, do-anything cheap-to-maintain vehicle.

Boulanger's brief was simple. 'Four wheels under an umbrella'; enough space for four people, all wearing hats; 50Kg of luggage; a basket of eggs to be carried on the back seat. The car not only had to have extreme comfort but would have to be capable of travelling at least at 50 Km per hour. When driven over a ploughed field, not one egg had to be broken. Boulanger demanded an absolute minimum of a car with the maximum of versatility.

The code name given to the project was TPV - Toutes Petite Voiture. Boulanger recognised that the population of rural France, on the whole, relied upon more primitive forms of transport than the motor car; those who were fortunate in owning a car seldom bought new which meant that more often than not, second hand cars were usually unsuitable for the demand placed upon them, considering the poor state of the roads. Social trends were beginning to change in France, there was a market for a small car, economical and able to traverse the poorest of surfaces. It had to be capacious and utilitarian. The rural farmer would expect to pack into it anything from a bale of hay to a pig. Moreover, it had to be cheap to buy, require the very minimal maintenance with repairs able to be undertaken by the owner. The market potential was therefore tremendous. With the auspicious reputation of the Traction Avant, a small Citroën built to the right design had every chance of success. There was a need, also, for Citroën to diversify into an alternative range of models other than the Traction Avant.

By 1936, the initial design was laid down and a full-sized wooden mock-up was prepared. A year later the first road-going prototype was ready. The engine design was far from complete and in the event the initial trials were carried out using a BMW 500cc motor cycle engine. Eventually, the BMW unit was replaced by a twin-cylinder water cooled engine of 375cc capacity. Extensive use was made of a light alloy, duralinox, for the body panels, although expensive it did help to keep the weight of the car to a minimum. The prototypes showed the little car to be a minimal vehicle in every way. It was stark. Simple hammock seats were suspended from the roof while protection from the elements was afforded by a canvas top that stretched from the windscreen as far as the base of the boot. The barest of instruments were supplied and a handle started the engine (originally it was intended to have a pull-cable start), ignition was provided by means of a flywheel magneto whilst a single headlamp provided frontal illumination.

The suspension system for the TPV proved troublesome; a system of torsion bars, it was far too complicated and did not work well. André Lefebvre, who was placed in charge of the initial design work, was persuaded to install strengthening bars in the sub frame even at the expense of extra weight. Pierre Boulanger was anxious that the prototype be developed at great speed; it was becoming almost impossible to keep the project secret. Finally, Boulanger could wait no longer, he was confident the car was ready and ordered that it be shown at the 1939 Paris Salon and that 250 cars should be ready for the launch date. Apart from Boulanger's confidence, the state of readiness of the car was not shared by all the design team. In many respects it was 1934 all over again. As it happened, the TPV never had its debut; the outbreak of the Second World War prevented the Salon from taking place. Had it not been for the War, the future for Boulanger's TPV would have looked bleak.

With hostilities, the order was given for all 250 prototypes to be destroyed. One car was saved however and successfully hidden throughout the War. Although car production was halted during the War years, the design team at Citroën continued their work. It was recognised that once fighting had ceased there would be more need than ever for a minimal car. In secret, work was carried out developing and perfecting the design brief that Boulanger had ordered; the body became more rounded, the single headlamp was replaced by two lamps and the starting handle was supplemented with an electric motor. The interior received a facelift and seating improved whilst the problems concerning the suspension were satisfactorily overcome by the utilisation of a unique inter-connecting system. Up to this point, the Citroën designers had gone along with the idea of a water-cooled engine but now, Walter Becchia, an engineer who had joined Citroën from Talbot designed an air-cooled, flat twin-cylinder engine again of 375cc. This coupled up to a four-speed gearbox, which in reality was a three speed box with overdrive, fulfilled the original requirements of the car quite satisfactorily and began the long history of the use of air-cooled engines in small Citroën cars.

The detail features of the 1939 prototype version of the 2CV were as strange as its general appearance. The canvas top extended down to the tail of the car. The interior was even more 'basic' than the post-war production versions — note the seat squab suspended from the roof framing and the bent-strip door handles. What other concern could have designed what were virtually semi-cicular rear door outlines? Yet even more radical ideas were considered — such as bodywork entirely in canvas on an aluminium skeleton. The 375cc horizontally-opposed water-cooled two-cylinder engine was short enough to fit in front of the combined gearbox and differential, unlike the existing Traction Avant range — the engine developed 8 b.h.p. By May 1939, 250 examples of the prototype design were ready at the Levallois factory for the Paris salon de l'Auto that was never held, due to the outbreak of war in September of that year and the order was given to destroy them — but one was kept and is shown in these photographs.

Citroën's design team continued to work on the concept of the TPV during the war years knowing that the need for a basic go-anywhere, do-anything, cheap to buy car would be even greater once hostilities were over. The design of the TPV changed somewhat, the 375cc water-cooled engine was replaced by an air-cooled engine of the same capacity, the shape of the car was smoothed out a little and a second headlamp provided. Whilst extremely basic, the car gained electric starter and the minimum of instruments, interconnecting suspension and comfortable seating. The TPV became known simply as the 2CV.

With the War over, the TPV was ready for production. Boulanger planned that the car be displayed at the 1948 Salon. But what to call the little car? Designed to be simplicity itself and powered by a two-horse power engine, it was referred to merely as the 2CV.

The 2CV was unveiled at the 1948 Paris Motor Show and at once created a ferocious storm. It was denounced by the motor traders and critics alike; derisory comments were shouted from the press, Citroën were asked whether they gave a can-opener with every car they sold. It was called the worst car ever produced. Crowds gathered around the Citroën stand to look at the cars in amazement, nowhere had anything like it been seen before. Citroën agents shook their heads in disbelief at the Company's practical joke, how on earth, they asked, could this car be expected to sell? But sell it did. The French loved it and at once Citroën were inundated with orders.

Production of the 2CV did not commence until 1949. One hundred cars a day came off the production line at the Levallois plant in Paris, then 150 cars but even this was not enough. The waiting lists grew and up to 750 cars a day were being produced at one stage. Naturally, the 2CV was powered through its front wheels; any other form of transmission would have been unthinkable in view of Citroën's pioneering work with the Traction Avant and developing its qualities of roadholding. As it turned out, the roadholding on the 2CV was beyond all belief. The four-speed gearbox, fitted behind the engine instead of in front as with the Traction, had a top ratio that was more like an overdrive and once in top gear the car could lope along all day at a steady speed and return an incredibly high mileage from a gallon of petrol. The soft suspension, capable of off-road driving just as well as on normal surfaces, allowed passengers all the comforts of a large car. The front wheels were inter-connected with the rear by means of spring loaded cylinders placed longitudinally on each side of the chassis.

The 2CV was designed to go anywhere, and it did. Perhaps after the monocoque frame, as used on the Traction, it was strange to see the 2CV using a chassis, this

Unveiled at the 1948 Paris Salon, the 2CV was at once ridiculed by the press and the motor industry. Yet the French loved it, and orders poured in far faster than cars could be produced. In this view, taken as the President of France visited the Citroën stand, the rival Renault stand with examples of the rear-engined 4CV on display is also visible.

was utilised for ease and cheapness of manufacture as well as permitting all the body panels to be bolted on to it. In the case of body repair, there was no easier car to mend.

The 2CV had to be either a complete success or complete failure. Its design was such there could be no half-measures and Boulanger's shrewdness had told him the 'umbrella over four wheels' was a recipe for outright success. After hostilities had ceased, there was a situation in France much the same as had been prevalent after the First World War. Then André Citroën had presented his Type A, now after the Second World War when the need was for a 'minimal' car, the Deux Chevaux appeared. Certainly, the 2CV was unlike any car on the market; its eccentricity appealed to the French - the poorer and richer alike. Anybody driving in a 2CV could travel incognito, such was the way the car was accepted. From the bumper to the tail light, unconventionality was the Deux Chevaux. With canvas roof and simple hammock seats, the barest of instruments and a gear lever that sprouted oddly from the fascia in even more whimsical style than that of the Traction Avant; with instantly removable seats and flip-up windows, this was the 2CV. With a pull on the piano-wire starter cable, the engine cackled into life and from then on the minute air-cooled flat-twin engine and accompanying transmission powered the car along with a series of agricultural noises that at once became music to the Deux Chevaux owner. The 2CV looked like no other car. With its nose-down attitude and rear-end uppermost, there was no helping but to smile at it. The rounded features belied the amount of space the car offered and when seen at speed it could easily be mistaken for a boat pitching in the waves.

Recognisable anywhere, the 2CV with its almost singularly crude bodywork with two small round headlands protruding starkly from the bonnet on stalks, gave the assurance that it pretended to be nothing it was not.

The success of the car in its native France prodded the decision it should be built at Slough. The Factory was equipped with the necessary tooling and assembly lines ready for production to commence during October 1953. The major problem was to whether the 2CV would attract the same popularity as it had managed in France; certainly there was a requirement for a a small economical car, the home market was somewhat starved of choice and supplies due to the high volume of exports, but, nevertheless, the curious and unfamiliar 2CV had to compete against the Morris Minor, Austin A30, Ford Anglia as well as a choice of second-hand vehicles. The outcome was that the British were just not ready for the miracle car that had become a way of life in France and sales in the main went to the British manufacturers.

*The original production 2CV engine, of 375cc and with two air-cooled horizontal cylinders, one on each side of the centre line. The output was 9 b.h.p., giving a top speed on the level of 40.9 m.p.h., according to **The Motor** road test of an early Slough-built car published in December 1953. The modest weight of 10 cwt unladen helped in returning a fuel consumption of 54.7 m.p.g. 'driven hard' — it was difficult to avoid doing so with such modest power. At that date it cost £565 in Britain, including purchase tax, which was expensive by comparison with the lively-seeming Austin A30 with its smooth-running engine at £476 or the Ford Popular at £391, the later admittedly old fashioned and 'basic' by British standards.*

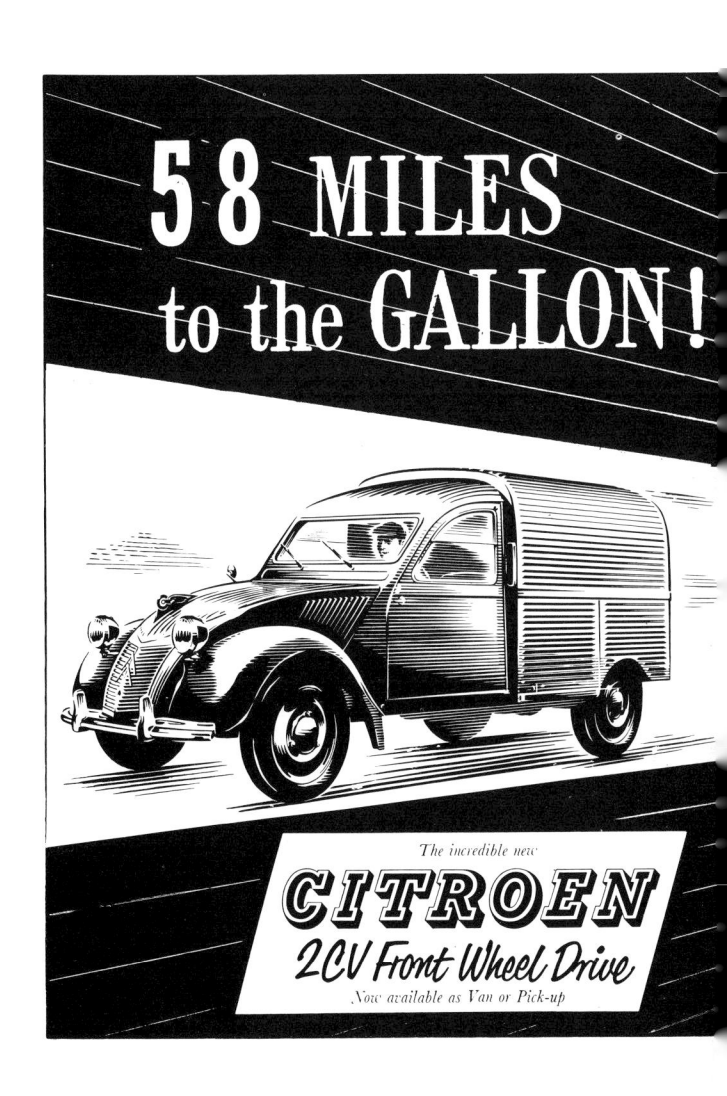

The fuel economy was emphasised as the key selling point for the 2CV van when introduced in Britain, but few were sold in this country. The bonnet emblem peculiar to Slough-built 2CV models is clearly shown.

THE CITROEN 2CV VAN

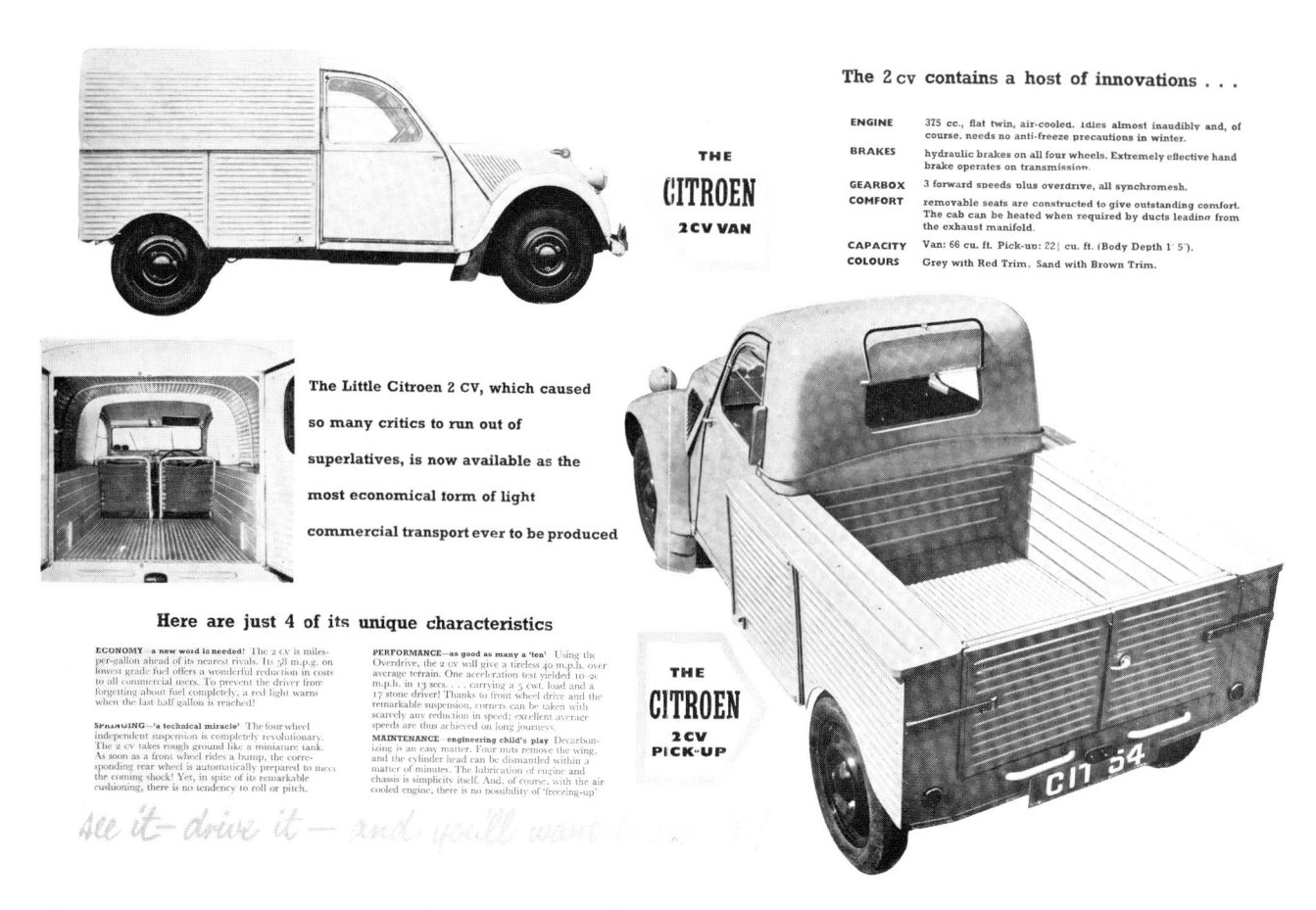

The 2 CV contains a host of innovations...

ENGINE 375 cc., flat twin, air-cooled. Idles almost inaudibly and, of course, needs no anti-freeze precautions in winter.
BRAKES hydraulic brakes on all four wheels. Extremely effective hand brake operates on transmission.
GEARBOX 3 forward speeds plus overdrive, all synchromesh.
COMFORT removable seats are constructed to give outstanding comfort. The cab can be heated when required by ducts leading from the exhaust manifold.
CAPACITY Van: 66 cu. ft. Pick-up: 22½ cu. ft. (Body Depth 1′ 5″).
COLOURS Grey with Red Trim. Sand with Brown Trim.

The Little Citroen 2 CV, which caused so many critics to run out of superlatives, is now available as the most economical form of light commercial transport ever to be produced

Here are just 4 of its unique characteristics

ECONOMY—a new word is needed! The 2 cv is miles-per-gallon ahead of its nearest rivals. Its 58 m.p.g. on lowest grade fuel offers a wonderful reduction in costs to all commercial users. To prevent the driver from forgetting about fuel completely, a red light warns when the last half gallon is reached!

SPRINGING—'a technical miracle'. The four wheel independent suspension is completely revolutionary. The 2 cv takes rough ground like a miniature tank. As soon as a front wheel rides a bump, the corresponding rear wheel is automatically prepared to meet the coming shock! Yet, in spite of its remarkable cushioning, there is no tendency to roll or pitch.

PERFORMANCE—as good as many a 'ten'. Using the Overdrive, the 2 cv will give a tireless 40 m.p.h. over average terrain. One acceleration test yielded 10-20 m.p.h. in 13 secs. . . . carrying a 5 cwt. load and a 17 stone driver! Thanks to front wheel drive and the remarkable suspension, corners can be taken with scarcely any reduction in speed; excellent average speeds are thus achieved on long journeys.

MAINTENANCE—engineering child's play. Decarbonizing is an easy matter. Four nuts remove the wing, and the cylinder head can be dismantled within a matter of minutes. The lubrication of engine and chassis is simplicity itself. And, of course, with the air cooled engine, there is no possibility of 'freezing-up'.

THE CITROEN 2CV PICK-UP

Both van and pick-up made extensive use of corrugated panelling. Quite contrary to the implications of the jocular comment this provoked, the various portions of the body were specially pressed into this form to give maximum rigidity with minimum weight. The interior view shows the level floor and tubular-framed seats.

Nevertheless, the 2CV did go into production at Slough, although only four or five cars a day were made on the small assembly line. It was marketed in three forms, Saloon, Light Van and Pick-up Truck. Just as in France, the concept of the little Citroën was thought to be eccentric and stories emerged of the car being born out of corrugated metal left over from the War. Nothing, of course, could be further from the truth. Enthusiasts of the Citroën marque naturally loved the car, even if they were the privileged few to recognise the car's qualities. Specification of the 2CV was Anglicised to meet the requirements thought necessary for the British market. Driving controls were fitted to suit right-hand drive; modifications to the trim were made by fitting wheel embellishers where there were none on French models, trafficators were fitted just ahead of the front doors and rear windows were made to open. British-built 2CVs were fitted with a metal boot-lid with 'Citroën' written in script upon it similar to that found on the boot or spare wheel cover of the Light Fifteen, this is in contrast to the Paris-built 2CVs which at that time had a canvas boot cover with a metal lift-up hatch being available only after 1957. On the bonnet was adorned a striking emblem, circular in shape, with an outline of a Traction Avant in the form of a flying Light Fifteen. Engraved around the emblem were the words 'Citroën Front Wheel Drive'. The badge was unique, being fitted to Slough-built 2CVs only.

Mechanically, the car was ingeniously simplistic. It could do all that was asked of it and more besides. Production commenced using the 375cc engine, a tiny unit developing a mere 9 b.h.p. at 3800 r.p.m. The air-cooling ensured the car never had to suffer frozen radiators and resulting in less service maintenance. The horizontally-opposed twin cylinders were never happier than being pushed to their full potential, the oil-cooler made sure the engine never overheated. A further means of reducing maintenance resulted from the way the engine was constructed; the need was alleviated for cylinder head gaskets as the heads themselves were machined to such fine limits as to make the fitting of them unnecessary. Looking at the engine compartment one could be forgiven for thinking there was something missing, so much space prevailed. All that was visible, apart from the battery and a few cables and wires, were the engine, which had a cooling fan built into the cowling, the gearbox fitting snugly behind it with drive shafts connected to the front wheels.

The braking system was almost as quaint as the rest of the car. Lockheed hydraulics were fitted to both the front and the rear assemblies with a mechanical parking brake acting upon the front wheels using separate shoes. The front brake drums were inboard mounted and fitted to the gearbox and not the wheels; the rear brakes were, however, relatively conventional. By having front inboard

*One of the few surviving Slough-built 2CV's. Note the half-hinged front and rear windows peculiar to Slough cars. Paris-built cars had the opening windows confined to the front only. British 2CVs had trafficators mounted externally by the front door pillars and chrome bumpers as well as a specially designed 'Front-Drive' emblem on the bonnet. No other Citroën used the emblem although it was used on advertising material. The boot lid on Slough 2CVs were metal whereas French cars had a canvas hatch cover. This particular vehicle, belonging to David Conway, featured in the **Motor Sport** road test of the 2CV in April 1954. In that road test report, William Boddy fell victim to the 2CV's charms, 'it is a fascinating, splendid little car, to which I would gladly give permanent shelter in my garage' he wrote. Ending the report, W.B. noted in the following short paragraph —*

'Certainly from now on I shall look with scorn at cars of low power output which employ heavy lumps of cast-iron surrounded by water for engines, and I shall refuse to regard as an economy car any vehicle which does not give a genuine 60 miles per gallon on cheap grade petrol.'

drums, the brakes were not affected by water and as the majority of braking was concentrated at the front, the design and layout can be appreciated. Rack and pinion steering helped to increase the already outstanding roadholding for which the car had received wide acclaim both in its native France and elsewhere. Although there was very little vibration transmitted through the steering wheel it remained a trifle heavy and required deliberate handling on sharp turns especially at low speeds.

The gear change was a delight. The configuration of the gear pattern appeared at first to be peculiar and this was accentuated by the odd push-twist-and-pull operation. In fact, the gear positions followed a normal gate layout as found on other vehicles. The layout of the gearbox did, however, allow second and third ratios to be in a straight line and as these were the two ratios most required under normal driving conditions, all that needed to be done was to push the gear-change lever backwards and forwards in a single plane.

Instrumentation on the 2CV was abnormally basic, yet, all the information the driver needed to know was supplied with the minimum of equipment. The steering wheel was set at an angle that afforded maximum driver comfort, and with the soft canvas hammock seats slung on crude tubular frames reminiscent of deck chairs, a surprisingly high degree of support was provided. Immediately in front of the driver where the unsuspecting might expect to find the speedometer, a small trapezoid nacelle housed an ammeter together with a switch controlling the interior light and a panel illumination lamp. On the right of the ammeter an indicator light warned of low fuel. One can be forgiven for thinking that such a device unnecessary until it is realised the car did not have a fuel gauge; the driver was expected to undo the fuel cap on the rear wing and inspect

Slough-built 2CV models found themselves far and wide around the world. DSK 420 arrived in Tanganyika after being sold by Citroën Agents Messrs. Mithani in Dar-Es-Salaam. The van was purchased by the Rev. Father Fouguer of the White Father Mission who is pictured with his new vehicle. Note the chromium-plated hub caps fitted to 2CV models produced in Britain.

a long dipstick to examine how much petrol was in the tank! Such was the penalty for low fuel consumption. The speedometer, instead of being with the other instruments, was situated at the base of the windscreen to the left of the driver.

To the left of the speedometer, a knurled wheel operated the scuttle vent so increasing the amount of fresh air into the car. Such a simple device, it was retained until the demise of the 2CV thirty seven years later. The speedometer drive cable also drove the windscreen wipers. This presented a problem in as much as at low speeds the wipers hardly moved across the screen; to resolve this minor dilemma a manual override knob was fitted so that the wipers could be operated by hand-in wet weather it was advantageous to have a passenger in the car! A simple spring-loaded 'time-delay' switch activated the semaphore trafficators; an umbrella-type handle pulled the handbrake into action whilst to the right of the steering wheel another knurled wheel adjusted the headlamps, compensating to suit the load level of the car. The light switch was mounted on the steering column and also activated the headlamp dipping device as well as the horn. The 2CV had 'organ-stop' pedals for brake and clutch instead of the pendant pedals fitted to the Traction. Probably the most eccentric device on the Slough 2CV was the interior light installed above the windscreen, doubling as the speedometer illumination it shone a beam of light on to it-at the base of the windscreen.

Interior heating of the 2CV was grossly simple yet completely adequate. Warmth from the cylinder heads was allowed to enter the car at the base of the scuttle and when not required in summer could be easily diverted via a valve through venting tubes to the front wings. Opening the canvas hood and rolling it back provided copious fresh air transforming the the 2CV into a Cabriolet. A further advantage of the opening hood afforded the car to be instantly converted to a utility vehicle. Due to the rounded contours of the Deux Chevaux and the provision of a completely flat floor, the ample room inside the car was as if it were an illusion. The soft suspension caused considerable body-roll when cornering, the effect was witnessed by others rather than experienced by the 2CV's occupants. With such a diminutive engine, retaining the car's speed was important as the limited engine power took time for speed to be regained. The theory behind Citroën's suspension allowed the car to travel around bends faster than might have been thought. As the laws of physics dictated, something had to give, the enormous suspension travel permitted the car to lean but grip was maintained, aided by the front wheel drive. Considering the size of the engine, the 2CV could return surprisingly high average speeds especially over long cross-country journeys.

It was features such as the suspension and the clutch that made the 2CV a delight to drive. A centrifugal clutch had been designed which enabled gear-changing, at engine speeds less than 1000 r.p.m., without having to use the clutch pedal. This was much appreciated in driving conditions, especially in towns, when first and second gear would have to be selected at frequent intervals. The car could be left in second gear with the 'trafficlutch' taking up the drive as required. The suspension of the 2CV hardly changed throughout the entire production of the car; leading and trailing arms, interconnected by coil springs compressed into cylinders on the underside edge of each side of the chassis offered the smoothest and softest ride of almost any car. The system required only the minimum of maintenance save from occasional greasing. The Van and Pick-Up versions of the 2CV benefited from the same mechanics as the Saloon except for the clutch which was entirely conventional. The commercials had a

The attitude adopted by the 2CV when concerning sharply could be quite alarming to onlookers but was much less so to the driver or passengers. The enormous suspension travel allowed considerable roll, yet the margin of safety enabled the driver in a hurry to keep up speed to a greater extent than appearances suggested. The car shown dates from 1955.

5cwt. payload, the suspension on these vehicles being invaluable in transporting loads with ease and less chance of damage.

A year after its introduction to the British market, the 2CV received an increase in power. The 375cc engine was replaced with a motor of 425cc providing 12 b.h.p. at 3,500 r.p.m. On a road test carried out by *The Motor* over a distance of 1,200 miles, the car returned a fuel consumption of almost 50 miles per gallon. The test duration included both long and short journeys as well as around London when the car was made to work hard. Apart from the increase in power little else had changed; the 2CV was instantly conspicuous by its steeply drooping 'rippled' bonnet, prominent headlamps and large air-intake at the front. The narrow windscreen complimented the equally small rear screen and the fabric roof facilitated open-top motoring. The six-volt electrics were adequate enough for the limited equipment and the dynamo fitted to the crankshaft charged the small battery at sufficient rate. Behind the cooling fan the ignition circuit-breaker points required to be re-set and checked every 36,000 miles. With the absence of a distributor, the coil on top of the engine provided the current to the two sparking plugs.

Perhaps it was too much to expect such a modest car as the 2CV to be supplied with an engine revolution counter. In any case special marks on the speedometer showed the most appropriate speeds gear ratios should be changed; the twin-cylinder engine was designed to be used to its capacity without fear of causing any harm and the maximum speed was, therefore, the car's cruising speed. *The Motor* when commenting on the progress of the 2CV reported:

'It can be said that the Citroën driver in a hurry overtakes more people than overtake him. Driving solo on a cross-country journey from the Midlands to East Anglia, a run of rather over 100 miles was completed at an average speed of over 34 miles per hour with a fuel consumption of fractionally better than 55 miles per gallon. In one sense it may be said that the cruising speed on open roads is anything between 35 m.p.h. and 45 m.p.h., but it is in fact normal to drive flat out when the going is good, there being no sign of distress if speeds between 50 and 60 m.p.h. are sustained downhill.'

Throughout the World, the 2CV has collected many names - 'Ugly Duckling', 'Ragamuffin' and so on. The British never took the car to heart in those early days; when one of the employees at the Slough Factory took a 2CV home one night, a boy looked at the car carefully before asking whether it was a 'home made job'!

When considered against its rival cars on the British market, the 2CV was not cheap. On its launch it sold for £398 plus purchase tax of £166-19s-2d, making a total of just under £565. This was at a time when the Austin A30 could be purchased for £476 and the Ford Popular at £391. Alas the 2CV was too utilitarian, underpowered and lacked aesthetic appeal for the British market. The finer qualities of the car were never realised by the British motorist whose quest for economy not so keen as their French counterpart. Despite continued marketing and enthusiastically favourable press reports from motoring journalists, the 2CV refused to sell. During its span of production some 1036 vehicles were built at Slough with just under half the number being exported. All of the 72 2CV Pick-ups were destined for the British market although most of these found service with the Royal Marines and were air-lifted from Royal Naval Commando vessels for use in rough terrain areas abroad. It continued in production for a relatively short time at Slough and by 1959 the decision had been taken to halt production.

With the cessation of the 2CV assembly at Slough, the Company were left with the dilemma of what to do with 350 2CV chassis that remained unused. The decision was taken to produce a car adopting the same ideals as the 2CV but with a modern two-door body with separate boot which would appeal to the housewife and two-car family. Under the auspice of Nigel Somerset-Leeke whose brainchild the new car was, the design team got to work with Peter Kirwan-Taylor of Lotus Elite fame who was employed for the particular project to produce a glass-fibre bodied car, utilising the redundant chassis, that would appeal to the motoring public where the 2CV had failed.

Thus the Citroën Bijou was born - the British 2CV. The car was unveiled at the Factory on 17th October 1959 before an audience of invited guests and Citroën Agents to preview that year's Motor Show. The car had been kept a close secret with only a few people close to the Factory's affairs knowing of its existence. The Bijou exhibited, gleaming in ivory paint, was driven into the preview area amidst applause and enthusiasm for the small new car.

The last 2CV to be built at Slough leaves the finishing shop. Latterly the model was marketed in Britain as the 'convertible saloon', endeavouring to take advantage of the readily-opened canvas top, which gave a fresh-air facility offered by no competitor saloon model in Britain at the time. However, the price was still against it, even though it was back to the original £565 after a period when increased purchase tax had pushed it up to £598, for from August 1959 it was faced with a new rival, marketed in basic form at £497 — the Mini, originally sold as the Austin Seven or the Morris Mini-minor. The standard 2CV saloon was officially discontinued in Britain in January 1960 — in this view, a row of the Bijou model that sought to give the basic chassis a new lease of life follow behind.

This photograph of the Bijou prototype appeared in the brochure issued for the Motor Show in October 1959. The new glass fibre body completely altered the appearance, only the style of wheel giving a clue to its being based on the 2CV chassis.

Later at the Motor Show, the car was also well received. For the first time a totally British-bodied Citroën had been built at the Slough works. The Bijou as a car was unique, it was solely manufactured at Slough with only a handful being exported. If a success, it was intended that it should replace the 2CV entirely for the British market. The prototype appearing at the Slough preview and at the Motor Show differed from the production cars that were delivered from the middle of 1960. Modifications had been made to the bonnet line and to the shape of the air-intake making the car appear somewhat sleeker.

Externally, the Bijou certainly attained the appearance of a British-styled motor car; a two-door, four-seat saloon, the car really only provided enough room for two adults with two children on the very cramped rear seat. The hammock chairs closely resembling those found on the 2CV were comfortable enough but were fitted low to the floor leaving the driver and passenger seated with their knees almost under their chin. The tubular seats, as with the 2CV, could be easily removed for the occasion of the family picnic. The dashboard had the benefit of circular dials in place of the sparse instruments of the Deux Chevaux and the lift-up boot lid gave access to a cavernous luggage area. At this point the differences to the 2CV ended although many of the fitments on the car were used from other Citroën models.

The front-hinged bonnet, which was secured by a key, allowed easy access to the engine compartment and provided generous space for maintenance. Beneath the glass-fibre bonnet could be seen all the running gear and engineering qualities of the 2CV, even to the inner wings which looked as if they had just come off the 2CV production line. The 425cc air-cooled flat-twin motor boasted of supplying 12 b.h.p. at 4000 r.p.m. and the gearbox with four speeds was in reality a three speed box with overdrive. The suspension system and brakes were directly taken from the 2CV, usefully using up stocks of parts, as well as ensuring low maintenance and running costs. The interior of the car was light and airy thanks to the large window space; there was no provision for a fabric hood as the plastic body did not allow for the stresses this would have produced but the body styling did reduce the absolute starkness making the Bijou more acceptable and homely to the British motorist.

The gear lever vanished into the hidden depths of the fascia panel and like the 2CV retained the pull-twist-push action. The centrifugal clutch was appreciated by at least one journalist who described the system thus:

'For people who do much of their motoring pottering about town, there is one big attraction. Apart from the orthodox clutch there is an ingenious centrifugal clutch which, in first and second gear, automatically disengages when the engine speed drops to below a few hundred revs. per minute.

Rear profile of the Bijou. The general similarity to the the D Series cars described in the next chapter is evident. Running gear was pure 2CV but the instruments, steering wheel and body embellishments came from the DS.

THE UNIQUE CITROEN BIJOU

The complete change in the market at which the Bijou was aimed by comparison with the 2CV is conveyed by the cover of the brochure issued when it was introduced. This was a car for the lady driver dropping her husband off for the 8.15 train to town, collecting the children from school or picking up the shopping (brought out to the car by a suitably deferential shopkeeper), with no trace of the utility machine in which the small French farmer was expected to take his pig to market.

A pristine example of the Bijou, Citroën's attempt to sell the 2CV in more glamorous form. Peculiar to Slough, the Bijou was not manufactured anywhere else although a few cars have found their way abroad. It is reported that the Bijou was so named by Mrs. J. Somerset-Leeke, wife of the man responsible for the idea, who compared the car to a jewel.

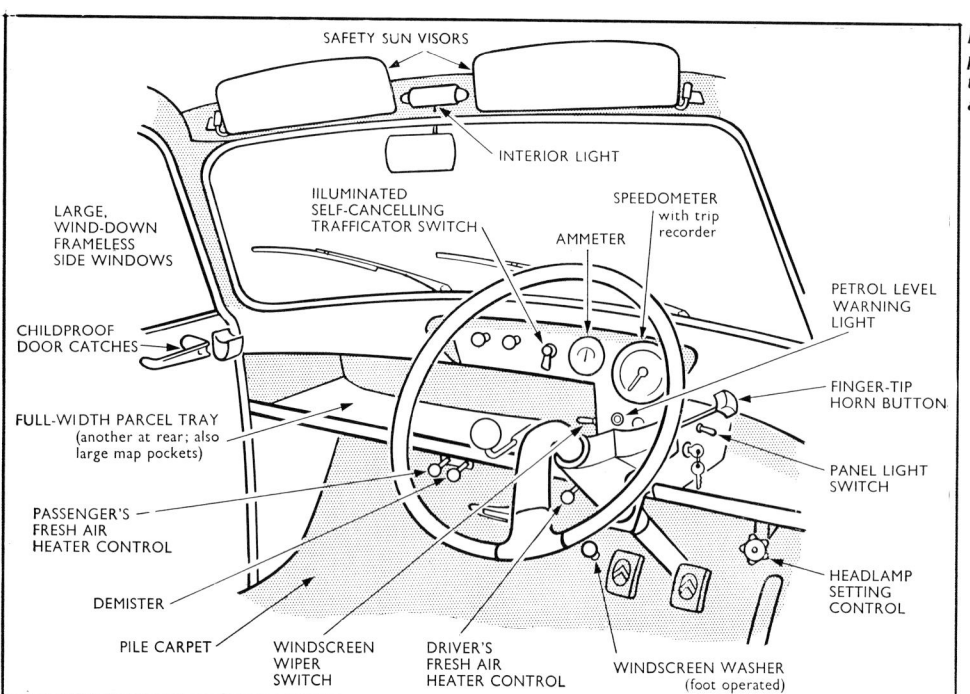

Driving position of the Bijou. The push-pull gear lever was retained but apart from that the controls were a mixture of 2CV and DS.

This is a great saver of patience and left-leg work in a traffic queue. So long as you are in second gear, you can do all the stopping and starting you have to with only one foot working the brake and accelerator. In such circumstances the car has all the virtues of automatic transmission.

And it's foolproof. I tried to beat it by some vicious stamping alternately on accelerator and brake, but the Bijou wouldn't stall. Lady drivers please note!'

For many people the brake pedal was situated rather closely to the base of the steering column making for some a little discomfort; the parking brake was situated under the parcel shelf and an adjacent knob allowed headlamp adjustment from inside the car. The heating system, as on the 2CV, was quite adequate with a demister being incorporated. The choke, starter button and turn indicators were all housed on the dashboard while the windscreen wiper and light switch were attached to stalks either side of the steering column. Instead of the flat windscreen and flip-up side windows, these were replaced with winding windows and curved screens back and front. One item had been lost in the design of the Bijou - the manual override for the windscreen wipers.

The Bijou still retained one important visual look of the 2CV, the famous nose-down attitude. To try and disguise this, it is reported that for publicity photographs and some of the occasions when on display, the boot was laden with sandbags. A story came to light about the Bijou which is totally in keeping with the car. Just before the press review when a siege of reporters descended upon the Bijou, the assembly staff were experiencing difficulty in successfully securing the rear window. Several attempts were made to perfect the job resulting each time in failure. Finally, an old hand was called for who at once set to work completing the task just as the press group arrived in the workshop. The mechanic stood back to admire his work, slammed the door at which point the pressure blasted the entire window clean from its frame to shatter at the feet of the embarrassed officials conducting the party.

Bodies for the Bijou were originally produced by James Whitson of West Drayton, Middlesex, who had previous experience in the manufacture of plastic bodies for cars. Grave problems occurred in the form of severe crazing of the bodywork which ultimately led to a number of bodyshells being exchanged. Later, manufacture of the bodies were carried out by a company in Crowthorne, Berkshire, specialising in fibre-glass products. Towards the

Under the skin of its glass-fibre body, the Bijou retained the 2CV chassis virtually unaltered. This view of the front-end mechanical assembly is taken from the rear and shows how the 425cc two-cylinder air-cooled engine, gearbox, differential and brakes were in one unit — the conventional-looking gear lever was linked to the dash-mounted push-pull control. With the Bijou, about 1½ cwt heavier than a standard 2CV, the 12 b.h.p. output gave performance that was very limited by 1961 standards and the outstanding fuel economy was offset by relatively high cost of £674, later increased to £695. The cheapest car in Britain at the time was the Ford Popular, by then in more modern 100E form, at £494, and though much less economical on petrol it would probably have taken an average driver four or five years or so to recover the extra cost at contemporary prices.

end of manufacture of the Bijou, stacks of completed bodies could be seen waiting for orders. Against the British cars of the late fifties and early sixties, the fifteen inch wheels of the Bijou look over-large but nevertheless complimented the suspension and assisted further in ironing out the bumps. The Michelin X tyres existed on surprisingly low pressures, 15lbs. p.s.i. at the front and 17 lbs. p.s.i. at the rear. With air-cooling, starting naturally was instantaneous and servicing kept to the absolute minimum; as with the 2CV, the Bijou could be easily identified by its pleasantly peculiar high pitched engine note which, if allowed to, would burble along all day and maintain a fuel consumption in excess of 50 miles per gallon.

Where the 2CV failed to gain a foothold and an impression upon the British market, all hopes had been pinned on the success of the Bijou. Citroën's little jewel received some excellent notices in the motoring press and journalists took to its eccentric ways whereas they had scorned the 2CV. To the media, the Bijou was an acceptable car even allowing for its pedigree. Yet, just as the 2CV had failed so did the Bijou. Just 211 examples of the car were produced, all except seven were destined for the home market. After the initial surge of orders sales of the Bijou were slow. The colour schemes offered by Citroën were not attractive, middle green, beige and orange. When it was realised the car was not to be the success as had been hoped, the customer was given the choice of having the car sprayed to whatever colour of their choice.

The Bijou was well worthy of success. It had its shortcomings but was a brave attempt to continue in the economical small-car market. It was never a cheap car, the price on its launch was £674-0-10d including purchase tax. A year later it had risen to £695; the Morris Minor cost £590 and the new Ford Anglia £589. The Bijou was launched almost at the same time as the Mini which cost £497 and was immediately overshadowed by its unconventional design and the furore created at its launch.

Another oddity to appear from Slough was the H Van. Although never produced for the British market or built at Slough, three examples were imported from France and converted at the Factory to right hand drive. Suffering from incredible gallic charm, it is highly unlikely these vehicles would ever have sold in the United Kingdom. Two of the H Vans were supplied to Citroën Agents whilst the third was purchased by a company in Bristol. The vans, which were of 35cwt. capacity, boasted of a flat floor made possible by front wheel drive and enabled a six foot person to stand upright in the cargo area. Based upon the running gear of the Traction Avant, with 1911cc engine and three-speed gearbox, the vehicle had a corrugated style body with 2CV headlights on short stalks at the front. Whilst being popular and highly practical as the mainstay of the French commercial market, there was no room in Britain for it alas.

The production of the 2CV did not meet with complete failure. Those who dared buy the Deux Chevaux fell in love with it admiring the fine qualities of the car. The 2CV quickly won a reputation for ruggedness and soon became an explorer's car turning up in the most inhospitable locations usually where no other car could reach. Its simple toughness let it cross the most obdurate terrain with its Meccano style mechanics letting the owner care easily for all its needs. A proportion of the cars went for export to Australia, New Zealand and South Africa; the climates which would have been detrimental to most other cars had hardly any affect on the 2CV. The Pick-up also found a new role; the Royal Marines experimented with lightweight cross-country vehicles capable of being airlifted from aircraft carrier or supply ship to be dropped into areas inaccessible by road. The Pick-up fitted the requirements exactly as the ideal vehicle to cope with hazardous conditions and sixty five Slough-built models, less doors and windows, were supplied to the Royal Marines for operational use with HMS Bulwark and HMS Albion. Sadly only a few Slough-built 2CVs have survived around the world and it is ironical that a considerably greater number of Bijou's (fewer than fifty) have endured the course of time.

Following the return to peacetime car making, motor manufacturers design teams at once started planning for the future. Citroën were no exception. A lot of secret work was carried out in the early years on planning for a new car to replace the Traction Avant, already twelve years old at the time of re-starting car production. Whatever was to replace the Traction would have to continue the qualities

The Citroën H Van. Though a familiar sight in France, this was never built at Slough or commercially imported. However, three examples were brought over from France and converted to right hand drive. Powered by the 1911cc petrol engine, and running gear from the Traction Avant, it was popular on its home terraine by virtue of its capacious loading and carrying ability. Two of the three H vans were sold to Citroën Agents and the third sold to Rowe and Company, Builders Merchants in Bristol. Worthing Motors passed on their H Van to the Citroën Car Club, in whose possession the vehicle was at the time of the photograph.

of this fine car and it would have to create a tremendous impact just as the Traction did in 1934. By 1950, designs of the new car had been drawn up although still in blue-print stage. Late during that year the drawings were sent to Slough. Speculation existed in the motoring world of a new model from Citroën but at each motor show there was no sign of the Traction replacement. The 6H had been introduced as a test-bed for something new. In July 1955 it was announced the Slough Factory would close from August for a period of some six to eight weeks for the purpose of rebuilding the painting ovens and carrying out reorganisation of the assembly lines should a new model arrive at a later date.

The 2CV's new role; 65 2CV Pick-Ups were purchased by the Admiralty for use in inhospitable areas where ruggedness and reliability were the key requirements. Helicoptors air-lifted the vehicles from aircraft carriers and supply ships, dropping them ashore for operation. In the photograph, 2CVs from HMS Bulwark are prepared for action.

Like a thunderbolt, the DS created a storm upon its introduction at the Paris Salon in 1955. Its styling created great controversy; the uniquely aerodynamic lines were claimed to signify space, power and technological supremacy. Queues of spectators rushed to see the new car which the magazine L'Auto Journal referred to as 'La Bombe Citroën'. On the first day of the Paris Motor Show no fewer than 12,000 orders were taken for the DS. Citroën's new car extended the use of hydraulics that had first been seen on the Traction Avant 6H; in addition to full hydropneumatic suspension, hydraulics powered steering and braking as well as the gear change. On announcement, it was said of the DS. 'A manufacturer has introduced for 1956 the motor car for 1966'.

The designation DS sounded like the French for 'goddess' — déesse — when pronounced with a French accent, a clever and appropriate allusion for so remarkable a car.

Chapter ten: The Goddess

The demise of the Light Fifteen, together with its stablemates the Big Fifteen and the Six, were lamented by many. With some four hundred orders still outstanding, British customers felt somewhat aggrieved especially the Traction Avant was still being manufactured in France. The last Traction Avant rolled out from Slough in August 1955 but it was not until the 25th July 1957 that the very last Traction left Javel.

The question of a replacement for the Traction Avant had been spoken of since 1950; rumours and counter rumours abounded in the motoring world and Citroën agents anxiously waited for news of what promised to be a Supercar. Stories of an audacious new design that would shake the world were talked of; cars of outlandish shape and specification to match, novel gearboxes and inboard mounted brakes were said to be ready to sweep the market. On more than one occasion L'Auto Journal published articles and drawings upon information they had received concerning a new 10CV Citroën, they even showed some photographs, which the course of time suggests were authentic. Over the years, pictures of early prototypes have come to light, one of them not unlike a prototype Saab from their Project 92, even to sharing a split windscreen. Another reveals a breathtakingly streamlined car, with obvious Citroën connections and displaying four headlamps built into a recess in the bonnet. The really interesting story concerned that of a proposed engine design, an air-cooled flat-six. There is no reason to believe such an engine was not considered at one time by Citroën; certainly many extravagant and daring designs for a body structure for the new car were put on the drawing board, so why not the power unit? The idea of a flat-six cylinder would have no doubt been a serious development in view of the flat-twin as used in the 2CV, later, when the GS was announced in 1971, an air-cooled flat four was utilised.

Porsche favoured the air-cooled flat-six concept from 1964, firstly with a two-litre engine, gradually rising to a 3.6 litre unit, whilst the Czechoslovakian Tatra received a rear-mounted air-cooled vee-eight engine.

There was no question as to whether the hydropneumatic suspension installed on the rear wheels of the Citroën 6H was going to be adopted for the new car and it was widely accepted that the Six Cylinder was a test-bed in this respect for the new model. There was also little doubt the new car, when it did arrive, would be as breathtaking in design as the Traction had been in 1934. Post-War Motor Shows passed without any sign of the new Citroën, then, immediately before the 1955 Paris Salon, news came that the Company were to drop a bombshell and announce the long-awaited car.

During the Spring of 1955, the ailing Panhard company reached a marketing policy agreement with Citroën. In exchange for Panhard taking over the manufacture of the 2CV Van in France, Citroën would market their cars. In real terms, the agreement meant that Citroën had effected a take-over of the Panhard company. Whilst the Panhard factory remained in operation it did allow their cars to be sold in Britain via Citroën at Slough. The Panhard bore no resemblance to the Light Fifteen whatsoever, yet was just as unique and technically advanced. There was some similarity with the 2CV in as much as the Panhard was equipped with an air-cooled flat-twin cylinder engine, somewhat larger than the 2CV's, at 850cc. The wind-cheating aerodynamic design of the car together with its gearing ratios allowed a top speed approaching 80 m.p.h. With front wheel drive, soft suspension and sports saloon handling, it managed to hold the road as if the wheels were glued to the surface. There was little doubt that such a car might have appealed to the Light Fifteen owner and rumours were rife when production of the Traction had

Panhard et Levassor was one of the world's oldest-established car makers, production having begun in 1891. The Dyna model in production at the time of the agreement with Citroën was of advanced design, remarkably light at 14 cwt unladen, largely because of extensive use of aluminium alloy, yet 15ft. long and capable of seating up to six on bench seats. Its 850cc air-cooled flat twin-cylinder engine developed 42 b.h.p. at 5,300 r.p.m., well above average for the size at that period and tuned versions were class winners at Le Mans. It was available in Britain from 1954, via Citroën Cars at Slough from 1955 up to the early 1960s — but few were sold, doubtless partly because of the price of £1,000 being seen as very high for a two-cylinder 850cc car even if of high technical merit.

been withdrawn this was the car to take its place on the British market.

The Paris Salon opened to the news of Citroën's new car. The rumours had been well founded and what appeared from Javel was perhaps the most extraordinary car the World had ever seen. The DS was a thunderbolt. It was incredible. The whole concept of the car caused sheer amazement—and the motoring public loved it. Citroën had done it again; in 1934 when the Traction Avant created a sensation with its advanced ideas, the DS went even further. The mechanical heart of the car centred upon its hydraulic system which powered not only the suspension but also the brakes, transmission and steering. Futuristic was hardly the word—it was space-age.

The pure aerodynamic lines of the DS resulted in a highly unusual body shape with large areas of glass and thin pillars, wide doors and a spacious boot, the absence of a visible radiator air-intake and above all, an astonishing amount of interior space for the driver and passengers. In front of the driver, the dashboard had the style and futuristic approach in keeping with the mode of the car. The steering wheel, a single-spoke affair created much consternation; Citroën have been credited with this fascinating invention since the DS appeared but ironically the original idea was not theirs. The single-spoke steering wheel had first made its appearance on an early Talbot. Previously unknown comfort was provided by sumptuous seating and the unique suspension which allowed the car to travel over the poorest of roads at almost unimaginable speeds.

The DS was unique in so many ways. Had André Citroën been alive, this was the car without doubt he would have designed. The architect of so many publicity stunts, The Patron would have successfully staged the greatest coup purely by launching this new car. Although Citroën had been dead for twenty years, the DS preserved the Patron's philosophy for technical advancement and total engineering efficiency. In a word, the DS was a tribute.

On the first day of the Salon no fewer than 12,000 orders had been taken for the car. Crowds flocked through the turnstiles, their first and only thought was to see this new creation. There was only one headline in the Salon edition of L'Auto-Journal—VOICI LA BOMBE CITROËN—. The DS was raised upon a large dias adjoining the Citroën stand; around it crowds of interested spectators were often as many as eight deep, all anxious to get a close-up view of this latest wonder. The crowds were even deeper surrounding the DS on an adjacent stand with Citroën's other models; piece by piece the car was feverishly examined in every detail and to get behind the wheel was to experience the vehicle's engineering phenomenon. The DS was also on show at Citroën's showroom on the Champs-Élysées. Even on a Sunday afternoon the queue of curious onlookers, four deep, stretched for half a mile to catch a glimpse of the car. Citroën had arranged for twenty DSs to be at the disposal of their guests to demonstrate its performance, the following extract is taken from a press report of the show:

'Twenty DS19s were made available for the further entertainment of the guests and what a thrill it was! We

For the crowds, there was no other car at the 1955 Paris Salon than the DS. Twenty cars were made available to take invited guests for a demonstration ride proving the car's suspension ability and roadholding performance.

The DS at once made others cars seem out of date, just as the Traction had achieved twenty-one years earlier. The distinctive styling was enhanced by the lack of obvious air intake, thin pillars and large windows.

were taken by bus to the outskirts of Paris where suitable roads brought out the salient features of the car. In spite of speed and what we might call mad and reckless driving, there was that feeling of security coupled with comfort. That one ride was worth the visit to Paris, it was something I never want to forget and something I shall never forget.'

The DS, as with Citroën in general, was a car that was either accepted and loved or rejected and despised. Motoring journalists were rapturous, they loved the audacity of its shape and its disregard for conventionality and conformity. The DS and 2CV were worlds apart yet their family resemblance so obvious. Between the two cars there followed a logical identity that could only arise by originating from the same design board. Jacques Ickx said of the DS: 'A manufacturer has introduced, for 1956, the motor car for 1966.'

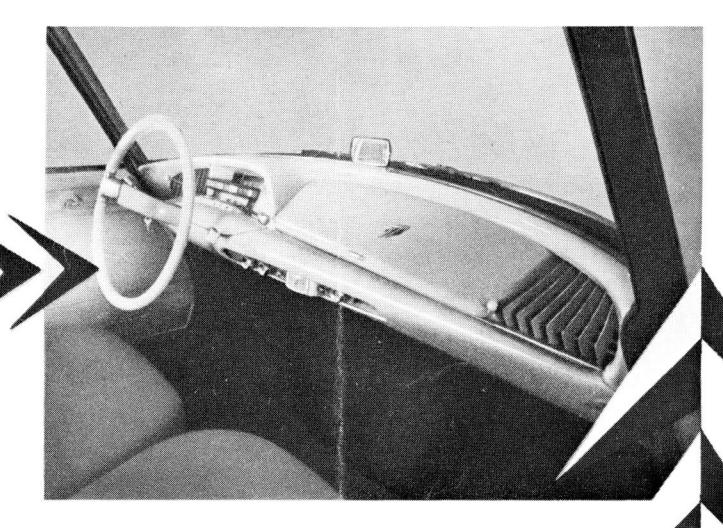

Even that statement did not go far enough for, in 1966 the DS was still very highly advanced and even in 1976, when the last DS had already been produced, there was not a car that could claim such technological achievement.

With the announcement of the DS in Paris there was an almost instant reaction to the car in Britain. Just as in its native France, the DS was admired and considered to be outstanding. Naturally there were those who viewed the car with some suspicion, it had taken the Traction Avant a long time to become firmly established and at once a wholly new concept had to be examined. Nevertheless, the rather humdrum lines of British cars of the mid-fifties were put to shame when seen beside the bold and provoking French creation. Attention was drawn to the Slough Factory to ascertain when the DS might be produced at the works. Alas, it was to be some eighteen months before the first British-assembled DS would leave the Trading Estate.

There was some criticism directed at Citroën Cars for discontinuing the Traction Avant as soon as the DS had been announced in Paris. A vacuum had been created in both home and export sales; during 1956 just 359 cars were built of which 155 were exported. The main assembly

The futuristic dashboard of the original DS. Note the single-spoke steering wheel.

This photograph of an early right-hand drive DS19 appeared in the owner's manual. It illustrates how the 'wheel at each corner' concept was continued, there being very little overhang at the rear in particular. The continuation of the weatherstrip above the windows, suitably enlarged, to provide housings for the flashing turn indicators alongside the rear window was particularly neat. The total price on introduction was £1,486, substantially more than the final price for the Big Fifteen of £1,064 and slightly above the Six H at £1,474.

lines fell silent and the factory resorted in the main to a stores and servicing operation. In fact, the question was asked as to whether the Company would ever get back into the business of building motor cars again.

As usual the British were sceptical of any unusual design or technology and evidence showed attitudes had changed little from the days when the Citroën front-wheel drive made its first appearance. *The Autocar* commenting on the debut of the DS in France had the following to say:

'The 11CV (the French equivalent to the Light and Big fifteen) has been in production for twenty-one years without any basic changes. It was a fairly short-odds bet, therefore, that when it was replaced the new car would be equally advanced in its conception, and the impact which the new DS19 made at its presentation the night before the Paris Salon was opened was quite staggering. It will take some time to prove whether the innovations offered will be acceptable to the buying public. There is a complicated system of hydraulics, controlled from a master pressure pump and accumulator. The system is ingenious, but there is a complimentary degree of complication which may present problems in maintenance.'

Citroën's rivals appreciated this form of commentary and there was a campaign between some of them to produce advertising denouncing the car in the light of its so-called complicated machinery. Fortunately, none of this found its way into the press. The state of shock the motoring industry had found itself following the launch of the DS was slow to recede and British motor journals constantly kept their readers in touch with the car's development until it was finally ready to be assembled at Slough.

Production of the DS19 was very slow to get started in Britain. At regular intervals statements were put out from the Factory that the car was ready to be put into assembly. The anniversary of the announcement of the DS passed by and still the manufacturing lines lay idle. Outwardly the DS would virtually resemble the French model, the main differences were to be the interior trim and level of finish. In general, it was considered the interior style of the Paris model to be far too futuristic for the British motorist and therefore had to be Anglicised. For customers having to endure the wait to obtain a right-hand drive DS, the car's arrival in Australia in its original and French attire but with right-hand steering, was looked upon with frustration. The cars which were used for road testing and publicity reports had been built in France and were never available in the United Kingdom.

The Paris Salon in 1956 again drew tremendous crowds. The Bertone-designed DS attracted fanatical attention but there was an added feature, that of the appearance of a cheaper and less complicated version of the car, the iD19. Care had been taken in its design to retain the advanced features of the DS, its styling and facilities, but it was constructed without full use of hydraulics for all major engineering functions. The suspension was fully hydraulic but the steering and gearchange were manually operated. The introduction of the iD signified two models of the D series available on the French market but still there was no word from Slough. A serious rumour circulated that the DS was not planned to be marketed in Britain. The 1956 London Motor Show was watched with great interest and with much relief a press report was issued from Slough confirming a British-built DS would be on show. When the doors opened at Earls Court, there, shining under the glare of spotlamps on stand 148, was the DS. It had arrived in Britain.

There were a number of reasons why production at Slough took so long to get under way. Following Citroën policy over previous years, it was decided that as many components as possible should be supplied from British manufacturers. With a car so novel and complex as the DS this was not such an easy task to achieve as technology that had been developed in France was not yet available in the United Kingdom. There were a multitude of technical problems that faced the design and engineering team at Slough, the car had been under development in its native country for a considerable time and many of the early difficulties had been overcome by the time the car's introduction made headline news. Much of the information on the DS had been kept a closely guarded secret, so much so that it was as much of a surprise to the Company in Britain as it was to the rest of the World. Even after the announcement of the DS very little information flowed into Slough concerning the technicalities of the car; the hydraulics were almost an unknown quantity with the only experience being gained by that of the 6H, with constant trial and error providing the means by which knowledge of the DS was slowly built up.

Space-age technology had reached the motor industry. This fanciful advertising drawing with wheel apertures omitted drew attention to the smooth body styling of the DS as well as the smooth underside which played its part in the car's high-speed performance.

The early DS models that found their way to the British Factory for evaluation were a constant source of headache to the engineers. A number of parts had to be redesigned for the British market models, contracts placed and the components eventually manufactured and supplied. Not only did the principles of the car's hydraulics have to be understood but the practice of actually building them into the car had to be mastered.

The Motor on December 5th, 1956, ran the following headline:

'The most complicated car made anywhere in Europe, the most comfortable car made anywhere in the World.'

This statement could hardly have been nearer to the truth.

Not for the faint-hearted. Some idea of the complexity of the DS is conveyed in this sectional illustration from a 1962 catalogue. The iD version simplified matters slightly by using a conventionally controlled gearbox and clutch and unassisted steering, but the hydro-pneumatic self-levelling suspension remained.

For 1957, the DS was still revolutionary; the shape and concept of the car was alien and on more than one occasion it was likened to a spacecraft. The long, deep sloping bonnet and absence of air-intake; sharply raked windscreen and large all-round glass area with frameless windows on the doors; lack of wheel arches on the rear wings together with the capacious boot and the huge rear window, all gave rise to a desire to know just what the new-fangled wizardry was all about. Inside the car, deep leather upholstered armchairs provided the most satisfying comfort, there was an amazing amount of room for rear passengers who could recline back and stretch out their legs. Design and construction of the DS meant that driver and passengers sat inside a protected shell allowing hitherto unknown luxury. If all this was not enough, the mechanics of the car were not for the faint-hearted; twenty years earlier, it was a brave man who had purchased a Light Fifteen, now a lion-heart would have to contend with hydraulic suspension, gear-change, brakes and steering. All this coupled with front wheel drive and disc brakes eulogised the virtues of the Citroën bristling with new features and ideas.

In place of a conventional steering wheel, the strange single-spoke device was simply an extension of the steering column, curved at the end and forming the shape of a wheel. The brake pedal had disappeared and in its place a mushroom shaped valve on the floor, requiring only the lightest feather touch, to bring the car to an almost instant stop. Also gone were the handbrake, gear change lever and starter button. Sitting in the driving seat, the DS owner was at once confronted with an entirely new layout. From the orderly array of controls, as found on the Traction, a new generation of ideas had come of age; the dashboard lacked dials, in their place numerous switches were situated to the left and right of the steering wheel while immediately ahead a neat nacelle housed the speedometer, fuel gauge, mileometer and trip recorder. A rectangular clock flanked the left hand side of the instrument panel whilst at either end of the fascia fresh air distributors aided the ventilation.

Just as the Traction Avant had done in 1934, so the DS achieved over twenty years later by making, at a single stroke, all other cars outdated. The high performance, coupled with equally performing braking and suspension outshone other makes of cars, many of which still heavily relied upon immediate post-war styling. The appearance of turn indicators positioned at roof level at the rear of the car together with a suspension system, seemingly thinking for itself, raising and lowering the car at will, proved a new era of car design had arrived. To some people, the DS represented a venture into the field normally dominated by American cars with their large passenger capacity and novel ideas and gimmicks. Once the DS had been driven opinion usually changed to the agreement it was a highly sophisticated motor car.

The publicity department at Slough had constituted a fine marketing policy towards the DS.

'Slip gently behind the wheel of the new Citroën DS19 — sink deep into its soft, luxurious comfort and you'll be all set for the thrill of a lifetime, for a ride thats a glide in a car of the future — a car that virtually thinks for you and almost drives itself.

Just a flick of the finger on the gear selector and the engine starts automatically, the gear is selected, the clutch automatically engaged and you're away. Another flick, another and another and you're in top, without the touch of the clutch, and accelerating fast.

The power assisted steering is as light as a feather, as effortless as a dream, yet so responsive and so very accurate that you know at once that complete control is right there at your fingertips.

You sit back and relax, only to realise that you're doing more than eighty. But where are the bumps, the jerks, the lurches, the rolls? The're simply not there — you're not just riding, you're gliding!

You urge her round bends, you corner fast and she clings to the road like no car you've ever driven. So small is the gravitational pull yet so great the grip between tyres and road that you are almost unaware of the demands you are making.

You try the brakes — just a gentle touch — and you feel them bite and hold. Then comes an emergency and your foot goes down, but real pressure is unnecessary — just one quick, easy movement and the car stops in a dead straight line — no jerks, no jars, no judders and, as you come to rest, the clutch automatically disengages — you cannot stall the engine, and there you are, ready to pull away again, without bother back to the eighties, back to the smoothest, safest car glide you've ever enjoyed.'

To the driver of 1956, such a description of a car could only be descibed as emotive and mouthwatering. Thirty years on, a car capable of such easy and safe motoring is still a dream.

The roadholding of the DS was remarkable beyond all doubt. Full credit is due to not only the ingenious suspension and the essential front wheel drive, but to the aerodynamic styling which incorporated the DS having a virtually smooth underside resulting in the car effectively being pulled down onto the road surface. Such was the performance that first place was awarded to the car in the two-litre category of the 1956 Monte Carlo Rally — and within just four months of being introduced upon the French market. The Citroën hydropneumatic suspension had its critics as well as devotees. Many of the critics little understood its technology and theory that made it a class

The DS had legendary road roadholding capability as demonstrated in this picture of a car taking part in the East African Rally. Citroën notched up many rally victories with the DS, the combination of front-wheel drive and hydraulic suspension being the Company's recipe for success.

apart. Of admirers, there were many, possibly none so prestigious as Rolls-Royce who adopted Citroën's suspension for the rear axle on some of their cars. Mercedes Benz also realised the virtues of self-levelling suspension devising a similar system.

By the time the DS was put into production at Slough, so much had been said of the car it was instantly recognisable and had become a legend and wonder of the motoring world. It was not merely the unique hydropneumatic suspension that had been responsible, neither was its unusual but efficient styling, it was the whole concept of the car from the first nut and bolt to the last degree of comfort. In Citroën's own words the car was simply described thus:

'This car, of entirely new conception, solves the problem of providing maximum comfort, safety and speed according to present day requirements equally on the smooth modern roads as on the corrugated tracks of underdeveloped countries.'

To achieve this ideal, Citroën engineers worked hard and long. As with the introduction of the Traction Avant in 1934, problems were experienced. The knowledge gained in producing the Traction was invaluable, especially the 6H, but for the Slough engineers part of the dilemma was to adapt an already technologically advanced car to British requirements. Even more difficult was the task of convincing Citroën agents the car was not as complicated as they had been led to believe.

The main engineering principles pioneered with the Traction were retained in the specification of the DS. The monocoque body provided built-in strength and allowed panels to be bolted on which enabled repairs to be carried out rather more quickly in cases of accident. Lifting the huge bonnet, the owner of a DS was immediately confronted by a mass of equipment that appeared to be crammed into the space with a shoe-horn. The engine was installed tightly against the cabin bulkhead and the radiator, instead of being at the very front of the compartment, where it would have been expected to have been found on other cars, was positioned mid-way back leaving a large area at the front of the bonnet for the spare wheel and tool kit. As on the Light Fifteen, the gearbox was placed ahead of the power unit providing direct transmission with the front wheels. The four cylinder 1911cc engine was, essentially, the same as that installed to the Light and Big Fifteen. The formula was already there for a well-tried power unit and it was considered practical to develop it rather than pursue the experiments with alternative configurations.

The engine now provided 75 b.h.p. at 4,500 r.p.m., largely due to a new cylinder head cast in aluminium with hemispherical combustion chambers, large diameter inlet and exhaust valves which were angled in vee formation at 60° with an entirely new design of rocker assembly. Carburation was produced by a twin-bodied Weber unit allowing the second butterfly to open at a later and more progressive stage so giving a valuable boost to the acceleration where it was most needed. The Floating Power principle had not been forgotten, it had seen life throughout the Traction era and again this unique way of stabilising the engine was employed on the DS. As with the Light Fifteen, the complete engine assembly was mounted on rubber blocks with positively no metal contact with the chassis. The exhaust system was designed to be quiet and highly efficient. Firstly, the exhaust gases were passed through an expansion chamber before being released to the silencer. Also for quietness, the engine fan was constructed from nylon instead of metal. Improved water cooling for the engine was devised for the DS; as well as a water pump the system was also fitted with a thermostat. The ignition differed from other cars, instead of a distributor there were two coils and two contact breakers, each coil being wired to two of the sparking plugs. This method had obvious derivations from that of the 2CV, however, instead of there being only one cam providing a low-tension current to the two sparking plugs, there were two cams within a single contact-breaker case operating each contact breaker. In addition, a separate advance and retard control was situated on the dashboard.

The design of clutch installed on the DS created almost as much controversy as the car itself. Operated entirely by hydraulics there was no need for a clutch pedal. In fact, there was nothing different about the clutch plate, it was a normal single dry disc. The differences occurred in the method of operation. Replacing the conventional pedal was a hydraulic cylinder that operated the clutch mechanism; a valve either admitted fluid under pressure from the main accumulator into the cylinder which activated disengagement of the clutch, or, it released fluid from the cylinder allowing the clutch to engage under action of the return spring. The clutch was operated by two control mechanisms in series, i.e. one was connected to the change speed control which caused withdrawal of the clutch before engagement of the gear and followed with the re-engagement of the clutch after the re-engagement of the gear. The second was operated by engine speed which automatically disengaged the clutch when revolutions dropped to idling speed.

Among the DS safety features, Citroën drew attention to the all-round visibility given by the slender windscreen frames and 'frameless' door windows and the front mounting of the spare wheel.

A modulator, or 'brain', controlled by the accelerator pedal, automatically varied the speed of clutch engagement allowing for the whole range of driving technique from moving off slowly to a quick get-away. In cases of emergency, there was a manual control capable of releasing pressure in the clutch cylinder. This was situated on the dashboard and permitted the engine to be started with a starting handle, turning the engine by hand, tow-starting the car and facilitating the adjustments of tappets etc. The operation of the clutch depended on the use of the column-mounted gear selector which required only the lightest of hand pressure for the mechanism to be effective. Having the starter motor control linked to the gear shift it was impossible to start the car when in gear and prevented stalling the engine.

Although the 'automatic clutch' formed part of the specification of the DS19, it did not imply the driver losing any control over the gearchange. It was still necessary to select the gear in the normal manner but the movement upon the gear lever ensured the operation was carried out easily, quickly and, moreover, very smoothly. Second, third and top ratios had synchromesh, these being the ratios normally in constant use. The gearbox was quite conventional, however, the levers normally required to operate the selector forks were replaced by hydraulic cylinders which allowed the right amount of fluid into the system to change the ratio selected on the steering column. Safeguards were built into the system in order to prevent the possibility of either the incorrect gear, or two gears being simultaneously selected.

Gear ratios were provided at convenient intervals; 25 m.p.h. was available in first gear, 50 in second, 72 in third and the high-geared top managed an impressive 90 miles per hour. Evidence suggests that this particular system of gearchange was far less wearing on the clutch mechanism as against a manual system. A drawback, however, depending upon which way the system is viewed, was the necessity for the driver to ensure some positive synchronisation between engine speed and gear ratio. Failure to do so resulted in a considerable jerk when the clutch re-engaged.

Apart from the styling of the DS, the one major factor to create unprecedented controversy was the suspension system. Seen previously on the rear axle of the 6H, the full potential of hydraulics had not been appreciated until the appearance of Citroën's D series cars. Where other cars rocked and pitched over poor surfaces, the DS literally glided along providing driver and passengers with a completely stable ride. At the touch of a lever the ground clearance was adjustable to accommodate almost any terrain. While the 6H had been under development the Citroën design team had been busy furthering the practicalities and resources of the car, the result was that the system had been perfected well enough to be extended to an entire system. At this stage, it is interesting to note that between the time the 6H was put into production and the DS launched, there does not appear to be any record of 6Hs being tested with full hydraulic suspension as a test-bed for the forthcoming car. Perhaps this can be put down to the DS as being one of the best-kept secrets.

Citroën's pneumatic suspension rapidly gained recognition as the most advanced and practical suspension found on any car. It consisted of a system utilising a mixture of special fluid (LHS) and nitrogen with the LHS contained in a cylinder and and the nitrogen in a sphere. The result gave greater flexibility and by varying the volume of fluid under pressure between the wheel and the gas, ground clearance could be kept constant whatever the load in the car. Ground clearance could be kept at a constant level by varying the volume of LHS contained in the cylinders and the spheres. By means of anti-roll bars and height correctors the fluid, under extreme pressure, was able to flow between the suspension cylinders.

As the load of the car increased and the vehicle sank under the weight, so the height correctors were activated by the anti-roll bars having the effect of increasing the pressure of the fluid in the cylinders which in turn raised the level of the car to a neutral position. When the load level of the car decreased so the ground clearance would increase

The diagram illustrates the principles of hydropneumatic suspension. By keeping the body at a constant height above the road under varying static loads it ensures the minimum movement of the body and displacement of the centre of gravity when moving on uneven surfaces. Each wheel is linked to the piston working in a cylinder attached to the body. Vertical movements of the wheel are transmitted to a piston and through the medium of hydraulic fluid acts on a diaphragm in the sphere containing compressed gas above each diaphragm. By the means of a lever inside the car, the ground clearance can be adjusted to cater for all surfaces whilst the system can be used a means of jacking the car in the event of wheel changing.

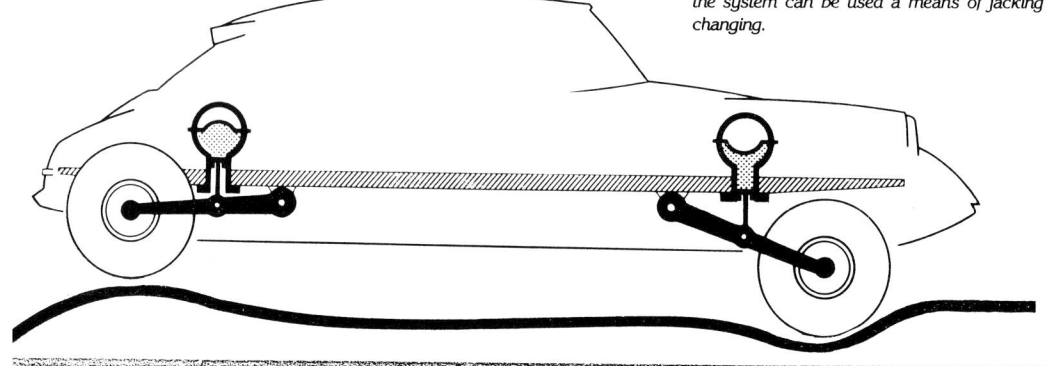

so decompressing the nitrogen, sending the hydraulic fluid back to the reservoir and lowering the car back to normal operating position.

The braking system of the DS also received a considerable amount of comment. Gone were the days when great foot pressure needed to be applied to the brake pedal to slow or halt the car. For many years the Westinghouse servo system had been employed to improve the braking performance of the Citroën over many other cars. This had saved the driver from having to utilise excessive pedal pressure and therefore it was only natural to assume that some positive thought had taken place over the drawing board to make the DS the car with the most responsive braking. In designing the DS, Citroën had revolutionised the brake pedal. In its place a floor-mounted mushroom shaped valve appeared. At first, use of this device took some getting use to and for the unwary a trial braking could quite easily result in unexpectedly severe braking, with the driver being thrown forward almost out of the seat. Such was the potential severity of power available. The mushroom required only the lightest of touch to retard the car's speed.

The front and rear braking circuits were designed to be fully independent, with the front circuit supplied from a pressure accumulator connected to the front suspension system. It was for safety there were two independent circuits, the rear braking being supplied direct from the rear suspension. As the brake mushroom was operated, the slide valves sent fluid under pressure to the brake cylinders, when released, the fluid returned to the reservoir. When controlling the braking pressure, the pressure acting on the brake cylinder pistons also acted on the slide valves, the effect of which made the pressure acting on the brakes proportional to the effort applied to the pedal. To increase braking power it was necessary to increase the force applied to the mushroom pedal and in this way the device operated as a normal pedal.

Those expecting to find a hand brake on the DS were disappointed for it lacked such a contrivance. What it did have as an independent mechanical brake was a foot-operated device in the position where the clutch pedal was normally found on other cars. This was the cause of unlimited confusion especially to owners new to the Citroën marque. The mechanical brake could be applied with the left foot for holding the car momentarily such as at traffic lights or on a hill but if required for parking it was necessary to lock the mechanism by means of a special chain and switch lever under the dashboard. The DS19 had inboard mounted front brakes, the principle of which had been developed from the 2CV. Instead of drums, the DS had the benefit of disc brakes with cooling achieved by collecting forced air from special vents placed either side of the front number plate.

The steering of the DS was also unique. Apart from being power operated it was coupled to the main hydraulic system as with the suspension and braking systems. Whatever the road surface the rack and pinion mechanism ensured effortless steering and there was almost a total lack of vibration transmitted through the column. Winter conditions, ice or dusty pot-holed surfaces meant nothing

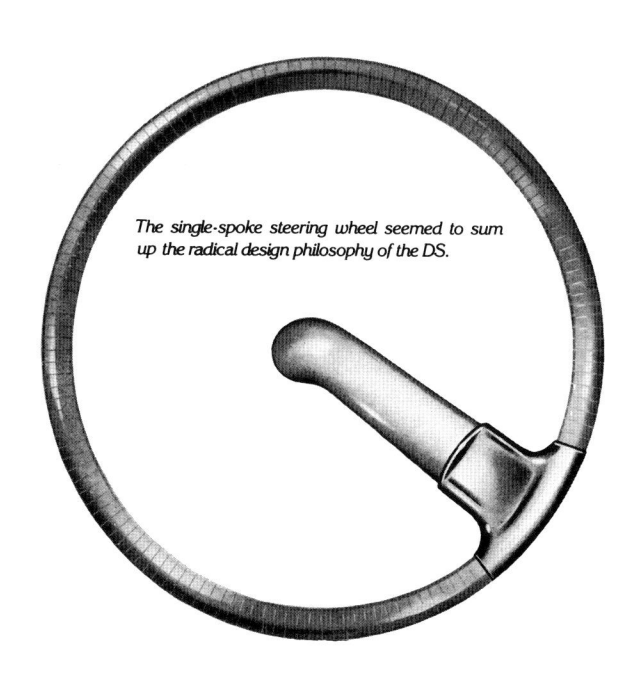

The single-spoke steering wheel seemed to sum up the radical design philosophy of the DS.

to the DS, the hydraulics took the strain. The mechanical action of the pinion on the rack was replaced by a piston moving in a cylinder fed by fluid from the main accumulator via two valves operated by the steering column. The valves admitted fluid to either one or the other side of the piston according to the movement of the steering wheel; with one side of the piston under pressure, so pressure on the opposite side was released. In normal use no mechanical contact existed between the steering wheel and the rack, with the pinion only following the movement of the rack. Should the hydraulic system be out of action, the striking plate operating the valves came into contact with the body of the valve which allowed full mechanical control of the steering.

The eccentricity of the DS was not just confined to the car's hydraulic system. The built-in jacking device, glass-fibre roof and the highly controversial dashboard were all part of the package. The jacking device is of interest in as much as it was possible to lift the car without any of the effort required on conventional cars. Firstly, the car had to be raised to the highest suspension level and a stand, supplied with the tool kit, slotted into a special housing located on the floor pan. With the lowest suspension level then selected the offending side of the car was lifted off the ground. The styling of the car did not allow for cut-away wheel arches on the rear wing. In order to change a rear wheel, therefore, it was necessary to remove the wing completely. A much easier operation than it appeared as the wing was secured by just one bolt. By using a special spanner it was a simple task to detach the panel. In the case of a rear tyre puncturing at the worst possible moment, it was feasible to raise the suspension to the highest level, so taking the weight off the offending wheel and continue driving on three wheels only. Numerous experiments were carried out whereby a rear wheel was completely removed and the car travelled perfectly well on three wheels, the suspension ensuring the car was kept quite level and safe.

The DS afforded extraordinary amounts of space for back-seat passengers. Note the sumptuously cushioned seats.

A further curiosity was by way the wheels were fixed to the hubs; on most other cars the wheels were retained by normal hub nuts, but not so the DS. A single hexagonal bolt secured the wheel of the DS19 requiring a special tool to undo it. The operation to change a wheel may have appeared clumsy, nevertheless, it took no more time to change wheels on a DS than it did on any other motor car.

The interior of the DS earned a reputation for being fully equipped. 'Wall to wall' carpeting graced the car as did the softly trimmed supple seats. Arm-rests upon the doors added to comfort; good visibility and four interior lights provided as much convenience as possible. The facilities offered to both driver and passengers were second to none with there being very few manufacturers who could match the specification. The heating and ventilation were interesting for the period as it allowed fresh air to enter the car through ducts on the fascia panel. Warm air was directed both to the front of the car as well as to the back for the comfort of the rear passengers, a provision normally only found only on the most expensive of cars. The dashboard layout of the first cars from Slough utilised the same format as the French-built models, the neat array of dials and switches usually installed in British cars gave way to extreme unconventionality. The use of instruments on the dash of the DS19 was kept down to a basic level. Switches abounded all over the fascia in what can only be termed as a haphazard manner, but the system worked well with the owner soon coming to terms with the French-orientated approach.

The car was full of little surprises that made owning a DS so pleasant. With the bonnet and boot open it was still possible to have full forward and rearward view from the driving seat; the lower edges of the panels being deeply curved, together with the strategic positioning of the hinges gave an uninterrupted line of vision so amplifying the car's safety aspect. Ignition timing was adjustable from the dashboard, this inheritance from the Traction prevented the car's performance suffering should a poor grade of petrol be used. The superb interior lighting with lamps in the door pillars and on the rear panels, fully reclining seats and luxury deep pile carpets made the DS just about the most comfortable car on the market.

The DS19 made a huge impact in Britain. Following the success of the Light Fifteen, the name of Citroën had become synonymous with technical advance. Car design had been revolutionised; the question as to whether the motor car would ever be the same again was being asked. Even accounting for the DS being proved at home and on the rally track there was the suggestion it was over-complicated. In truth, the car was too much ahead of its time. Just as the DS went into production at Slough so a simplified version of the DS was announced in France. The iD19, with its little less technical wizardry would have been welcomed on the British market.

It was not until March 1958 that the 'less complicated' hydropneumatic Citroën was put into production at Slough. Outwardly indistinguishable from the DS19, the iD19 was much more conventional. Instead of using hydraulics for all of its major functions, only the suspension remained, the gear-change, steering and braking being completely conventional. Had the iD19 been the first of the D Series to appear, the shock of the DS might not have been so great, nevertheless, the iD was still every bit as much an advanced car and shared many of the other car's finer points. In France there were two versions of the iD, Standard and De Luxe. In Britain the iD resembled the De Luxe version but in an Anglicised form.

The iD19 was considered by Slough to be an important addition to the D Series. Whereas the DS19 obviously deterred potential customers shy of its bristling technology, the iD offered a compromise between straightforward automobile engineering and a taste of the exotic. Citroën badly needed to boost sales as the delay between the demise of the Traction and the emergence of the DS had cost the Company sales of new cars to their competitors. Production of the DS was running between fifteen and twenty cars a day, this reflected a relatively poor performance when considered that the golden age had been reached when just over a million cars were built in factories around the country. Competition from wholly British and American owned companies constituted a major threat but their cars lacked Citroën's attributes of front wheel drive and comfort. Although the iD was less elaborate than the DS, it was still way and above almost any other saloon car on the market in performance and specification.

The interior design of the Slough-built iD differed considerably from that of the DS. In place of the strangely contoured dashboard there featured a polished wood fascia with the controls neatly set in a panel immediately below it. Housed in the dashboard, a glove box provided concealed stowage space and at either end of the fascia vents directed fresh air into the car. Directly in front of the steering wheel a tidy nacelle contained the speedometer,

SUPERLATIVE CITROËN

The car that has driven a gap in the English language

Futuristic power was the theme behind many of Citroën's advertisements for the DS. The question must be asked as to whether the DS was too advanced for the time, especially for the British market, and perhaps whether such an aggressive approach might have been self-defeating for a car of which the appeal was one largely of great comfort and lack of effort in driving. The British motorist in the mid-1950s was certainly not used to such aerodynamic styling and high technology. Even when the D Series were superseded in the mid-1970s, it was still outstanding in these respects.

ammeter and fuel gauge, the whole affair resembling more of a typically British style of dash arrangement. Without power steering it was necessary to increase the diameter of the steering wheel which retained the single spoke design as fitted to the DS. In place of the hydraulic gear change a manually operated gear shift was attached to the steering column following the trend in design at the time. A conventional clutch connected the four speed gear box, necessitating in doing away with the foot controlled parking brake which was replaced by a customary hand brake installed on the right hand side of the driving seat. The mushroom foot brake was sacrificed in favour of a normal pedal operating a straightforward braking system.

A curious feature of both the DS and iD19 entailed the suspension height control lever being positioned on the left hand side of the front passenger seat. This resulted in the driver having to leave the seat to alter the suspension height should there not be a passenger to operate the lever. This was a direct casualty of converting the car from left hand to right hand drive. In later models the problem was rectified with the lever being installed to the right of the driving seat.

Although a cheaper car, the comfort afforded by the iD did not suffer; the seats were as comfortable and were covered in best quality leather, but did not recline. Carpets were denied the thick foam underlay but apart from material changes there was little difference between this and the more expensive DS.

The engine fitted to the iD had a lower compression and coped more easily with lesser grade fuels than the DS although a manual ignition control was provided. The twin-choke carburettor fitted to the DS was replaced with a single choke unit but accounted for little difference in performance between the two cars. The manual gear change was quicker than the hydraulic change and the seven-piston pump fitted to the DS took more power from the engine than the smaller pump fitted to the iD. There was some question as to whether it was beneficial spending the extra money on the DS when nearly the same luxury motoring could be achieved with the iD. A governing factor were the running and maintenance costs; whereas many owners might contemplate self-maintaining the iD, few considered this on the more complicated DS.

The main differences showed up in the handling of the two cars; where the DS was easy to park with the power steering taking all the strain, at low speeds the iD was extremely heavy but in contrast was quite light at speed on the open road. Braking also suffered on the iD; whilst adopting the same configuration as the DS with discs at the front and drums at the rear, considerable foot pressure was required to halt the car within the same distances as the DS with its power brakes. The independently controlled hand brake operating on the front wheels acted exactly in the same manner as the foot-type parking brake. Michelin X radial-ply tyres complimented the soft suspension which provided the iD as good a ride as the DS. The low pressures helped grip the road with the same tenacious support experienced with the Traction. To confirm the qualities of the iD, the car was outright winner in the 1959 Monte Carlo Rally. Third place went to a Panhard DB and fourth place to another iD Citroën.

DS Production at Slough

The period between the cessation of production of the Traction Avant and commencement of the D Series was not a happy time for the Company. With diminished production of cars there was need only for a much reduced labour force. Apart from Chargehands the majority of

The Citroën iD was brought onto the market to cater for the customer who wanted the styling and suspension of the DS but required more conventional braking, steering and gear change, as well as lower cost. This suited a large number of British customers and in an effort to Anglicise the car still further, a dashboard more in keeping with contemporary preferences was designed. The instruments of the iD were mounted within a veneer fascia giving the car a feel of the 'establishment'. When introduced in Britain in January 1958, the iD19 was priced at £1,498, the DS19 by then costing £1,726.

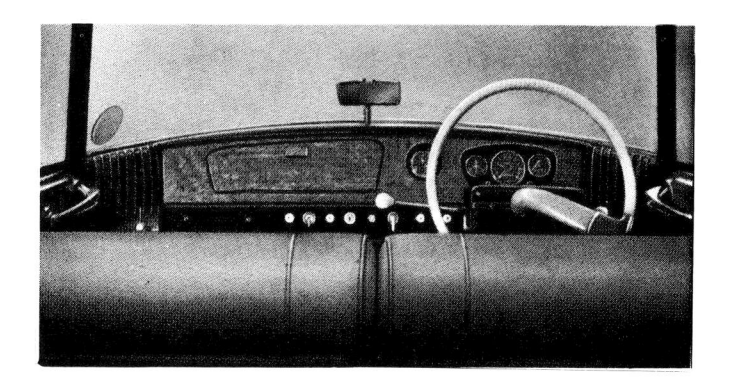

In the Finishing Shop, DS body panels receive attention after the process of filling and stopping has been completed following delivery from Paris. Panels were sent to Slough in their greased state and therefore underwent treatment before assembly could take place. A guide has been applied to the panels which underwent rubbing, scuffing, wiping and were then blown dry.

assembly staff were laid off. Many found alternative employment never to return to the Factory. These were sad days, no longer did the noise of machinery dominate all else. It was a relief, therefore, when production of the DS finally got under way and machines burst into life, arc-welders lit the workshop with flashes of vivid blue and the trim shop came alive with the singing of sewing machines and the screaming of cutters.

The major components of the D Series were manufactured in France. Floor pans, body panels, engines and transmission units were exported to Slough in kit form. On arrival at the Factory by rail all parts were checked, unloaded and put into the relevant store. With the body pressing laid onto the assembly line, panels were bolted into place with the framework immediately taking the shape of the car. In the main, Citroën's policy of using British components was retained although this applied only to such items as electrical equipment, etc.

Body panels were delivered to Slough in their greased state from Javel and had to undergo preparation before assembly could begin. For this operation a finishing plant had been installed during 1958 by Heat and Air Systems Ltd. for the pre-treatment, priming, filling and finish coating of all the body parts. The system was designed to cater for approximately fifteen cars a day. Panels were loaded onto purpose-built trucks attached to the conveyor system which transported the components through a series of ovens designed to operate at differing temperatures providing the optimum results at each stage. The initial procedure was to coat each piece of body equipment with a sound deadener which was applied to the under parts and interior of doors, wings and bonnet. Following this came the process of Deoxidine treatment where the entire body, its accessories, front wings and valances were cleaned, de-greased and de-rusted. It was necessary for all the panels to go into the oil-fired oven at a temperature of 310°F before being allowed a flash-off period of four minutes prior to returning to the oven for a further forty minutes at 315°F. Once completed, the items were brushed off, wiped and finally blown-clean.

The priming stage came next. The body and accessories were brushed with a solvent before being sprayed with a synthetic primer coating. After ten minutes flash-off period the primer was stoved for forty-five minutes at 285°F followed by a cooling time of eight minutes. For rubbing down, a guide coat was applied which enabled the body finisher to see what parts needed attention. The panels were then rubbed, scuffed, wiped and blown dry in order the filling and stopping processes could be undertaken. The only part of the body not to pass through this process was the glass-fibre reinforced plastic roof.

The parts of the bodywork attached to the conveyor trucks at this stage were ready for their first colour coats. Paint was applied followed by a twelve minute flash off period before force drying at 180°F for thirty minutes and a cooling-off for eight minutes. Further stopping-up and facing-down, colour flattening, wiping and blow drying then took place. With the process almost finished, two further cellulose coats were applied. A twelve minute flash off period was allowed followed by more force drying at 180°F for forty minutes with twelve minutes cooling-off after which, final assembly and polishing were completed. Management at Slough claimed the paint finish of their cars to be superior to those built in France. There is no reason to deny this considering the modern equipment, techniques and experience employed at Slough. Mass production ensured cars built at Slough were engineered within the finest of tolerances. Since its earliest days the Citroën Company had earned a reputation for perfection.

The main body frame of the DS and iD completed, accessories were installed as the car passed along the assembly line. The 12-volt electrics, instruments and controls were, in the main, supplied by Lucas; Connolly produced the fine quality leather hides and Michelin the tyres. With the suspension fitted and connected, the engine, gearbox and transmission units were lowered and

The same body panels emerging from the stoving oven where they have remained for twenty minutes at a temperature of 220 degrees F. Stopping-up followed by facing-down and wiping dry took place in this next stage of the finishing process.

bolted into place. Both the engine and gearbox were delivered from Paris already assembled complete with the braking mechanism, radiator, cooling fan, sparking plugs and distributor. After installation and connection to the main components, the car was ready to run. Finally, bumpers which had been chromium plated in the extensive plating shop within the Factory were fitted before the completed car was sent to the Final Test Shop where the Citroën underwent a rigorous test with necessary adjustments being made. Satisfied that the car had passed every stringent test it was sent to the despatch area to await collection by the agent.

It was the responsibility of the Citroën Dealers to collect their vehicles from the Factory. At Middleton Motors, Citroën Main Agents in Hertfordshire, the young salesman caught the Green Line coach from outside the garage direct to Slough where he collected the car and returned to Potters Bar with it. One Saturday he collected three cars which meant three separate journeys by coach! Such was the personal interest and dedication of the Citroën Agent.

The iD and DS were not the type of car normally to be associated with sports tuning. With a fine pedigree in their own right and with a performance to match, *Motor Sport* magazine considered the cars to be in the sporting saloon class. Connaught Cars, of Send, Surrey, who were recognised for their sports conversions, were able to supply the DS and iD in GT form capable of a top speed in excess of 100 m.p.h. For the price £1,598 a prospective owner could purchase a new iD Connaught Citroën with a full conversion package. Power steering and brakes were fitted and in place of the standard iD seats, fully reclining individual bucket competition seats were supplied. The Kenlowe thermostatic cooling fan was fitted and the original flywheel changed for a lightweight type with a twin-choke Solex carburettor replacing the single choke type as fitted to factory models. Additional soundproofing, stainless steel body stripes, Brooks retractable seat belts were all specified and the whole package was neatly finished off with a Stirling Moss wood rimmed steering wheel and Connaught GT body motifs. Connaught claimed a much improved performance and smoother acceleration. As optional extras there was provision to supply and install a rev. counter, centre armrest with glove or map locker, door mounted map pockets, radio and twin S.U. carburettors. There is no evidence the conversion sold in any large numbers and it is doubtful whether any examples survive to this day.

The 1959 iD produced some minor changes in the design of the interior layout. A clock was added to the fascia and the heating and ventilation controls were more comprehensive. Space was allocated for a radio on the dashboard in front of the passenger but at the expense of a reduction in the size of the glove box. The design of the fascia altered to account for a somewhat improved aesthetic appeal with a greater emphasis on curves rather than severe straight lines. The corresponding model of DS still retained all the features that made the car so famous on its introduction. By the end of the year, the 1960 models were announced, the iD cost £1,415 tax paid and the DS19 a little over £1,630. When compared to similar sized cars on the market, the Citroën was expensive. The Vauxhall Velox cost £929 tax paid while the better trimmed Cresta sold for £1,014. The same money required to purchase the DS could buy either a Jaguar 3.4 litre, Rover 100 or the Vanden Plas 3 Litre Automatic.

The self-levelling suspension of the D Series allowed heavy loads to be carried without having any affect upon the car's handling and led to the potential development of an effective load carrier based upon the same principles as the saloon car. In October 1959, Citroën announced the introduction of the Safari Break. At once, the Safari offered the ultimate in estate cars, but at a price. At £1,765 it was £600 more expensive than the Ford Zodiac Estate and a little over £100 more than the Humber Super Snipe Estate Car. The Safari had the most distinctive lines though; from the front it had the appearance of the iD and DS, the roof line was level over the entire length of the car and extended way beyond the rear door pillars ending in a curved shape with a huge wrap-around rear window. Based neither directly on the iD or DS, the Safari utilised features from each model and was built upon a strengthened floor pan seven inches longer than the Saloon to accommodate the heavier bodywork and increased carrying capacity. The benefit of front wheel drive was clearly demonstrated by the completely flat loading area which enabled the rear seat to be folded flat into the floor space of 7ft. in length.

In an instant the Safari could be converted into a people-carrier. Seven passengers, including the driver, could be carried in absolute comfort, two in the front, three on the rear seat with a further two on folding seats at the back of

The estate car version of the range was introduced in Britain in October 1959. Its name in France was the Safari Break (a quirk of language is that the spelling of what in Britain might be called a shooting brake takes on the spelling we associate with a quite different meaning of the word of the same sound) but the version offered from Slough was simply the Safari. Its specification incorporated a combination of the iD's engine and transmission with the power-hydraulic brake system of the DS as well as, of course, the self-levelling suspension. Wheelbase length was unchanged but extra length at the rear — 16ft. 6ins. overall — gave immense internal space.

the car. The two occasional side-facing folding seats were far from being designed merely for children and provided surprising comfort even on long journeys. These folded into a well when not in use leaving a perfectly flat stowage area. The Safari naturally retained the hydropneumatic suspension and ease of height control; however, the control lever was still positioned on the passenger's side of the car. The suspension proved exceptionally useful when heavy or bulky items were being loaded as the car could be made to sink to its lowest level and then raised to its normal running height. Hydraulics were used to power the braking system with disc brakes at the front and supported by larger diameter drums at the rear, controlled by the mushroom button. Manual steering was fitted which caused the Safari to be excessively heavy when parking or driven at low speeds. The gear change and clutch were also manually operated with the gear shift mounted on the steering column.

Leather upholstery was supplied for the Safari and individual front seats were replaced by a bench seat. The dashboard received minor modifications to that of the iD with a clock fitted between the instrument nacelle and the glove box. The generous capacity of the Estate Car was supplemented still further by the provision of an excellent roof rack fitted as standard. At the back of the car, the tailgate opened at two levels for ease of loading. The rear wings of the Safari had cut-away wheel arches as it was not designed the wings should be removed in the event of wheel-changing due to the longer floor pan and construction of the body. In its test of the Safari, *The Motor* had several criticisms ranging from the length and width of the vehicle to the styling of door catches. In the event, however, *The Motor* concluded there was not a vehicle on the market that could match it.

The D Series Citroën has always intrigued motoring journalists; they have never, that is apart from self-confessed Citroën admirers, fully come to terms with the car, its ability or potential. In the wrong hands the car could be a frightening machine, it made a mockery of those nervous of it. The D has always been capable of returning very high averages without having the necessity of above average top speed. It has always been at its best when having to work whereas some motor cars are only good for fast motorway driving. This view is upheld by the D's remarkable rally successes. A well-known journalist once commented that while testing a new car (a non-Citroën) that was supposedly capable of high speeds, he was often confronted with the situation of a battered DS roaring past well above the speed the car should have been able to reach. The speeds and power obtained from the four cylinder engine could only be a tribute to Citroën engineers and designers. There were calls for a six-cylinder DS, this never came and there really never was a need for it. The gears of the D were long-legged and were sufficient to cope with every eventuality that arose.

The Ami 6

The success of the 2CV in France led Citroën to introduce the Ami 6. Almost 159,000 2CV's were built in France during 1961 and it was considered potential existed for an up-market version of the car. The Ami also served in part to fill a gap in the Citroën range; between the 2CV and the iD there existed a void in which Citroën's competitors found their niche. Renault gained ground with the Dauphine and Fregate whilst Simca sold their Aronde in large numbers and Peugeot found favour with the 203 and later the 403.

The Ami 6 shared the same logic as the 2CV, it still offered minimal motoring but with greater comfort, more power and a heavier but strangely aerodynamic body yielding increased space on the same chassis. A new air-cooled flat-twin engine of 602cc pushed the fiscal rating from 2CV to 3CV. The demise of the 2CV in Britain left a gap the small-car end of the market and the decision was taken to build the Ami at Slough.

Launched onto the British market in time for the 1961 Earls Court Motor Show, the Ami 6 was displayed on stand 96 alongside the iD, DS and Safari. The Bijou was not on show but Citroën assured the car was still available. Where both the 2CV and Bijou had failed it was hoped the Ami 6 would succeed.

Designed around the chassis of the 2CV, the Ami 6 followed many of its attributes; with a heavier body and glass-fibre roof, it offered much more in the way of large car comfort and facilities than its predecessor. With its sharply dipping bonnet with protruding headlamps and inward sloping rear window, a design Ford also adopted on their Anglia and Classic Saloons, the Ami was considered by many to be just about the ugliest car on the market. Citroën found the design of rear window prevented the screen becoming obscured by rain and grime and that glare from headlamps did not affect it. As with the DS and iD, all door

The Ami 6, launched in Britain for the 1961 Earls Court Motor Show, gained the unfortunate title of the ugliest car in Britain. The wrap-over bonnet protruding over the edge of the headlamps gave the car a hooded-eyebrow appearance. The Ami 6 also featured a reverse-slope rear window much akin to that already established on Ford's Anglia models of the time. Powered by a 602cc flat-twin air-cooled engine, it shared much of the running gear of the 2CV. Where the original 2CV and Bijou had failed, alas, so also the Ami 6 failed to appeal to the British motorist.

pillars were slim and the four doors opened wide enough to allow easy access to the car's interior. The curved front windscreen provided more space in the front of the cabin and helped in giving the impression the car was larger than it actually was. Several features of the DS were found on the Ami such as the door handles, the single spoke steering wheel as well as various control knobs and switches. Sharing the same running gear as the 2CV, the Ami sported the push-pull-and-twist gear change with the gear lever sprouting from the fascia panel. Naturally, the Ami received the same suspension as the 2CV affording supreme roadholding and passenger comfort.

The 602cc engine managed to propel the Ami at a top speed of 65 miles per hour with four people and a full quota of luggage as well as returning 50 miles to the gallon of 2 star petrol. The suspension, due to the heavier body, was extremely supple and under load, softer than the Deux Chevaux. All the body panels were of lightweight construction but lacked nothing in strength and safety. The bonnet dipped away between the front wings with their built-in headlamp assembly resulting in a hooded or 'eyebrow' effect at the front of the car. The seats in the Ami were sublimely comfortable with arm rests fitted on all the doors. Sliding front windows and vents on the dashboard provided ample fresh air. The Ami 6 personified the nose down attitude of Citroën's small flat-twin cars, this time the manufacturer did nothing to hide this attitude as they had tried with the Bijou.

A small assembly line was constructed at Slough for the Ami 6. The first ten cars to leave the Factory had been built in France, imported to Britain but converted to right hand drive. At £820, the Ami 6 was considerably over-priced, the Renault Dauphine cost £690 and the Ford Anglia £589. With its robust and proven mechanics, low maintenance and superb comfort, the Ami 6 failed to sell and completely lacked the success it should have had. Only seventy cars were built at the Factory before production was abandoned. In France it sold well, so well that thirty years after its introduction there are still thousands in daily use.

There were by far a greater number of Estate versions sold in Britain, these were never built at Slough but were imported from France in right hand drive form. It is sad to note that as far as is known, not one Ami 6 Saloon exists today with right hand drive. The last accounted car was sold cheaply due to a simple fault that had not been correctly diagnosed and later the car was broken up.

D Series Success

The popularity of the D Series was recognised with a marked increase in production of cars at Slough. During 1959 deliveries of new cars returned to the level of pre-1955; over 1,400 cars were built with 246 exported. In 1960 the figure rose to 2000 and of these 1,720 were for the British market. The Slough Factory had always built cars destined for Commonwealth countries so aiding Britain's export trade, however, between 1959 and 1961 Citroën decided to open assembly plants in South Africa and Australia. The decision had been taken in light of

The power output of the DS was increased to 83 b.h.p. in 1961 so allowing the car a higher top speed — 93 m.p.h. The advertisement for the new version depicts a DS at speed with the artist certainly doing the car justice.

changing world trading standards together with Britain's associations with the European Common Market. The drop in export production and change to supplying, in general, purely for the home market had a significant affect on the Factory as will be seen later. Meanwhile, production of the DS and iD in France dramatically increased; from under 29,000 cars in 1957 to almost 67,000 in 1959, 83,000 cars were built in 1960. During 1963 over 93,000 left the production lines.

The Motor when reviewing the DS19 in a road test published in July 1961 eulogised over its qualities and found the combination of ride, roadholding, stability, brakes and ventilation 'probably unequalled in the world'.

The 1911cc engine produced a timed mean maximum speed of 93.3 m.p.h. and it was pointed out that as the top (fourth) gear was effectively an overdrive, giving 23.1 m.p.h. at 1,000 r.p.m., this represented only 4,000 r.p.m. which could be held indefinitely for motorway cruising. In favourable conditions over 100 m.p.h. was reached. Even so, it was felt that an engine of this size, in conjunction with very high gearing, could not be expected to give outstanding acceleration and suggested a larger engine would bring this more into line with the car's other high-speed capabilities. This, in due course, proved to be a prophetic comment.

W. O. Bentley, the designer of the vintage cars bearing his name, in his book *The Cars In My Life* acknowledged the worth and originality of Citroën. He had owned and driven a Light Fifteen over many thousands of miles and so impressed with front wheel drive he worked on a prototype which, had the car gone into production, would have been sensational. The car was designed with a five cylinder radial engine driving the front axle, later Bentley experimented with an air-cooled flat-six engine using Citroën transmission layout and torsion bar suspension. Financial reasons prevented the project maturing but it did leave Citroën to have another attempt at the flat-six concept if they so wished.

During 1962, changes to the specification mainly affected the interior styling of the car with a water temperature gauge fitted to the dashboard and the mushroom brake pedal increased in size. Improvements to the heating and ventilation allowed warm air to penetrate into the rear compartment from beneath the back seat and, with adjustment, would demist the rear window. The price of the car increased from £1,646 to £1,738 of which £522 was purchase tax.

The price of the DS dropped in 1963 to just under £1,569. Minor specification changes saw the suspension lever moved to the side of the driving seat and the fitting of non-cancelling direction indicators on the steering column. Previously, Citroën had fitted an indicator time-delay device to the fascia which in effect, was automatic. The 'British' dashboard as fitted to the iD was dropped in favour of the DS type fitted to French built cars. The most significant change was the replacement of glass-fibre for the roof in favour of steel. This applied to Slough-built cars only with Paris-made vehicles retaining the glass-fibre roof. There does not appear any particular reason for the change except for cosmetic purposes as the steel roof remained unstressed.

In addition to the DS, iD and Safari, there were a number of other models supplied from Slough based on the Citroën D Series. These were notably the DS Convertible, known in France as the Decapotable, the DW, Safari Ambulance, Tourmaster and Countryman. Also built in small numbers, the DS Executive and a number of special vehicles such as hearses and specially adapted Safari models for use with research and the media. The DS Executive found a market within diplomatic circles; it retained all the luxury specification of the DS but in addition was supplied with a glass partition between front and rear seats, radio telephone, intercom and separate heating and ventilation.

The Safari Ambulance, Tourmaster and Countryman were all based on the standard Safari Estate Car but with alterations in design for each model. The Ambulance represented a revolutionary new concept in patient care; throughout France little else was used for medical purposes. The Safari Ambulance was sold mainly to private ambulance companies such as the Inter Counties Ambulance Service, it was fully equipped and provided fast, safe transport with the hydropneumatic suspension ensuring the smoothest ride for the patient. The Tourmaster, announced in October 1963 had been designed for the hire trade. It was a full eight-seater with all seats facing forward. Three folding seats immediately behind the driver's and front passenger seat could be made to collapse into the floorwell while the rear seats were positioned further back than normal over the back axle.

The power output of the 1911cc engine in the iD19 and Safari models was increased slightly to 69 b.h.p. in 1961. An iD of this period is seen in London in company with some Horse Guards and, just visible behind, a Ford Consul Classic.

The Ambulance derived from the Safari offered as smooth a ride for the patient as possible, together with outstanding roadholding for high-speed travel. Widely used on the Continent, in this country the model was often specified for private ambulance service where long-distance journeys were to be undertaken. Noteworthy in this view in addition to the bell, roof lamp and illuminated ambulance sign are the extra driving lamps in streamlined fairings. Among the D series cars in the background at what is evidently a south of England dealer's premises is a pre-war Traction Avant model.

Together with the full seating capacity there was room for eight large suitcases and the built in roof rack carried a further 75lbs. of luggage. The Countryman benefited from the same principles as the Tourmaster but instead of being factory furnished it was adapted by coachbuilders Harold Radford. Everything was provided for the true sporting man; gun racks, fishing rod retainers, built-in picnic table, drinks case and ice container. The suspension allowed off-road and rough country driving. The BBC used a number of specially adapted Safari's for their Outside Broadcasts division which proved extremely satisfactory as mobile platforms for the televising of horse racing events.

The Slough Factory offered hearses produced to order, based upon the Safari Estate Car. It is unlikely that Citroën prepared the bodies at the works but would have sent them to specialist coachbuilders for conversion. These vehicles featured coffin bier, built-in wreath rack and pillarless rear side windows. Note the rear side doors are fixed. The advantage of the Citroën Hearse allowed automatic constant ground clearance which could be adjusted to suit placing the coffin. Standard DS or iD cars could be used to match the hearse so providing a most graceful cortege. The scene shown here is evidently in the Manchester area, judging by the registration numbers of the hearse and most of the cars, though the second car has a Bolton number.

In October 1962 Citroën Cars announced that the Decapotable was to be available in Britain. This, Citroën's most elegant motor car combined all the luxury of coach-built bodywork with the added feature of the advanced DS technology. The Drop-Head Coupé with its hydropneumatic suspension and power-assisted steering claimed a 100 m.p.h. plus maximum speed and 95 m.p.h. in third gear. The Decapotable when announced was the most expensive car in the Citroën catalogue at a fraction over £2,541 it was almost £1000 dearer than the DS Saloon.

Designed by Henri Chapron, who was also famous for the Presidential DS and, later, SM, the Citroën Decapotable was the most exciting car on the market in its class. A thoroughbred sporting machine capable of carrying four people in majestic style, comfort and safety, its low sleek lines accentuated by the two-door coachwork and partially enclosed rear wheels. Lighter than the DS by a hundred-weight and with slightly different gear ratios, the Decapotable's 1911cc engine delivered 83 b.h.p. at 4,500 r.p.m. On its introduction, the Decapotable received the dashboard layout of the iD. A year later, in time for the Motor Show, the DS fascia was specified, a change in keeping with the car's special charisma. Coachwork for the Decapotable was offered in a choice of twelve different colours all in polychromatic finish. To match, the high grade leather upholstery was available in eleven shades.

At the 1963 Earls Court Motor Show, Citroën displayed yet another variant car, the DW. In effect, this was a compromise between the DS and Decapotable; there was a requirement for a sporting saloon in the form of the DS but with the 100 m.p.h. plus performance of the Convertible. The DW was a product particular to Slough and was marketed alongside the iD, DS and Safari models. Hydraulics powered the suspension, steering and brakes but the transmission was manually operated via a conventional clutch.

Inside the DW unabashed luxury reigned. Deep, comfortable front seats trimmed in quality leather, fully reclined. Carpets with deep pile and thick foam underlay adorned the floor while a twin heating and ventilation system, independently controlled for front and rear, satisfied creature comforts. The layout of the DW was similar to that of the DS; it shared the same style of dash with round dials clearly visible through the single spoke steering wheel.

The acceleration of the DW in lower gears was not as impressive as might have been hoped and certainly acceleration in top gear at low speeds did not show the car to its full advantage. The lack of fast acceleration in lower gears was compensated by a high top speed. A figure of 104 m.p.h. had been claimed, together with very reasonable fuel economy figures. An overall petrol consumption of 28 m.p.g. and 32 m.p.g. touring could be obtained. At a little under £1,600 inclusive of tax, the DW represented excellent value for money.

On the whole, the British motorist did not take to the hydraulic gear change as well as European motorists. Had not Slough produced the 'Anglicised Citroën' many sales may have been lost to other manufacturers. The Safari had, until the introduction of the DW, been based mainly on the specification of the iD. There had been, therefore, some sacrifice in respect of comfort and technology over the DS. Recognising the need for an Estate Car with similar specification to the DS, Citroën announced a Safari with the same equipment as the DW. No longer did the Safari have that slight utilitarian air but boasted leather-trimmed fully reclining seats, two-speed windscreen wipers and sublime comfort.

In many ways the advent of the DW spelled change. It was the last of a line of famous Citroëns utilising the original D Series engine and although the 1911cc unit continued to be installed in the iD19 and iD19 Confort imported from France. On the horizon were new engines which were to power the cars for the next ten years. With the change in power there was to be a change in direction, a change that would have significant effect upon the British Factory.

Following the decision to open assembly plants in Australia and South Africa, car production dropped at Slough in 1962. In that year 813 cars were built of which 145 were exported. In 1963 and 1964 production levels rose again with 1083 and 1035 cars respectively. 174 cars were exported during 1963 and the following year just 74 cars were sent abroad. On the bonus side, it did mean that more cars were being sold to the home market.

(Opposite page: top) The Decapotable, with special coachwork by Chapron, was arguably Citroën's most elegant motor car. With a maximum speed of over 100 m.p.h., the DS Convertible afforded luxury with open top motoring; it retained most of the technical features of the DS but had a manual four-speed gearbox. When announced, the Decapotable cost a little over £2,451, almost £1,000 dearer than the DS. It offered special quality leather trim and a polychromatic paint finish in keeping with the high standard of the car.

(Opposite page: lower) A particularly impressive Slough-built DS19 in concours condition. Note the attractive driving lights fitted to the DS; these were a feature of cars produced from 1965. At the 1963 Earls Court Motor Show, Citroën announced the DW, a car peculiar to Slough and somewhat of a compromise between the DS and the Decapotable; the DW enjoyed all the trim and comfort of the DS but the running gear of the Decapotable making it a 100 m.p.h. plus, sporting saloon.

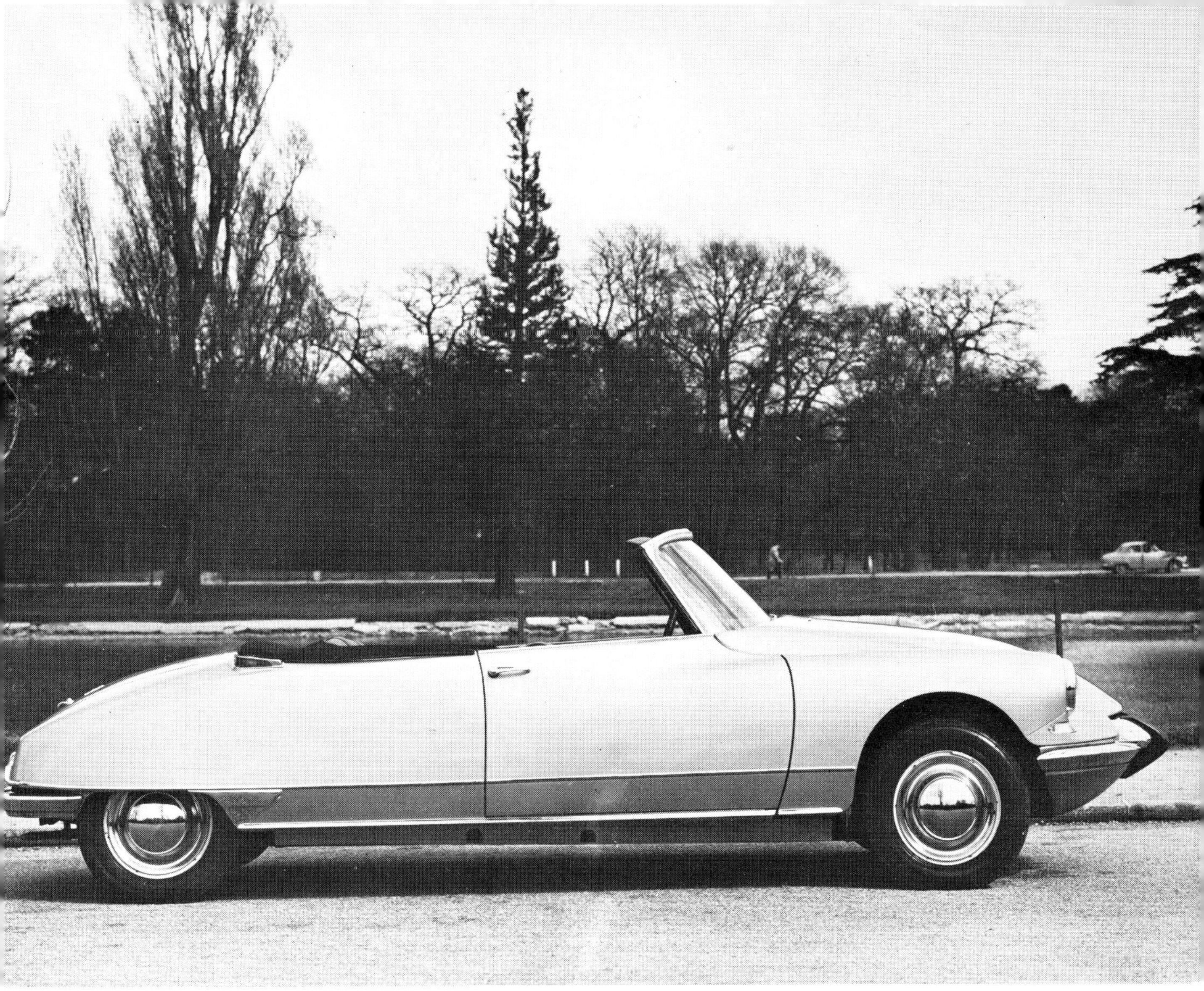

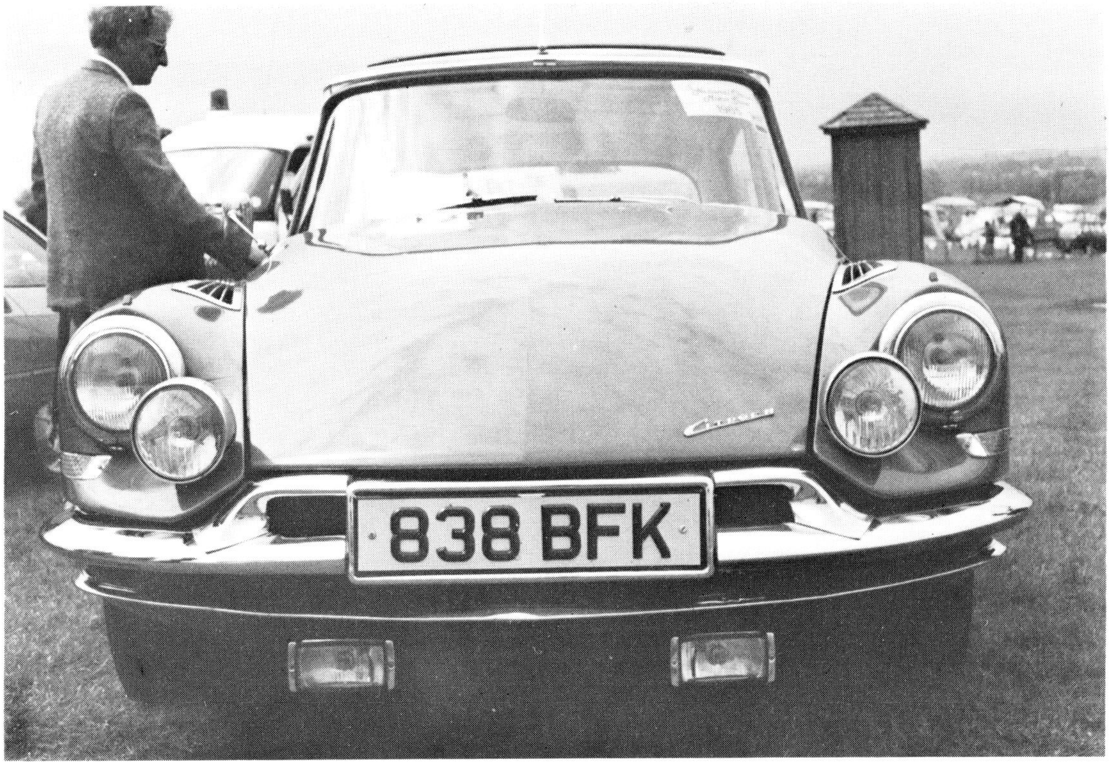
838 BFK

Chapter eleven:
The sun sets at Slough

Since those early days of Citroën, when during the early 1920s the Company laid its plans to open the Factory at Slough; when the formation of the Trading Estate was taking place with Citroën at the hub of activities; when the clatter of machinery and efficiency of mass-production resulted in the first cars rolling off the mechanised assembly lines under the roof of the largest factory building in the Country; great strife had been known and a war fought and won, the scars remained, not only upon Citroën, Slough and its industry, but upon the entire nation.

The full potential of Citroën's Slough Factory was never realised, despite the whole aspect of building cars was being British orientated even, though many of the major components were built in France and imported for final assembly. In France, the Citroën represented a nationalistic car, very Gallic and individualistic and as such very much opposed to British values. The Citroën was fit for a President and yet could be owned by a peasant, it represented all classes of life within the nation. Never throughout its history have Citroën designers ever bowed to normality; André Citroën pursued his desire for eccentric logic and even after his death his ideas were carried forward by his successors.

It was a brave man therefore that ventured into Citroën motoring with the climate naturally opposed to the French way of life. Those early Citroën owners were pioneers in a land that was steeped in conservatism and shunned the unknown and untried. The Traction Avant was viewed with the utmost suspicion while the DS was considered with total bewilderment. The British Citroën did much to reverse the distrust of the new into an acceptance that cars could be a logical, safe and highly reliable mode of transportation. The Citroën turned a chapter in the motoring history of Britain and in many ways became part of the industry as any other truly British motor car.

Within the workforce at the Factory, there was a great sense of loyalty with the staff proud to be building cars acknowledged to be unique and amongst the finest in the World. In all aspects of manufacture, pride in the extreme was taken over the product whether it were in the trim shop, body assembly or the finishing shop. The Factory personnel developed good relations with Citroën owners who often relied upon them for assistance in keeping their cars running. Few garages kept spares for Citroën and often Citroën dealers were few and far between. It was usual, therefore, for the stores staff to come in contact with owners and over the years built up friendships completely unprecedented in most other car manufacturing plants. Confronted often with a bare description of a customer's requirement, the correct part would be produced in no time at all with the storekeeper often knowing the long part number off by heart.

Behind the loyalty there was a fear. Towards the mid 1960s it was clear that with restrictions on imports being lifted as well as a spiralling increase in labour costs, changes would have to be implemented in the organisation of the Factory. Local assembly of cars in Australia and South Africa together with a greater number of cars being exported from both Paris and Citroën's new Factory at Rennes, meant that fewer cars were being produced at Slough. During 1965 just 492 cars were delivered from the British Works with 7 of those going for export. Research and development by Citroën indicated that a replacement of the D Series was under review; an agreement with NSU resulted in the Comobil Company being formed with its headquarters in Geneva to explore the use of rotary engines. There was news also that an entirely new model was to be launched aimed at capturing the lucrative middle-sized car market which eventually led to the introduction of the GS. Citroën announced in 1965 that they expected the D Series to have a further five years of life but this figure doubled turning out to be ten years.

Citroën's forecast of the D range of models came at the time they announced the introduction of the DS Pallas. The new car made its debut at the 1965 Motor Show and denoted the ultimate in luxury. Initially, the Pallas appeared to be similar to the DW but further investigation revealed significant changes to the specification. Two quartz iodine auxiliary driving lamps graced the already impressively sleek front end of the car whilst the interior was trimmed to the highest standards worthy of the marque's flagship. Under the long bonnet lay a new power unit; the 109 b.h.p. engine whisked the Pallas up to 112 m.p.h. but managed to return 25 miles per gallon. To support the new surge in power, Citroën designed a new dashboard describing it as 'sportive'. A tachometer, cigar lighter and full array of instruments and warning lights embellished the fascia including an indicator warning of front brake pad wear. The Pallas was fully hydraulic so carrying on the principle with which the first DS established. A manual gear change version with conventional clutch was offered as an option but in each case the Pallas breathed supremacy which is acknowledged still to this day with many Citroën enthusiasts claiming this to be the finest car Citroën had ever built.

The significance of the Pallas, the new generation of D Series models waiting to be launched, together with Citroën's highly robotic manufacturing plant at Rennes, heralded the end of car production at Slough. It had

As the sun sets at Slough, a fitting photograph depicts three cars built at the Factory, together with later imported models. From left to right: One of the last Bijou to be built before the project was abandoned. Towards the end of the Bijou programme, Slough offered to paint the car in any colour to the customer's choice. Next to it, John Austin's magnificent 1936 Twelve Roadster which had a part to play in the television advertising of Citroën's GS models. The Fifteen 6 Cylinder contrasts well against the Roadster; this is a late car, note the louvres on the bonnet and the more substantial front bumpers. Fourth from the left, a post-1967 DS, note the faired-in headlamps. A GSA can just be seen on the far side of the D and at the end an Acadiane, left-hand drive van version of the Dyane. The Acadiane superseded the 2CV Van (AK400). In the background, to the left can be seen a right-hand drive 2CV.

become increasingly more expensive to build cars in Britain than it was to import from France. United Kingdom sales represented only a fraction of the total production of Citroën Cars which, in 1965, amounted to over 400,000 vehicles.

Early in 1966, Louis Garbe, Managing Director of Citroën Cars in Britain since 1936 addressed the workforce and announced the closure of the Factory. In future, all Citroëns sold in the United Kingdom were to be imported ready assembled from France and the Factory converted into a pre-delivery and storage depot supplying agents with cars and providing service and stores facilities for customers. During its years of operation, the Citroën Factory built 59,532 vehicles bearing the Double Chevron therefore valuably contributing to Britain's distinctive motor industry.

On the 18th February, 1966, the last car, a DS 21 Pallas, rolled off the assembly line and the Factory closed. Within the empty and silent building lay a history of cars so singularly unique and poignant. Ironically, it was forty years to the day that the Factory was officially opened by a jubilant André Citroën.

The D Series received a major facelift in 1967 with a revision to the frontal treatment of the car. Twin headlights, faired into the wings, replaced the single headlamp styling and, in addition, the driving lights on the DS were coupled to the steering mechanism enabling the car to 'see around corners'. The new styling of the D represented a much bolder appearance and as such won new customers to the marque.

Chapter twelve: Tomorrow

Following closure of their United Kingdom manufacturing plant, Citroën Cars took a long look at their role as British concessionaires of the largest volume producers of automobiles in France. Production of cars increased in 1965 by 4.4% over the previous year and the export market was up by nearly 15%, accounting for 26% of the total production. The demise of British manufacture signalled a new and aggressive policy in the marketing of new cars directly imported from France which, even in the short term, began to result in an increase in the numbers of Citroën cars appearing on British roads. Taking on the role as Distributors and Service Agents, Citroën undertook to keep adequate stocks of new cars at Slough, usually being able to supply vehicles within three weeks of order and hardly ever more than eight weeks.

The importation of cars from France allowed Citroën to extend their range of 1966 models for the British market; at the same time prices were reduced by an average of £80 per vehicle. Eight models were specified which included the iD19 'Confort', DS19 and 21 in Pallas trim, two options of Safari and the DS21 Decapotable as the marque's flagship. After the disastrous attempt to sell the Ami 6 Saloon in Britain, an attempt was made to market the estate version which had been introduced on the French market in 1963 and received with much success. The Ami 6 Estate made its British debut at the 1966 Earls Court Motor Show and was priced at £667 including purchase tax. The horizontally-opposed, air-cooled twin-cylinder engine of 602cc from the Ami Saloon powered the Estate, producing almost 70 m.p.h. and 42 miles per gallon. Even with increased space, the far from pretty Ami 6 was slow to sell but it did at least offer a car of the Citroën marque in the smaller vehicle market.

News began to arrive from France of the occasional D model sporting modified front ends. In place of the 'frogeye' single headlamps, twin headlamps were faired into the wings. It appears that an old-established coach-building company, Pichon-Parat, were given a dozen or so sets of pressings from Citroën to test on selected customers for consumer reaction and technical evaluation. The design, whilst retaining the overall image of the DS was similar to the new Panhard 24 Sports Coupé. Chapron also were also producing coach-built conversions of D's with faired-in twin headlamps and the assumption was made that Citroën were considering some redesigning of the DS, this being a sign of things to come.

In the Autumn of 1967, Citroën announced model changes that had a significant effect upon their sales in Britain. Since its launch over a decade previously, the styling of the D Series had not seen any momentous change. Certainly, there had been technical improvements, the LHS 'red' fluid for the hydropneumatic system had been changed to a green fluid, LHM, which assisted in the prevention of corrosion within the system, but the exterior shape of the car remained the same. Introduced at the 1967 Motor Show, Citroën displayed the new range of D models that changed the look of the car. The already sleek and aerodynamic lines of the D were enhanced and streamlined even further with a stunningly beautiful redesigned front to the car. The windcheating design incorporated twin headlamps faired into the front wings and shielded by glass covers which were contoured in such a way as to prevent impairing lighting efficiency or the car's streamlining.

Behind the glass covers lay a revolution in car lighting design. The four headlamp system of the iD consisted of two long range lamps and two dipping headlights with the long range lights automatically extinguishing when the dipping mechanism was operated. It was the DS and Pallas with their self-levelling and directionally-controlled headlamps that created so much attention, and rightly so as this system offered the ultimate in vehicle illumination. The inner quartz iodine lamps were connected to the car's steering mechanism enabling the Citroën to literally see around corners. As the driver turned the wheel for cornering so the lights automatically turned lighting the direction of the vehicle. The self-levelling device complimented the Citroën's suspension and any up or downward movement of the car over an uneven road surface allowed the headlamps to remain at a constant height so avoiding the risk of dazzling oncoming traffic.

The impressive styling of the D won new friends; the reputation of the car had by now become well established and as a result sales began to increase. The streamlining of Citroën's operations left its mark and prices of new cars were reduced. In the case of the DS19 and DS21 Saloons £100 was taken off the list price with the cars selling for £1,597 and £1,698 respectively.

The 2CV had been France's success story in automobile history. Its utilitarian styling had appealed, as had the car's desire to run on nothing but the smell of an oil rag. Everyone it seemed owned at least one Deux Chevaux. The Ami 6 had proved there was a market for a Super-2CV and gradually the Citroën engineers intended that the minimum motor car, the umbrella on four wheels, should be replaced by a more modern design. It was with this in mind that the Dyane was despatched onto the market at the end of 1967 for the 1968 model year. Citroën Cars at Slough were still licking their wounds over the 2CV saga and more recently the Bijou affair; the Ami 6 disaster was still fresh in everyone's mind and it was with some trepidation that the Dyane was displayed at Earls Court.

During its first year, the Dyane sold in greater numbers in France than the 2CV with 100,000 cars built to the 2CV's 57,000. The Ami 6, however, surged way ahead with over 145,000 cars leaving the factory. Renault had gained a lot of ground in the small-car market with the 4L which, with its relatively heavier body and full-height tailgate, offered a compromise between a saloon and an estate car. The Dyane was aimed at the market that the Renault 4 had found success, for it too had a hatchback, could go anywhere and was cheap to run. The family resemblance to the 2CV was instantly noticeable but the Dyane managed to adopt a more substantial and contemporary stance.

Where the 2CV, Bijou, and Ami 6 had failed to make any impression on the British market, the Dyane

The Citroën Dyane made its debut in 1967. With the 425cc air-cooled flat-twin engine it bridged a gap between the 2CV and the Ami 6. Within a year, the Dyane had been joined by the Dyane 6 utilising the flat-twin 602cc engine. Citroën had considered the age and sales of the 2CV and brought the Dyane in as an eventual replacement for it. The Dyane had obvious family connections with the 2CV but the more modern styling allowed a full height rear hatch and greater comfort inside the car. The Dyane when introduced had a four-light body, the car shown in the photograph is a late model with six-light styling, chrome bumpers and a redesigned grille. In the event, the 2CV outlived the Dyane, the car that was intended to replace it.

reversed the trend. While sharing so much of the 2CV's ancestry in way of running gear, chassis and suspension, the car had a new and different aesthetic appeal. The stark bonnet with headlamps protruding upon stalks gave way to a softer design with headlamps built into the slightly squared front wings; a fifth door at the rear of the car allowed more space to carry bulky items and the interior was somewhat more homely. Sliding front windows replaced the half-hinged flip-up type while a fabric roof retained the choice of having open-top motoring or a snug interior. On economy, the Dyane showed itself in its true colours by having little thirst for petrol. Maintenance proved just as straightforward as the Deux Chevaux, sharing in general the same mechanical features. The lack of radiator and absence of need for concern about antifreeze in winter was a bonus. Two versions of the Dyane were available, the 4, an out and out economy car with the 2CV's 425cc engine, which was soon uprated to 435cc, and the 6, utilising the larger 602cc flat twin air-cooled unit from the Ami 6.

The appearance of the Dyane in Britain gave an impetus to interest in Citroën Cars generally. The success of the D Series, especially with the new ultra-sleek design put the spotlight on their smaller cars. There was growing evidence that Citroën were realising their lacking of middle-range models for there was a complete gap between the 'economy' market and the luxury range of car. The demand was met in part by the introduction of the Ami 8 which was clearly developed from the Ami 6. Redesigned frontal and rear treatment made the Ami at once acceptable for the British motorist, the heavier bodywork had a pronounced effect upon the car's handling even with the flat-twin 3CV 602cc motor,
making the car feel a lot larger than it was. By 1970, sales of Citroën cars in the United Kingdom reached levels not seen since the Company's early days when the headquarters were opened at Brook Green. A steady increase from 1967 culminated in over 4,300 cars imported during the 1970 model year.

A deal with Maserati

During February 1968 news of an agreement was reached between Citroën and Maserati which destined the two companies to work in close collaboration. There were benefits for both concerns, Maserati had access to Citroën's marketing prowess while Citroën gained from Maserati's vast experience in the design of high quality sporting cars. There was suggestion that in the future the two companies might operate on a joint venture. By 1970 the collaboration between Citroën and Maserati was realised in the form of the Citroën SM. Without doubt, the SM must rank as one of the greatest cars of all time. In a way, the SM was born out of a progression of ideas; early during the Traction era Citroën's quest for a supercar in the form of the 22 had not materialised and again in the development of the DS the Company gave up the idea of using a revolutionary engine, returning instead to the reliable, even staid, four-cylinder 1911cc unit. Maserati's engineering and design ascendancy in sporting cars gave Citroën the chance to transplant and develop a vee-six engine into the DS.

A number of prototype DS types with the Maserati V6 were used as test-beds for the Citroën SM. The Maserati engine, which appears to have started out in life as a V8 but was too large for the DS body shell, only just about fitted into the D's engine compartment with a shoe horn and a lot

At the Geneva Motor Show in 1968, Citroën unveiled the Ami 8 which was to replace the Ami6. It did away with the totally stark styling and reverse-rake rear window, comfort level was increased and at once the car found a market in the United Kingdom.

The Citroën SM was striking in appearance and its performance lived up to its looks. Announced at the Geneva Show in March 1970, its combination of a Maserati vee-six 2670cc 170 bhp engine having twin overhead camshafts on each bank, three Weber double-choke carburettors and a five-speed synchromesh gearbox, together with Citroën DS-type suspension and brakes produced what was then the fastest front-wheel-drive car ever, according to the **Autocar** *road test of June 1971 — a timed speed of 135 m.p.h. was recorded. The power steering had an unusual feel but was praised for its responsiveness once this had become familiar. The Ligier racing-car factory was acquired to build the SM. Fuel injection gave even more performance in 1973 but that year's world fuel crisis cut the market for such a car, inevitably expensive to produce, at a crucial time — it survived the association with Peugeot in 1974 but not for long, the last examples being built in 1975.*

of modification. Naturally, Citroën had hoped they could develop the engine for use in a production model of the DS but in the event this was not to be. The development of the body was carried out by Citroën, the end result being a highly provocative design using hydropneumatic suspension and VariPower steering, self-levelling directionally-controlled lighting all packaged with controls and facilities befit of a legendary car.

Out of a total production of almost 13,000 cars, approximately 327 were imported to Britain. They were never available in right hand drive although it was intended they should have been, however, there is evidence that three cars were converted to right hand steering by a Citroën dealer appointed as SM specialist. The SM fell victim to the fuel crisis of the early 1970's, the market for the car evaporated and production was abandoned. Driving the SM is an experience never to be forgotten; with its 170 b.h.p. 2,670cc engine, the SM whipped up to 135 miles per hour (145 m.p.h. if the car was a later one fitted with electronic fuel injection). Road holding can only be described as unbelievable, front wheel drive saw to it that the car was exactly where the driver wanted it to be and the inboard mounted brakes, assisted by the car's hydropneumatic system ensured it stopped effortlessly and rapidly. The VariPower steering took a little getting used to and created some controversy amongst Citroën owners. Although hydraulically assisted the system incorporated a power-return of the wheels together with a gradual tightening of steering pressure when under speed. At low speeds therefore, the steering remained extremely light but as the car's speed increased it became proportionally heavier and effectively promoted its handling capabilities. The SM was luxuriously equipped and designed as a Grand Tourer in the fullest sense. In front of the driver a wonderfully asymmetric dashboard featured a fully comprehensive instrument layout. Leather upholstery adorned the interior which, although classed as a four-seater, was a 2+2.

France was the SM's biggest customer with Italy, followed very closely by the U.S.A., in second and third places. In January 1972 the SM was voted Car of the Year in America; 1973 saw the best year for sales to Britain when almost 160 were sold. The fuel crisis of 1973 when oil prices dramatically increased, speed limits were implemented and there was the risk of compulsory fuel rationing, resulted in the end of the road for the SM. Although

Citroën's GS of 1970 broke new ground when introduced. The car, of sleek design and with a sporting flair, combined an air-cooled engine with hydropneumatic suspension and braking. The flat-four overhead-camshaft engine of 1015cc capacity could be freely revved and produced an altogether new driving experience. The GS did much to bring the company's high profile engineering of the DS down to earth.

Citroën's dream of a supercar had come true it was alas shortlived.

The GS-mid-range challenger

The gap in Citroën's catalogue of a mid-range car was bridged in 1970 with the announcement of the GS. For Citroën, this represented a new adventure into a market previously dominated by other manufacturers and at once, in Citroën tradition, created intense interest and furore. The futuristic technology and engineering mastery of the DS was revered; to many potential customers, though, it was out of their league both in price and capacity and it was to this market, therefore, the GS appealed particularly. On its launch, the GS suddenly brought Citroën's ideology down to earth, it represented in a compact four-door, four-seat saloon, a technically advanced car bristling with new features and easily affordable.

At once the GS was hailed as a revolution in the medium-sized car market. The air-cooled flat-four engine of a little over a litre in capacity (1015cc, 61 b.h.p.) together with hydropneumatic suspension and power-assisted load-adjusting brakes signalled a breakthrough in motor car design. The smooth body reflected the car's performance, the air-cooled engine, front-wheel drive and road-clinging suspension was not only responsive but presented the feel of a sporting saloon. To match the GS's driving character the interior expressed plushness; comfort abounded and for the driver an exciting aircraft-style instrument layout exemplified the joys of motoring.

The GS offered a new experience in motoring, the flat-four engine worked like a turbine at the front end of the car, inexhaustible and seemingly to provide vast amounts of power than the cc's implied. It is no wonder the GS received Car of the Year award, sales rocketed and by the end of 1972 deliveries of Citroën cars reached the unprecedented levels of 17,617 vehicles-over 400% increase on the figure for 1970. Cars destined for the British market differed slightly to those for France in as much as right hand drive models were fitted with a modified dashboard. Circular instrument dials for tachometer, speedometer, fuel, ammeter and clock were displayed in an aerodynamic and stylish fascia whilst left hand drive models featured a somewhat untidy dash with a mixture of dials and warning lights headed up by a strange revolving drum type speedometer. The handbrake lever on the GS sprouted from the fascia panel while the gear change lever was positioned comfortably between the front seats. A year after the Saloon's appearance, an Estate version was offered which provided extraordinary carrying capacity enhanced by self-levelling suspension.

Most customers opted for the four-speed manual gearbox version of the GS. However, Citroën were also able to offer a three-speed 'convertisseur' semi-automatic gearbox with torque-converter which did away with the clutch pedal but required manual operation of the gear shift lever. As soon as hand pressure was placed upon the lever so the clutch automatically disengaged by electro-magnetic contact. Two years after the GS had made its debut an uprated engine was introduced to the car. Still employing the air-cooled, flat-four cylinder configuration, power increased to 65 b.h.p. with a 1222cc unit which secured higher torque at lower revs. so aiding overall performance.

Resulting from an agreement between Citroën and NSU, there appeared in 1969 a number of special-bodied two-door Ami 8 M35 prototype cars, fitted with a Wankel single rotary-piston engine. None of the cars were initially for sale but were distributed to selected dealers in France for evaluation. During October 1973, Citroën announced, for the French market, the GS Birotor with a twin-rotary-piston engine. Sporting the fascia normally reserved for right hand drive cars, the Birotor was never exported, sales of the car were slow and after two years the project was abandoned. Citroën tried to recover all the cars that had been sold — less than 900 — with a view to disposing all evidence of the car. A few have survived with at least a couple finding their way to the United Kingdom.

A further derivative of the GS appeared in the form of the Ami Super. The twin-cylinder 602cc engine installed in the Ami8 made way for the four-cylinder 1015cc engine of the GS making the lightweight car into a relatively high speed machine. The GS gearbox was also used with the fascia mounted gear lever relocated to the floor, anti-roll bars and the disc brakes from the GS1220 completed the package. The tardy performance of the Ami immediately transformed to a quick-accelerating 90 m.p.h. sports saloon. There were few takers for the conversion as the GS

The GS, launched at the Paris Motor Show in 1970, was intended to appeal to the market which lay between the twin-cylinder models and the D series. Of much more streamlined outline than the smaller cars, it was intended to offer comfort and lively performance for four people, with the 1015cc flat-four engine developing 55 b.h.p. at 6500 rpm and an unladen weight of 17½ cwt.

Right hand drive GS cars had a dashboard reminiscent of an aircraft cockpit. Key to numbers: 1. Ammeter; 2. Fuel gauge; 3. Speedometer; 4. Total mileage recorder; 5. Trip recorder; 6. Electronic tachometer; 7. Clock; 9. Oil temperature and brake pad warning light; 10. Sidelights on, indicator; 11. Main beam indicator; 12. Heated rear window warning lamp; 14. Torque converter oil warning light; 15. Oil pressure warning lamp; 16. Hydraulic system warning lamp; 17. Direction indicators warning; 20. Rheostat for instrument lights.

By fitting the 1015cc flat-four engine as introduced for the GS, and itself light, being largely of light alloy, into the Ami car, Citroën produced the Ami Super model, even lighter than the GS, with an unladen weight of 16 cwt. Seen here is the Ami Super Estate.

An original publicity photograph of the GS Birotor — on the reverse it bears a warning not to publish it before 27th July 1973. This car, with Wankel-type twin-rotor engine, can be identified from the standard flat-four GS of the time by its flared wheel arches and Pallas trim. The engine proved unsuccessful and Citroën attempted to buy back all the cars sold but more than a few were kept by enthusiasts.

afforded a sleek and handsome body style with all the resulting attributes at relatively little extra cost.

A little over ten years after the sight of the first GS, major modifications were applied to the car. Engine sizes were increased, five speed gearboxes fitted, new designs of dashboard and controls appeared but far the most significant change was the bodywork styling converting the saloon into a hatchback. Redesignated GSA, the first car to appear was the Special with a four-speed gearbox mounted to an 1129cc engine. This was followed by the 'Club' version with 1299cc engine and five speed gearbox. Four gears were retained on Estate Cars and the three-speed semi-automatic (C-Matic) gearboxes were also specified. Later, five speed gearboxes became optional on the Special and the Estate. Citroën designed a new dashboard layout for the GSA; instead of the aerodynamic cockpit style as previously, revolving-drum instruments and 'satellite' controls housing all the necessary function switches were devised. Although these worked well they received ridicule from the motoring press and were far from popular with customers.

Imports of Citroën cars continued to rise, and for the 1973 model year well over 20,000 cars were sold to the United Kingdom. The popularity of the GS and GSA proved Citroën's claim to quality and adroit engineering; for the first time the Company entered into the world of television marketing producing, through their publicity agents, some unique and controversial advertisements. Well equipped, demonstrating comfort to the extreme and adopting a careful pricing policy, it was this model that established Citroën Cars as on the road to being a high volume sales force on the British car market.

Increased attention to petrol economy due to the 1973 fuel crisis and furthering awareness of the Citroën marque led to greater sales of the smaller twin-cylinder cars. The Dyane enjoyed a growing proportion of Citroën's U.K. sales, the car represented value for money and since modifications, which included a six-light body, attracted a new market of customer. European travel and the sight of vast numbers of small Citroëns no longer led to the belief these cars were driven purely by the eccentric. The great motoring public searched frantically for any car providing over 40 miles per gallon, there was an added bonus if the car was easy to maintain and did not involve being garaged periodically for expensive servicing. So, the 2CV was rediscovered or, for many, discovered for the first time. 100,000 2CVs were produced in 1971, over 121,000 in 1972 and nearly 150,000 in 1974. Buyers looking for the 2CV in Britain were disappointed, they settled for the nearest alternative and ventured into the world of

After just over ten years of production of the GS a number of modifications were made to the range of cars. The GSA had a hatchback, and a replacement dashboard with 'satellite controls'. The basic models had only four-speed gearboxes but higher-powered cars such as the Club had 1299cc engines and five-speed gearboxes. The photograph shows a GSA Speciale with an 1129cc engine and four-speed gearbox.

In 1974, Citroën decided to market the 2CV in Britain again, though now in 602cc form, initially as a response to the fuel crisis and the subsequent sharp rise in the cost of petrol. During the period since 1960 when the 2CV had been withdrawn from sale in Britain after poor sales in 425cc form, the model had altered somewhat. A smoother-looking bonnet had appeared and the so-called 'suicide' rear-hinged doors had been replaced by front-hinged ones. Most significant in terms of appearance were the controversial rectangular headlamps adopted in place of the original.

motoring under an umbrella on four wheels. Citroën had been contemplating halting production of the 2CV since the introduction of the Dyane, the car intended to replace it. However much they tried, demand and public opinion would not let the car go and to prove the point it sold in ever increasing numbers.

Owning a twin-cylinder Citroën was a love-hate relationship with more love than hate. For some, even the Dyane or Ami were not good enough, it *had* to be the real thing — 2CV or nothing. A requirement manifested itself for the importation of used left hand drive 2CVs from Europe and entrepreneurs found a eager market for cars brought in from France, Belgium and Holland. Eventually, in 1974, Citroën decided to re-introduce the 2CV to the British market in 602cc guise. The 2CV6 immediately received great acclaim, most had forgotten its abysmal sales record when produced for the British market at Slough and for many motorists there was the excitement of discovering the Deux Chevaux for the first time. In an attempt to give the 2CV a 'modern' appeal the familiar

The introduction of the Special version of the 2CV6 in Britain in January 1982 was welcomed as a return to the basic concept of the Deux Chevaux, as well as appealing to a growing 'nostalgia' market. The beloved round headlamps re-appeared and the interior became more spartan, without even ashtray or interior light, while the instrument panel was similar to early 2CV models. Yet, driven intelligently, this car could often keep pace with much more powerful models over quite long distances on cross-country journeys unless the drivers of the latter exceeded speed limits. It became an instant success and the UK became the 2CV's largest export market.

round headlights were replaced by rectangular lamps. These 'modern' appendages did little for the appearance of the car and eventually the design reverted back to the beloved and original specification. From 1974 a number of 'special editions' were offered and in the main concerned special paintwork designs such as the 'Spot', 'Beachcomber', 'Charleston' and 'Bamboo'.

Upon its re-introduction, the 2CV6 whilst retaining the traditional interior and fascia layout, shared an instrument cowling similar to that of the Dyane. As a cheaper option, and in an effort to regain the youthfulness of the Deux Chevaux, the Special came onto the market. Round headlamps were back, a basic trim was specified which necessitated the lack of ashtray and interior light. The hood could no longer be folded back to a half-way position fastening onto the roof support but instead rolled back, clipped at a mid-way point or fastened down at the rear just above the back window. The instrument panel reverted back in time also, a trapezoid speedometer flanked by essential switches and indicators provided the driver with adequate information. To the purist, this was the optimum 2CV.

Departure of the D series

Two years passed following the re-designing of the D models. Further modifications were announced with the introduction of the electronic fuel-injection DS21. This was the first time electronic injection was specified for a standard production French motor car and it pushed the top speed of the DS up to 117 miles per hour. The iD19 was redesignated D Special and the iD20 with the 1985cc engine renamed D Super; a milestone in the history of the car was reached when on 7th October 1969, the millionth DS rolled off the assembly line at Javel. New to the DS range in 1971, the D Super 5 made its appearance; fitted with a 2175cc engine and coupled to a five-speed gearbox, the car afforded luxury motoring with all the benefits of hydraulic suspension, steering and braking but with a conventional clutch and manual gearbox. The 106 b.h.p. engine maximised performance enabling a top speed of 109 m.p.h.

The pinnacle of D series production was reached with Citroën uprating the capacity of their four-cylinder engine to 2347cc, installing electronic fuel injection to what had been the DS21 and as such introduced the DS23. Capable of 111 miles per hour for the optional 115 b.h.p. carburettor model and 115 m.p.h. for the 130 b.h.p. injected model, the Goddess reigned supreme. The D continued to be built until 1975 when, on the 24th April, the last car rolled off the assembly line, a DS23EFI Pallas, so ending twenty-one years of production. During those twenty-one years a total of 1,455,746 cars had been built. The sumptuous comfort, exquisite styling, technical ability and above all, the total aura of the car will ensure it remains an all-time classic. The only appropriate epitaph to salute the DS can be described in Citroën's own words:

'Beautiful as it is, the appearance of the Citroën is above all functional. It is the outcome of the most advanced study of aerodynamics, suspension and roadholding applied to motor engineering. And this has, beyond all expectation, met the demands of performance, safety and comfort. Already far in advance when first introduced, continual improvement has ensured that Citroën still remain years ahead.'

As an era ended and the DS gave way to progress, so another era also faded away into the twilight. Citroën's Factory on the Slough Trading Estate, since witnessing the demise of car manufacture, became unsuitable for the Company's operation in the role of marketing their cars in Britain. In the main, the vast area where once the 7.5 h.p. and later the 11.4 h.p., 12.24 and the Traction Avant had been built surrounded by the noise and clatter of machinery and pneumatic tools, there was silence. Slough was synonymous with Citroën and although the decision had been taken to move from the Trading Estate it was felt the Company should remain within the town. In April 1974, the gates of Citroën clanged shut for the last time closing not only an era but an entire epoch.

New premises were taken in Mill Street adjacent to the railway station and the move finally confirmed Citroën's new attitude to selling cars in an aggressive market. The Company's headquarters consisted of both offices and a highly modern servicing department, a technical school for training agents mechanics and apprentices as well as a research and development unit. The parts warehouse instead of being located at the same premises were re-established a few miles away at Runnymede alongside the River Thames.

The demise of the DS was indicated in the Autumn of 1974 when announcement came of introduction of the CX. The engineering symbol of the aerodynamics of a moving body suited the new Citroën especially well. Long, low, smooth and sleek, the obvious relationship to the SM was evident. For 1974 the CX represented a new dimension in design although clearly Citroën; the body supported large window areas with a huge front screen and a concave rear screen. The windscreen had just one wiper yet managed to sweep more effectively than two; the aerodynamics saw to it that the rear window kept clear even in the worst weather. Inside the car comfort and opulence, an ergonomically advanced dashboard housed

(Facing page) The fine profile of the D Series cars. This is a D Special, successor to the iD19, with 1985cc engine.

The DS Safari continued its role as not only one of the largest estate cars built in Europe, but also having all the special qualities associated with the hydro-pneumatic suspension. Among noteworthy users was the BBC, for the model provided an exceptionally steady platform for a roof-mounted TV camera for use while keeping pace with the leading horses at race meetings, often on uneven ground.

A fine gathering of Citroëns by courtesy of Allen Brothers, Northchapel, Sussex. From left to right: just visible post 1946 Slough-built Light Fifteen; a pristine SM; CX Pallas and a DS 23. The cars span thirty years of Citroën production.

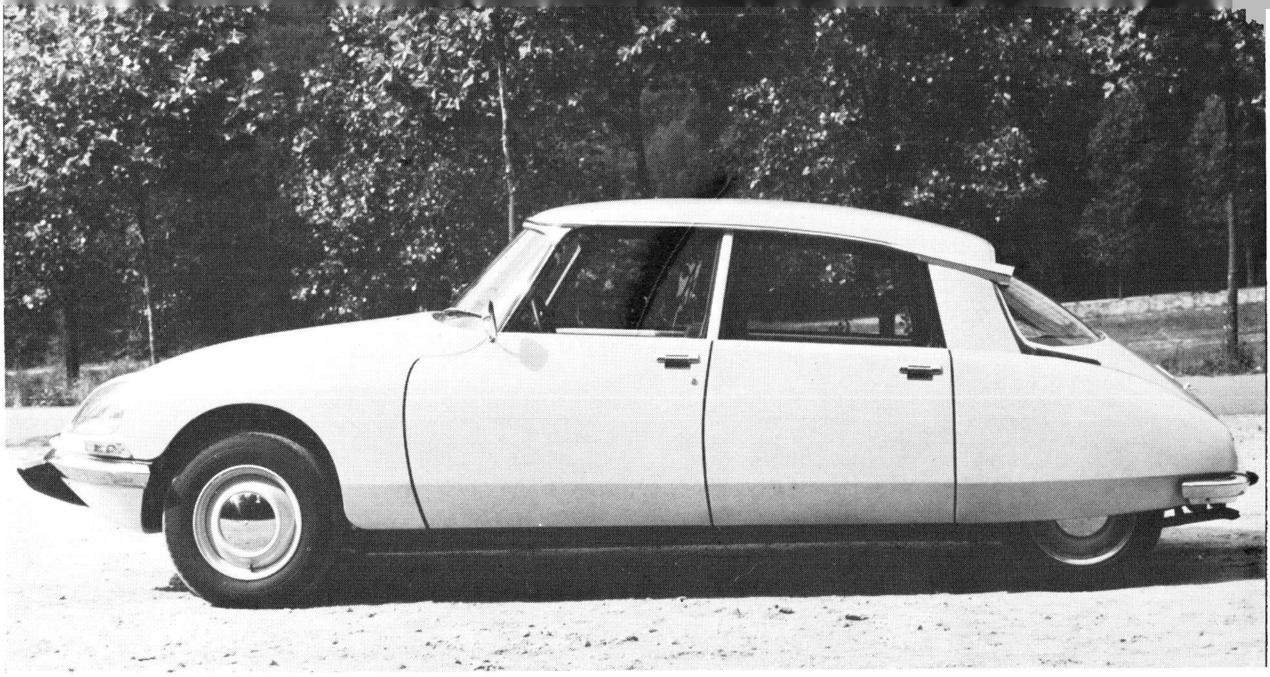

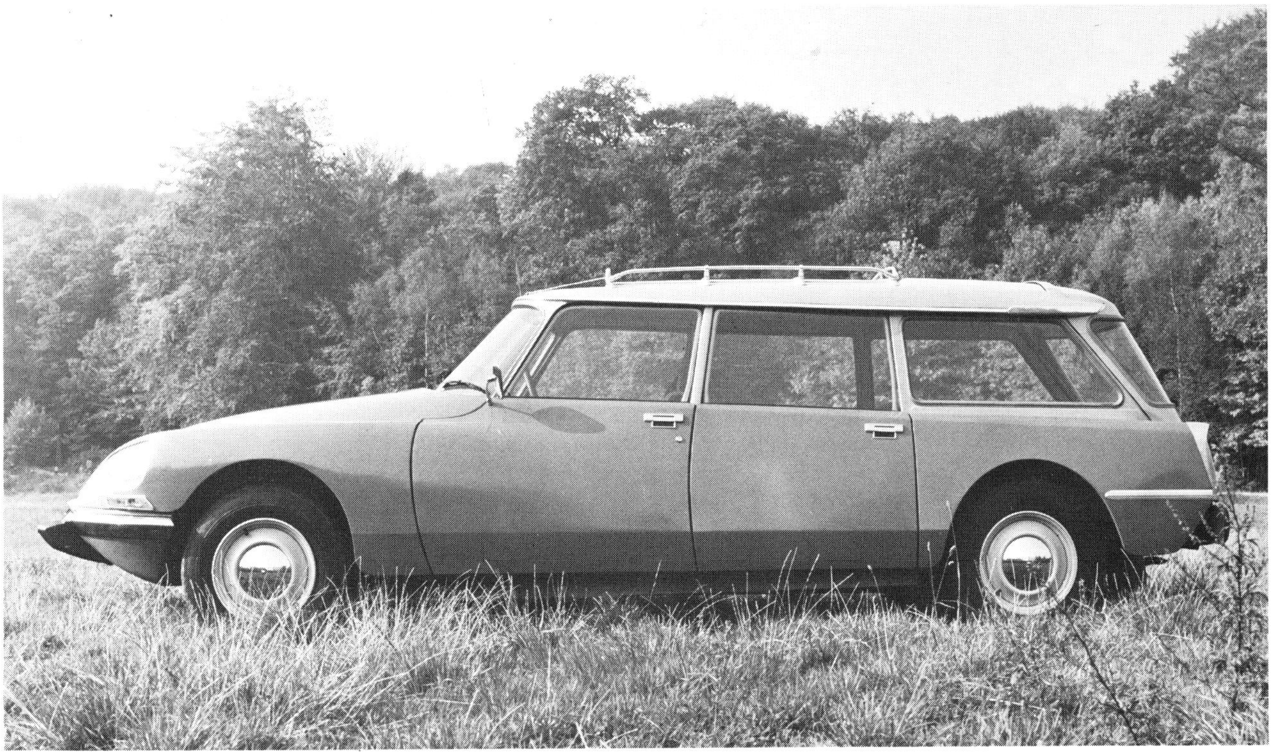

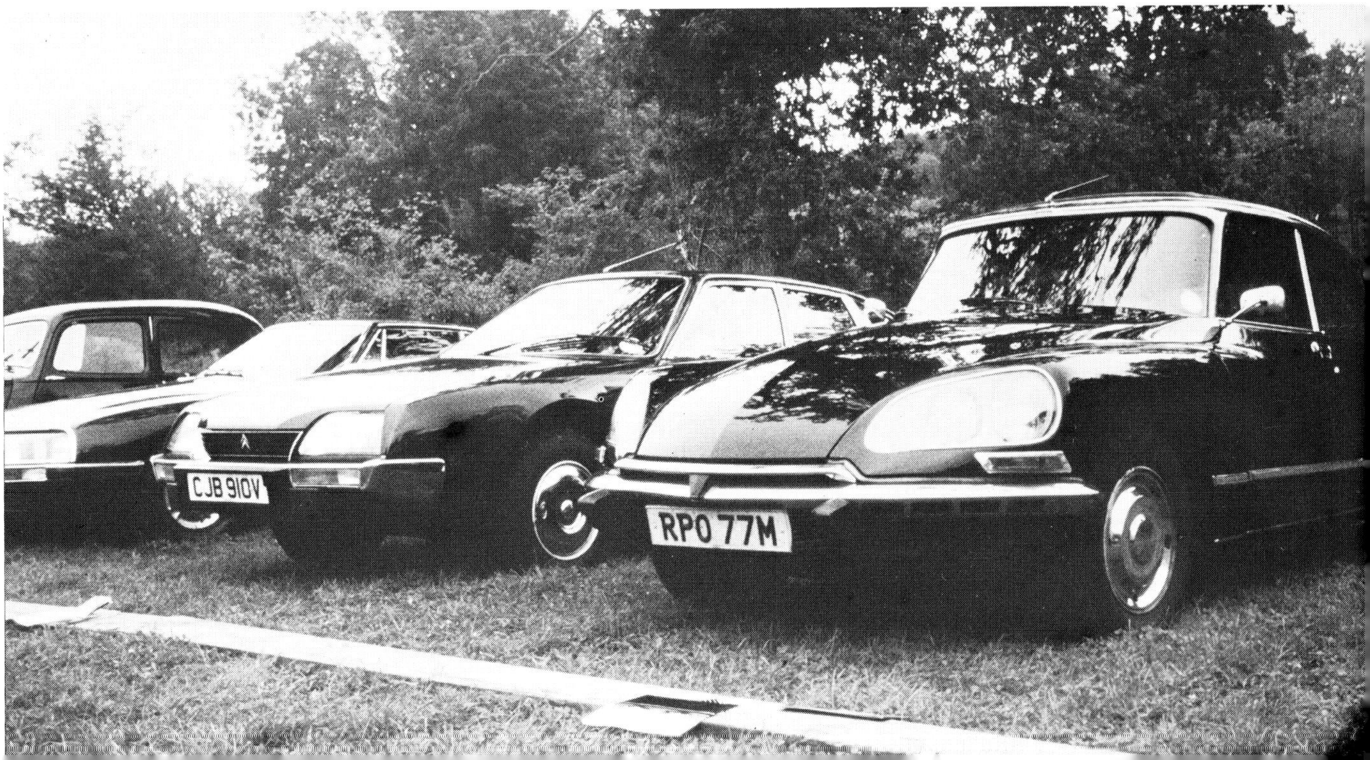
CJB 910V
RPO 77M

In the Autumn of 1974, the CX made its debut, resulting in the demise of the DS. In the CX there was much of the SM whilst the tradition of the DS also continued. Low and aerodynamic, the CX had huge areas of glass, comfort abounded but there was more conventionality than either the SM or the CX. There was some controversy over the adoption of VariPower steering, brakes were no longer inboard mounted and sadly the CX suffered from rust problems, especially before the 1980/1 models. Semi-automatic transmission incorporating a torque converter allowed smooth gear changing but the manual gearbox provided faster acceleration through the ratios. Top of the range models were eventually represented by the GTi Turbo, a classic grand touring motor car.

revolving-drum instruments, switchgear for lighting and indicators were so positioned that it was never necessary for the driver to take hands off the steering wheel. The CX adopted the VariPower steering from the SM on some versions, its powered-return often causing comment, controversy of course was to be expected. Hydropneumatic suspension kept the car level at all times whilst ensuring braking and steering were effortless in big Citroën tradition. The mushroom button, that had been the cause of so much contention with the DS, was replaced with a conventional pedal but that is where the difference ended. Often the CX was accused of having too good a braking system allowing the car to pull-up too quickly!

In principle, the engine from the D Series had been retained in the CX but instead of being installed in-line it was fitted east to west. Originally the CX arrived on the market with two engines specified, either a 2 litre (CX2000) or a 2.2 litre (CX2200). The 2-litre unit was in fact the well proven 1985cc engine seen in the D Special and propelled the car up to 108 miles per hour; the 2200 received the 2175cc engine pushing the speed up a further 3 m.p.h. but reaching it in quicker time with better performance. The 2200 was also specified in Pallas version equipped with VariPower steering and offering a more luxurious trim. The Safari in CX format soon became available and although equipped with the trim of the 2200 received the lower powered 1985cc engine.

Technical changes over the DS included the brakes which instead of being inboard mounted were installed on the wheel hub assembly. The body structure also changed; the monocoque sheet steel pressed body was attached to an underframe connected by means of special rubber mountings. The frame carried the complete wheel suspension assemblies as well as the steering, braking and engine and transmission systems. The construction had the advantages of allowing extra soundproofing, filtering of vibration and high steering stability.

Ensuing in the footsteps of the DS, the CX had a hard act to follow; for devoted DS owners and enthusiasts it was difficult to accept the new car. In retrospect, the same had been said of the DS when it was introduced following the Traction Avant. For the newly converted to Citroën motoring and engineering, the CX was a wonder; the shape of the car, comfort and feeling of sheer well-being when driving it was a totally new experience not found on other cars. *The Motor* said at the time of the launch of the CX:

'When Citroën introduce a completely new model it is an event of rare importance and interest'.

Considering the CX *The Motor* again commented:

'Surely one of the World's most beautiful production cars of all time.'

It is no wonder that Citroën's latest model was awarded 'Car of the Year' for 1974/5.

Changes in the CX line-up resulted in the 2200 petrol engine being discontinued and the appearance of the

2400 using Citroën's 2347cc engine. The CX2000 remained, but only in 'Confort' trim level, however VariPower steering was specified as standard with manual steering as an option. The 2400 was offered in both Super and Pallas trim but as an alternative the CX2400 Prestige, with only the most luxurious specification on a platform almost a foot longer than the normal saloon, could be obtained. A diesel version joined the range in 2200 format; this was a useful addition and provided economical motoring at almost 45 miles per gallon and a top sped of 91 miles per hour.

The appearance of the CX changed little over its years of production. New model specifications improved upon the level of trim culminating in the GTi and Prestige versions with leather trim and air conditioning. The C-Matic transmission made easy work of gear changing, the three-speed semi-automatic gearbox with clutchless and torque-converter operation ensured a smooth ride and when specified with fuel injection provided effortless but spontaneous performance. Later, fully automatic gearboxes became available as did the appearance of the GT Turbo. The final change in design affected the body trim resulting in giving the car a lower and even sleeker appearance. Towards the end of its life span the CX sold in disastrously low numbers, a new model was promised and suddenly the shape of the CX looked dated. Dated it was not, other manufacturers had emulated Citroën's design principles and had effectively sought to catch up. The CX suffered in part by never being offered as a five-door hatchback, the car grew up in the hatchback age and lost sales to such cars as the Rover SDi.

The takeover by Peugeot

Not for the first time in its history the Citroën Company experienced grave financial difficulties. In December 1974, an agreement had been reached between Citroën and Peugeot to work in closer association. By May 1976 the close association eventuated in Peugeot holding an 89.95% stake in Citroën and therefore effected a takeover of the Company. The takeover projected far-reaching consequences for Citroën who had always demonstrated extroversion against Peugeot's staid conservatism. Certainly there was the danger Citroën might fall victim to badge-engineering and this was seen in part with the appearance of the Citroën LN and LNA.

For a time, Peugeot had set up an association with Renault which failed to materialise to any consequence. A product of the affair was the Renault 14 which shared the same floor pan as the Peugeot 104. In turn, the 104 shared the same floor pan as the Citroën LN/LNA and later, the Visa. The Talbot Samba jumped into the fray as this was an identical car to Citroën's LNA, the differences appertaining to the motif on the brake and clutch pedals, Citroën orientated steering wheel and Chevron badges on the back and front of the car.

Peugeot's influence soon realised some rationalisation of the Citroën range. The Ami 8 and Ami Super were discontinued leaving the Dyane and 2CV to carry forward the air-cooled twin cylinder principle. The first new car under the Peugeot umbrella arrived in the form of the Visa. This was a hurriedly produced car based upon the floorpan of the 104 but was powered by an uprated version of

The CX Prestige, a luxurious version of the car built on a longer wheelbase. Note the single windscreen wiper on the CX models. The Prestige offered full leather upholstery, air-conditioning and extra space. The model was often chosen for official and diplomatic cars because of its high levels of comfort.

The Citroën Visa, introduced in 1978, was an early product of the Peugeot-Citroën consortium. It shared the floor pan with Peugeot's 104 and (due to a short-lived agreement between Peugeot and Renault) the Renault 14. Two engines were specified, a Citroën flat-twin air-cooled unit of 652cc or Peugeot's 1124cc water-cooled four-cylinder engine. The photograph shows an early model, distinguished by the 'plastic' snout which disappeared in later versions.

Badge engineering. The LNA, introduced on the British market in February 1983, was another early product of the Peugeot-Citroën enterprise and a successor to the LN which was never marketed in Britain. The LNA was bodily similar to the Peugeot 104 Coupé and virtually identical to the Talbot Samba apart from badges. The LNA never sold in large numbers; it was caught in a vacuum between the 2CV, which had a particular identity, and the Visa, which offered so much more in specification. Sadly, the car never seemed to gain recognition by the public, apart from enthusiasts of the Citroën marque.

Citroën's air-cooled flat-twin engine extended to 652cc. Instead of the interconnecting suspension of the Dyane and 2CV, MacPherson struts were specified. Alongside the Visa Club came the Super Version, a more powerful car with the Peugeot four cylinder water-cooled engine of 1124cc. Responsible for opening Citroën's market wider and appealing to customers who otherwise would not have bought a small Citroën in preference to other makes, the Visa presented good value for money and was a good performer. As the car grew up it was sold in GT and diesel guises, the GT competing in the hot hatch market. The diesel version was a winner, the 1.7 litre engine returned up to 60 m.p.g. obtaining a top speed of 93 m.p.h. A Citroën light van had not been available in Britain since production ceased of the 2CV at Slough although the 2CV AK and later Acadiane vans sold in huge numbers in France. The C15 van based on the Visa was introduced as a successor to the 2CV and Dyane Vans and was specified for the British market in right hand drive. Available in two colours, red and white, they were marketed as the Van Rouge and Van Blanc.

A further chapter closed in the history of Citroën when, on 22nd November, 1982, the Company forsook the original factory buildings at Javel. Sixty-six years earlier, the young André Citroën had set up his works manufacturing munitions for the Great War. The first Citroën motor car was delivered in June 1919 after the Factory had been converted to mass-produce automobiles and in 1934 the front-wheel drive revolution exploded. Twenty-one years later another bombshell, the arrival of the DS. On 9th October 1958 Paris paid its respect to André Citroën, the Quai de Javel was renamed Quai André Citroën. In mid-April 1975 car production ceased at Javel, the Factory no longer large enough to produce the demand for Citroën cars. Production transferred to a new factory to the north of Paris, at Aulnay-sous-Bois and to the modern and huge plant at Rennes. Between 1919 and closure in 1975, over 3,227,000 vehicles had been built at the Factory. Automobiles Citroën closed the doors on Javel and set up their new headquarters in the nearby suburb of Paris at Neuilly-sur-Seine.

The new face of Citroën unveiled itself in the Autumn of 1982 when, at the Paris Salon, the first of the completely new generation cars had the wraps taken off. The BX was exposed, a study of consumer surveys giving the motorist the car they would most like to see. At first the BX appeared rather angular; after the CX and GS it sported straight lines instead of a slippery and curvacious figure. Citroën showed some apprehension both towards their change in image and to their marketing policy for the future. With the BX, Citroën were keen the car should have a definite personality but at the same time maintaining a balance between run-of-the-mill styling associated with other manufacturers and, way-out originality synonymous with the name. The BX represented a combined effort within the Peugeot-Citroën group such as shared engines and transmission units, floorpan and technical qualities including hydropneumatic suspension, four-wheel power-operated disc brakes and body styling.

Citroën need not have worried. The BX, whilst a move away from the concept normally expected from them, retained enough charisma to make the car instantly identifiable and travelled the route into new ideas

The BX, introduced in 1982 as a range of 1.4 and 1.6-litre models, was the first completely new generation of cars under the Peugeot-Citroën regime. It was the BX that turned Citroën's fortunes on the British market; never before had the fleet sector considered Citroën due to their unconventionality, yet this car managed to convince fleet buyers it was a good proposition. Retaining hydropneumatic suspension, the BX offers an excellent ride with comfortable trim and attractive servicing schedules minimising time the car is off the road. The range has been expanded over the years to include diesel, fuel-injection, 16-valve and turbo-diesels of up to 1.9-litres as well as an anti-lock brake and 4 x 4 options. Seen here is a BX19 TZ1 as introduced in 1989.

concerning vehicle body structure. Use was made of composite polyester-glass fibre for the bonnet and rear hatch which had the rear window glass directly bonded on to it. Hydropneumatic self-levelling suspension and front wheel drive were the recipe for good roadholding and passenger comfort although the suspension system incorporated an integral pneumatic spring and damper without moving parts.

The BX was heralded with approval. The comfort and yet functional aspect of the car received praise, it fulfilled all the marketing requirements which were proven in the sales figures. The GSA had sustained criticism over its design of dashboard, the CX faired little better but the media had a field day with the fascia of the BX. It were as if Star Wars had been re-enacted, the dash was plasticky with angular satellite pods that looked as if they had come out of a corn-flake packet. With a change to a more aesthetic interior design, the BX settled down to sell in huge numbers becoming Citroën's best seller in the United Kingdom. Fleet buyers liked the car, they liked its service record and low maintenance schedule and what was more drivers took to the car gladly. Continuing from the GS and GSA in building public acceptance to Citroën's mid-market range of cars, the BX turned Citroën's fortunes.

Modifications in small degrees displayed careful thought and attention to detail and customer approval; 16 valve engines, electronic fuel injection, choice of power units, turbo and anti-lock braking as well as four-wheel drive have made the BX a formidable contender in a highly competitive market sector.

The Visa faded from the Citroën catalogue, the GSA had been phased out soon after the BX was unveiled and the Dyane was dropped at about the same time. Ironically, the 2CV survived the Dyane, the car which had been intended as a replacement for it. There is no doubt the 2CV has become a cult in Britain, never has the world shown such love and affection for a car displaying a following of adoration for its simple but logical form of transport. Demise of the Dyane, Ami and Visa left a gap in the small car market. The 2CV could not fill the void purely as it had its own peculiar niche quite unique of anything else. Citroën's quest for an eventual replacement of the 2CV led to several design studies one of the most singular being the ECO2000. The ECO was only a design study, a dream. Out of a dream came the AX, chic and stylish, practical and more than anything else, a Citroën.

At once the AX became a true Supermini, fuel-efficient and fun to drive. In contrast to the exterior size the AX manages extravagant amounts of space inside with comfort to match. On arrival upon the market it immediately took the lead over every other car in the market sector, setting new standards to which its rivals would have to strive hard to achieve. Three engine sizes power the AX, the economy 954cc which spins the car up to 90 m.p.h. and yet claims over 50 m.p.g. urban cycle while the Peugeot-Citroën engines of 1124cc and 1360cc are fitted into the mid-range and high-performers.

There was a gap in Citroën's catalogue for a small car, in the strongly-contested super-mini class. The AX came to the rescue; although a small car, the AX maximises every amount of space effectively and the designers have been resolute in reducing unnecessary weight. The result is a highly economical car utilising engine power to the limit. Introduced in 1987, the range includes 954cc, 1124cc and 1360cc engines, the largest available in GT form as shown here.

After forty-one years of production, the 2CV came to the end of the road. During its life, the 2CV never pretended to be anything but a minimal motor car, an 'umbrella on four wheels'. It signified tireless loyalty with the ability to go anywhere. The photograph shows the last 2CV coming off the assembly line on 27th July 1990, accompanied by the pomp and circumstance appropriate to so venerable a design. It had been over half a century since the model first appeared in prototype form.

Last of a famous line

As if to confirm Citroën's new direction with a final wave goodbye to the Citroën of yore, the Deux Chevaux after forty-one years finally folded down its umbrella.

The Morris Minor, Beetle, Mini, Fiat 500 and Renault 4 have all shared the accolade of a 'peoples's car' but none could quite topple the 2CV for its audaciousness, absolute commitment to minimal motoring and yet providing in an obtuse manner the most sophisticated engineering and recipe for long life and reliability. Probably one of the best reasons for the love affair with the 2CV is that it never pretended to be anything else than a basic form of motoring. It allowed superlative comfort from simple hammock seats, a relaxing and loping ride from large diameter but spindly tyred wheels on the end of incredibly long suspension arms; the capability of taking on any road surface; its cheapness to run and lack of unnecessary instrumentation , instant open-air motoring and bags of carrying capacity. Perhaps more than all, its love affair was afforded by its shape — its sheer, stark, beautiful curvacious body.

The real tribute to the 2CV is its own unpretentiousness and longevity created by the demand deserved of such initially clear and imaginative but simplistic design. The design was the product of an era and the commodity the resources available to a nation starved by war. So good the concept of the 2CV that over forty years from the first car rolling off the assembly line, thousands are seen every day on the roads throughout France, many of the cars older than the people driving them. Indeed, the 2CV is so much part of the way of life that the present generation driving them would not consider the original criteria for producing it. The 2CV will continue to be part of Europe for many years to come, it will continue to be loved and in return provide the simple pleasures of motoring in a sophisticated world. The sight of the 'Ugly Duckling' will bring back the smile to many faces, the whining and distant drone of the tiny air-cooled twin-cylinder engine be music to the ears. Who knows, one day in the future a designer may put down on the drawing board the blue print for a small family car, capable of crossing any terrain with four passengers in comfort, it might have to carry a cask of wine in the boot and provide such a supple ride as to carry a tray of eggs with not one being broken........

Another innovative big car

Back to the future! The European Car of the Year Award is no stranger to Citroën and therefore the XM carries on the tradition of the marque. The XM is another realisation of the Peugeot-Citroën partnership and is definitive of the route ahead. In every respect the XM represents Citroën idealism, technology and above all, personality. It is the development of the DS and CX that has engineered the XM as a futuristic car with a capacity for innovation and advanced engineering.

The XM follows Citroën's tradition of great cars, it bristles with technology and enjoys 'Hydractive' suspension that virtually thinks for itself. Computer-controlled, the suspension evaluates the surface of the road, movement of the body, speed and steering attitude, adapting the car to the conditions. The XM is a leader in car design perpetuating Citroën's quest for advanced technology. Introduced in Britain in October 1989, the initial range included 2.0-litre four-cylinder and 3.0-litre vee-six models with five-speed gearbox, but a year later a 2.1-litre turbo-diesel was added, claimed to be the world's first diesel car with a multi-valve engine — the XM Turbo SD is shown.

The Spring of 1989 saw the launch of the XM; it burst onto the market with vast aplomb. For the first time there was in a production car a 'thinking' hydraulic suspension, capable of deciphering exactly what was going on between the road surface and the wheels. The research into advance electronics and their marriage with hydraulic engineering culminated with the appearance of the Activa prototype in the Autumn of 1988. The Activa pioneered the way for the XM, developing its unique 'Hydractive' suspension which is computer-controlled, automatically and instantly adapting the car to road and driving conditions. Within a fraction of a second the car's suspension setting is determined from information gathered from five sensors which monitor steering, vehicle speed and body movement ,brake pressure and accelerator pedal movement. The safety features of the XM are further enhanced by anti-lock brakes, hydraulically powered steering and naturally, front-wheel drive.

From a driver's point of view, the XM is everything a Citroën should be. Comfort reigns supreme, the driving position has been carefully attended to, controls are logical and more than anything it is a deeply satisfying car. Even the quirks that Citroën are famous for are there; controversy has arisen over the parking brake which, following Citroën tradition and originating from the DS19, is foot operated. Apart from the furore, it is simple and straightforward.

The XM is a vast car with vast appeal. It follows on from André Citroën's dream of a supercar — the 22 of 1935, SM of 1970. Six power options are specified, even the most modest car in the range is a giant amongst the opposition; at the top of the range, the 3.0 litre, 24 valve V6 thunders up to 146 m.p.h.

The new ZX fulfils a need in the market between the AX and BX. Like the XM it is a car of the future confident of the direction Citroën are heading — forward!

Beyond the ZX and the current generation of cars, plans are already on the drawing board. As yet no one knows what holds for the future but for sure Citroën will be there, progressing forward with the same ideals and principles that led André Citroën to produce the Type A and Light 15. Those sharing his ideology produced the 2CV, DS and XM. The fascination for logic continues.

(Above) The Activa 2 Prototype, a design study in automobile engineering and technology. The work on 'active' suspension was combined with an exercise in modern styling and the publicity gained helped to publicise the technical step forward embodied in the XM.

The ZX, announced on the 25th of January 1991, is the newest Citroën providing a model in the niche between the AX and BX. In the manner now fashionable, a slender window is incorporated in each rear corner of the body, but an unusual feature is the way in which this directly adjoins the rear hatch.

The initial venture of Citroën into the taxicab business was this design complying with London requirements as supervised by the Metropolitan Police, dating from 1925. Though based on the 11.4 h.p. car model, it incorporated many special features to suit this purpose. The large-diameter disc wheels gave a stubby appearance, emphasised by the tall build of the body necessary to allow top-hatted passengers to enter and leave the vehicle without difficulty. The passenger door design resembled contemporary railway practice. The London General Cab Company had a large fleet of vehicles of this type.

Appendix One: Citroën taxicabs

The name of Citroën has long been synonymous with the taxi in Paris and throughout France but not so in recent times in London or the provinces. It would seem that the Citroën would be an unlikely vehicle to lend itself to the streets of England's capital city for hail and hire of the city dweller in a hurry, yet, it was just four years after André Citroën had launched the first vehicle to bear his name that the Citroën taxicab met with considerable success.

Ironically, it would appear that Citroën taxicabs were part of the London scene before they were fully established as a subsidiary of the manufacturer in Paris; Citroën entered the taxicab market in 1923 when their vehicles were supplied to the London General Cab Company at Brixton in South London. Until then, no other taxicab had been supplied with accessories as electric starting and lighting fitted as standard from the factory. The electrical equipment included headlights for country driving as well as side lamps and the latter were of a combination design capable of burning oil if required to do so. The Citroën taxicab was considered to represent a high class vehicle and as such with its level of equipment and technical adroitness achieved much acclaim on its introduction.

By 1923 over half of all taxicabs in the Metropolitan area were owner-driven, the increase in the popularity of the taxi meant that there was a new keenness within the trade but also a greater competition from motor bus and tram services. These were relevant factors appreciated by the main supplier of Citroën taxis within London, Maxwell Monson Ltd. who set about providing a comprehensive service. The price of the Citroën Taxi in 1923 amounted to £540 for a complete vehicle and £330 for the chassis. The cost of the Citroën was nearly £100 cheaper than the Beardmore which at the time was amongst the most popular vehicles for taxi fleets. From their garage in Halkin Place, Belgravia Square, Maxwell Monson not only provided vehicle spares at short notice but also a repair service. In addition they also arranged to supply vehicles on hire purchase with a deposit of £50 and monthly payments of £12. To assist the novice driver, Maxwell Monson undertook driving tuition as well as taking driver and vehicle to Scotland Yard to obtain a licence.

The specification of the Citroën taxi chassis as constructed to pass Scotland Yard requirements for service in London was based on the 11.4 h.p. car in having the 68 x 100 mm engine, single plate clutch and three-speed gearbox of that model, but the rear axle, though of helical bevel type, was a heavier-duty unit and the frame was of modified form. The wheelbase was 8ft. 1⅞in. and the wide-track (4ft. 8in.) axle had tyres of the same large-diameter 815 x 105 size used on almost all makes of London taxi of the day.

Citroën was almost the only volume-production manufacturer to venture into this specialised market at that time, the only other concern of comparable nature being Fiat, none of the major British makes later to become prominent in this field such as Austin or Morris having yet made their entry. The best-known British make was Beardmore, and another French concern, Unic, had been well established as a builder of London taxi chassis since before the 1914-18 war. The Citroën was noteworthy in having the smallest engine then on offer in a London cab,

In 1929, the London General Cab Company decided to update their fleet of Citroën taxis, modernising the body and fitting smaller-diameter wheels with larger-section tyres. The revised design is shown on the left, with an unmodified vehicle on the right for comparison. The tall build of the original had been reduced by the new wheels and by eliminating the roof rack. The folding roof of the landaulet body had given way to a fixed top and the door design modernised.

most of the British makes, including Beardmore, having 15.9 h.p. units while Unic favoured 13.9 h.p., though introducing a choice of 15.9 h.p. for 1924.

The vehicle had to meet the tight London taxi turning-circle requirements and the layout of the controls allowed the provision of an offside door for the driver, not always possible on some competitive models of the day due to their right-hand gear levers. Fuel consumption averaged at 26 miles per gallon though it was found possible to increase the figure to 30 m.p.g. on non-stop runs. A test drive on a new vehicle proved the Citroën to respond easily to London's traffic, be pulled up rapidly using either brake and having a ride quality equal that of a well-sprung touring car.

In 1926, Citroën reduced the price of their cab to £495 at a time when a new Unic taxi cost £625. The 11.4 chassis with English body enjoyed continuing success with Maxwell Monson providing a service for owner drivers while London General took considerable numbers of Citroëns into their fleet. When the London General business was registered as a public company in November 1928 it took over a fleet of 220 Citroën cabs.

The taxi scene in Paris was not a mirror image of London. Whereas over half of taxis in London were owner-driven, most of the taxicabs in the French capital were in the hands of large companies operating modern fleets of vehicles. The total number of cabs in service in Paris in 1928 amounted to over 15,000, of which approximately 7,000 were operated by five big companies having from a dozen to fifty cabs. Very few cabs were owner-driven.

The Citroën Company had seen the wisdom of direct involvement in the taxi trade and as a result formed the Société des Taxis Citroën in 1925. The aim of the company was twofold: a successful financial venture and as a means of direct advertising of the Citroën product, challenging the Renault-based fleet of the largest operating company. The Société des Taxis Citroën achieved their goal by conclusive demonstration of the reliability of a well-performing fleet of cabs. Goodwill was built up by introducing the company's cab drivers to go to the

Continental taxi designs tended to be more closely related to the standard car chassis of the period. This 1929 example appears to be based on the contemporary C4 model. Here the external roof-mounted luggage rack was still in favour. The rear quarter panels of the body appear to be fabric-covered, suggesting that it may have been of folding landaulet style originally, though evidently fixed and secured by polished beading in this view taken in the 'sixties.

149

A black and yellow livery was favoured for many Citroën taxis. This 11UA model of the mid 'thirties illustrates the style of painting echoing the type of body sometimes called a fiacre after the horse-drawn vehicle of that name.

assistance of Citroën car owners held up by punctures or breakdowns, and although this had to be abandoned under trade union pressure, they could still help voluntarily and cabs were provided with a tow line and hook to enable them to tow cars to a garage for repair, charging at the hourly rate shown on the meter.

On formation of the Société des Taxis Citroën in 1925 a fleet of pretty yellow and black landaulet vehicles on the B2 chassis performed outstanding duty from the 27,000 square foot garage at Levallois-Perret on the western fringes of Paris. During the early part of 1928 the fleet of 1,000 cabs were replaced by 1,400 new vehicles, based on the 12.24 chassis and representing a new direction in luxury and comfort for both driver and passenger alike. The new cabs, again painted in yellow and black had the benefit of an all-metal saloon and at once led the way in taxi design by being the first cab in Paris to be fully enclosed. There had been doubts as to whether this would be acceptable in place of the earlier style of body, with its facility for open-air travel in summer, but it proved successful. Another noteworthy feature was the Westinghouse servo brake system, which was being adopted generally by Citroën for its cars but of particular value on a taxi.

The new Paris cabs were noted for their remarkable comfort; apart from ample leg room and the provision of deep cushioned seats, they had tip-up seats for extra passengers. Cab prices were noted for their cheapness in Paris; passengers using the occasional seats were not charged and it was often cheaper for a party of four to take a taxi than ride on a tramcar. An interesting endpiece of a report in *Motor Transport* by a well-known English journalist, W. F. Bradley, on the new Paris cabs reads:

'The all-round vision is almost too good for the peace of mind of nervous visitors unused to the remarkable speed at which traffic flows'.

However, drivers had to be over 35 years old and were carefully selected. They paid for fuel out of earnings and petrol consumption under traffic conditions was quoted as between 29 and 31 miles per gallon, a remarkably good figure for brisk driving in urban conditions.

The London General Cab Company took the decision in 1929 to update their fleet of Citroën cabs by giving the vehicles a facelift with modifications to the passenger saloon and the driver's compartment. Apart from overhauling the mechanical equipment and fitting smaller wheels with larger-section tyres, attention was paid in particular to removing the roof-rack, redesigning the saloon door and replacing the hood with fabric covered coachwork.

As a further measure of their modification programme, The London General Cab Company undertook to purchase a number of Citroën 13/30 chassis with the 1629cc four-cylinder engine fitted and three-speed gearbox. In their workshops, London General fitted a lightweight landaulet body, the whole vehicle being designed by their chief Engineer, P. Geldard. There were several interesting features concerning these cabs which included the design of the front wings which were detached from the running boards to facilitate ease of repairs and work on the engine compartment; the cab weighed a mere 1¼ tons and used low-pressure tyres; the cab had an air-extractor in the roof and utilised a communication system — a Burovox device — in order that the passengers could talk to the driver by remote control.

Early during the 1930s a hybrid Citroën taxi appeared on the streets of London. Again operated by London General Cab Company, these taxis were dubbed the 'Chinese Austin' by the company drivers. Austin 12 chassis were utilised to support bodies from Citroën cabs that had been in store for some considerable time. A total of 196 'Chinese Austins' were put into service with the result of a cab that performed perfectly well but was never fully appreciated by drivers and passengers alike. By 1931, London General operated a fleet of 550 vehicles, 320 of which were Citroën.

By the mid 'thirties, the London taxi scene had turned to other makes, but Citroën taxis based on private car models of the final rear wheel drive types were a familiar sight in some other parts of Britain, notably Bournemouth where a sizeable fleet were operated under the appropriate name Citax.

Appendix Two: Delivery of vehicles in and from Britain

Year	Home	Export	Total	Comments
1919/1920	-	-	750	Imported by Gaston's
1921	-	-	1701	
1922	-	-	889	
1923	-	-	3009	Formation of Citroën Cars Ltd. Brook Green
1924	-	-	3080	
1925	-	-	6655	
1926	-	-	5299	Slough factory opened 18th February 1926
1927	-	-	5900	
1928	-	-	3650	
1929	1508	245	1753	Export of vehicles commenced
1930	1222	82	1304	
1931	898	60	958	
1932	497	80	577	
1933	1752	285	2037	
1934	1696	232	1928	Introduction of F.W.D.
1935	1056	197	1253	
1936	573	106	679	
1937	689	337	1026	
1938	690	531	1221	
1939	692	596	1288	
1940	208	221	439	
1941	21		12	
1942	2		2	
1943/1945	-	-	-	Factory requisitioned for war effort

Citroën made a feature of offering formal 'Town Car' bodywork on its chassis in the 1920s and early 1930s, thereby offering a style usually associated with expensive marques at low price.

Year	Home	Export	Total	Comments
1946	552	408	1050	Car manufacture resumes
1947	567	1373	1940	
1948	500	1809	2309	
1949	570	1686	2256	
1950	485	1910	2395	
1951	498	2407	2905	
1952	627	958	1585	
1953	695	1249	1944	
1954	442	1285	1727	Commencement of 2CV and 15 Six-H
1955	328	1032	1360	
1956	204	155	359	Demise of Light 15, Commencement of DS
1957	344	578	922	
1958	489	335	824	
1959	1172	246	1418	
1960	1720	279	1999	Demise of 2CV, Arrival of Bijou
1961	904	157	1061	
1962	668	145	813	
1963	909	174	1083	
1964	961	74	1035	
1965	485	7	492	
1966	726	3	729	Closure of Slough factory, all cars imported
1967	1078	-	1078	
1968	1040	-	1040	
1969	1297	-	1297	
1970	4304	-	4304	
1971	6992	-	6992	
1972	17617	-	17617	Introduction of GS
1973	20565	-	20565	
1974	16099	-	16099	Reintroduction 2CV
1975	22049	-	22049	
1976	21001	-	21001	
1977	23974	-	23974	
1978	31957	-	31957	
1979	34015	-	34015	
1980	27006	-	27006	
1981	27383	-	27383	
1982	24149	-	24149	
1983	25721	-	25721	
1984	24562	-	24562	
1985	27479	-	27479	
1986	34427	-	34427	
1987	46013	-	46013	
1988	66937	-	66937	
1989	66409	-	66409	
1990	60899	-	60899	Represents 3.03% of market share

This example of the DS Convertible dates from 1966, the year that marked the end of the Slough factory as a manufacturing facility. It is owned by Joe Judt, President of the Citroën Car Club.

Appendix Three: British and French designations

British designation	French designation	Comments
10 H.P.	Type A	
11.4 H.P.	B2	
7.5 H.P.	Type C	
12-24 H.P.	B14	
13-30 H.P.	C4	
2½ litre	C6	Six-cylinder
12.8 H.P. Chiltern/Clarendon	C4F	
Buckingham/Berkeley	C6F	Six-cylinder
Big 12	C4G	
Twenty	C6G	Six-cylinder
Ten	8	
Light 12	10 Legere	
Big 12	10	
Light 20	15 Legere	Six-cylinder
20	15	Six-cylinder
10	8NH	
Family Fifteen	11UA	
Diesel	11UD	
Super Modern Twelve	7	1302cc, FWD
Super Modern Twelve	7C	1628cc, FWD
Twelve Sport	7S (Sport)	1911cc, FWD
Light Fifteen	11BL/Legere	1911cc, FWD
Fifteen	1B/Normale	1911cc, FWD
SIX (6 cylinder)	15-Six	2866cc, FWD
Six (Hydropneumatic)	15-6H	2866cc, FWD
2CV	2CV	
Bijou	-	Slough only
Ami 6	Ami 6	
D Series	As French models	
DW	-	Slough only
Dyane	As French models	
Ami 8	As French models	
GS/GSA	As French models	
SM	As French models	
2CV	As French models	
CX	As French models	
LNA	As French models	
Visa	As French models	
C15 Van	As French models	
BX	As French models	
AX	As French models	
XM	As French models	
ZX	As French models	

The British and French horse-power ratings as used for taxation purposes, were both based on theoretical assumptions that were outdated in relation to actual power output even in the 1920s but were different from each other and this was an almost endless source of confusion. These entries in a French leaflet of about 1934 show 'Commerciale' versions of the 8 and 10 models known in Britain as the Ten and Big 12 respectively.

850. Berline Commerciale sur châssis " 8 ".

1052. Conduite Intérieure Commerciale sur châssis " 1

Appendix Four: Production of Traction Avant cars at Slough

Model	Super Modern Twelve & STD	Light 15	Big 15	Six Cyl.	LHD Light 15	6H
Year						
1935	Exact Figure Unknown Max 1350	Exact Figure Unknown Max 650	-	-	-	-
1936	Max 650	Max 350	-	-	-	-
1937	500	300	-	-	-	-
1938	900	350	-	-	-	-
1939	Max 1700	Max 1450	Max 300	-	-	-
1940	Unknown	Unknown	Max 50	-	-	-
1946	1199	-	-	-	-	-
1947	1838	-	-	-	-	-
1948	2484	-	-	7	-	-
1949	-	1852	-	235	68	-
1950	-	1963	-	370	110	-
1951	-	571	2	313	97	-
1952	-	1225	77	130	35	-
1953	-	1599	428	95	7	-
1954	-	971	411	29	-	2
1955	-	716	110	-	-	74

Note: Production ceased during World War II

*The Slough-built Traction Avant cars were given a distinctively British look by the retention of radiator grille used on early examples, rather than that with painted shell soon adopted in France, and by the use of standard Lucas lamps as found on many British makes and models. This Light 15 is a post-war example, identifiable by its louvred bonnet sides; it dates from 1946. Of such a car **The Autocar** said 'The Citroën is essentially a machine for motoring in ... robust and rugged ... not spoiled by any desire to remind its occupants of either a gin palace or a stately home. It is happiest on the open road with long distances to cover in as short a time as possible ...'.*

Appendix Five: Total production of Traction Avant cars

British model	Super Modern Twelve		Twelve Sport	Twelve	Light Fifteen	Big Fifteen	Light Fifteen	Big Fifteen	Big Fifteen	Six	Six H
French model	7A	7B	7 Sport	7C	11 Legere	11	11BL	11B	11 Normale	15 Six	15 Six H
Year											
1934	7000a	20620	1500a	6700b	1500b	3300b	-	-	-	-	-
1935	-	-	-	14700	1900	4100	-	-	-	-	-
1936	-	-	-	30000	5400	9200	-	-	-	-	-
1937	-	-	-	11300	-	-	6700	10700	-	-	-
1938	-	-	-	6245c	-	-	36526d	13207e	-	90	-
1939	-	-	-	8120f	-	-	27473g	14394h	-	2309j	-
1940	-	-	-	1133	-	-	445	2405	-	25	-
1941	-	-	-	154	-	-	2038	678	-	202	-
1945	-	-	-	-	-	-	1525	-	-	-	-
1946	-	-	-	-	-	-	10931	-	-	-	-
1947	-	-	-	-	19348	-	-	-	1697	118	-
1948	-	-	-	-	20091	-	-	-	7423	2730	-
1949	-	-	-	-	22700	-	-	-	13750	6100	-
1950	-	-	-	-	24700	-	-	-	17800	11000	-
1951	-	-	-	-	26000	-	-	-	16600	11500	-
1952	-	-	-	-	29800	-	-	-	24500	8550	-
1953	-	-	-	-	24900	-	-	-	34200	2060	-
1954	-	-	-	-	15600	-	-	-	33800	1240	1680
1955	-	-	-	-	14900	-	-	-	27640	440	1382
1956	-	-	-	-	8505	-	-	-	30890	-	-
1957	-	-	-	-	3862k	-	-	-	-	-	-

Remarks and key to explanatory letters
a) Vehicles produced from May to September 1934
b) Produced from October to December 1934
c) Comprises 6153 saloon, 71 roadster, 21 coupé
d) Comprises 35774 saloon, 671 roadster, 81 coupé
e) Comprises 6903 saloon, 2544 conduite interieure, 2315 familiale, 219 roadster, 37 coupé, 1189 commerciale
f) Comprises 8093 saloon, 27 roadster
g) Comprises 26915 saloon, 558 roadster
h) Comprises 7460 saloon, 2136 conduite interieure, 3029 familiale, 291 roadster, 1478 commerciale
j) Comprises 1818 saloon, 277 familiale, 213 conduite interieure, 1 roadster
k) Last Traction produced and left works 25th July 1957.

Total number of cars produced — 715,367

Traction Avant cars from both sides of the Channel: from the left, a Paris-built post-war Familiale seven-seater, a 1936 Slough-built roadster and a 1954 Six, also a product of the Slough works.

Appendix Six: Production of the 2CV and Bijou at Slough

Year	Chassis Numbers	Type
1953	8/530001 — 8/530026	Saloon (A)
	8/53001	Pick-up (AP)
	8/537001 — 8/537003	Van (AU)
1954	8/530027 — 8/530176	Saloon (A)
	8/535002 — 8/535005	Pick-up (AP)
	8/537004 — 8/537069	Van (AU)
1955	8/530177 — 8/530186	Saloon (A)
	8/535006 — 8/535012	Pick-up (AP)
	8/537070 — 8/537081	Van (AU)
	8/551001 — 8/551177	Saloon (AZ)
	8/556001 — 8/556010	Pick-up (AZP)
	8/558001 — 8/558052	Van (AZU)
1956	8/561001 — 8/561061	Saloon (AZ)
	8/566001 — 8/566009	Pick-up (AZP)
	8/568001 — 8/568013	Van (AZU)
1957	8/571062 — 8/571126	Saloon (AZ)
	8/576010 — 8/576019	Pick-up (AZP)
	8/578014 — 8/578032	Van (AZU)
1958	8/581127 — 8/581207	Saloon (AZ)
	8/586020 — 8/586043	Pick-up (AZP)
	8/588033 — 8/588054	Van (AZU)
1959	8/591208 — 8/591288	Saloon (AZ)
	8/596044	Pick-up (AZP)
	8/598055 — 8/598072	Van (AZU)
1960	8/596045 — 8/596079	Pick-up (AZP)
	8/600101 — -------	Bijou (BJ)*
	8/601289 — 8/601309	Saloon (AZ)
	8/608073 — 8/608098	Van (AZU)
1961	8/86080 — 8/86109	Pick-up (AZP)
1964	------- — 8/600313	Bijou (BJ)*

* Commencement of Bijou chassis numbers shown in 1960 and finishing in 1964 as information as to numbers of cars produced each year is not available. The table does not include Ami 6 models built at Slough.

INDEX

AEC 82
Albion, HMS 107
Allen Brothers 139
Alvis 71
Armstrong Siddeley 67
Audouin-Dubreuil 53
Austin 15, 25, 35, 37, 50, 52, 65, 66, 67, 70, 86, 88, 96, 99, 103
Autocar 42, 43, 48, 80, 82, 83, 112, 133
Auto journal L' 109, 110

Banque Lazard 52, 68
Becchia, Walter 97
Bedford, 60, 61, 85
Bendix 82
Bentley 70
Bentley, W. O. 124
Bertone 112
Bijou production 156
Billancourt 8, 68, 72, 74
Blue Cruise 68
BMW 97
Boddy, William 101
Boulanger, Pierre 80, 96-99
Bradley, W. F. 74
British Broadcasting Corporation 125
British Motor Corporation 81, 88
Brooklands motor racing circuit 65
Brook Green 18-20, 35, 37, 41, 47, 55, 80, 132
Brooks seat belts 121
Budd 27, 28, 29, 71, 72, 75
Bulwark, HMS 107, 108

Canadian Forces 85
Central Asia Expedition 75
Chapron, Henri 126, 130
Chevrolet 60
Chrysler 62
Chrysler Corporation 62
Churchill Tanks 85
Citax 150
Citroën, Amelia 6
Citroën Car Club 25, 107
Citroën Cars Ltd 14
Citroën Exhibition Hall 73, 74
Citroën Gear Company 7
Citroën, Hughes 7
Citroën
  Type A: 8-9, 11-12, 14, 15, 17, 18, 21, 99, 146; **Acadiane:** 143;
  Activa: 146, 147; **AK:** 143; **Ami6:** 122; **Ami8:** 130, 132, 134, 137, 141;
  Ami Super: 134, 135, 141; **AX:** 144, 146; **B2:** 21; **B12:** 25, 35;
  B14: 36, 38, 48; **B18:** 38; **Berkeley saloon:** 47, 48, 60;
  Bijou: 103-107, 123, 127, 131; **BX:** 143, 144;
  Buckingham saloon: 47, 48, 49, 60; **C15:** 143;
  CX: 138, 140, 141, 143, 144, 145; **C4/C6:** 40, 48;
  Chiltern saloon: 47, 48, 49; **Clarendon saloon:** 47, 48;
  Commercial vehicles: 58-61; **Diesel car:** 82;
  D Series: 109-126, 127-130, 134, 138, 139, 140, 145, 146;
  Deux Chevaux (2CV): 96-109, 117, 122, 123, 131, 136, 141, 143, 144, 145;
  Dyane: 131, 136-138, 141, 143, 144; **GS/GSA:** 128, 134, 135, 136, 143, 144;
  GS Birotor: 134, 136; **H van:** 107; **LN/LNA:** 141, 142;
  Six: 85, 89, 91, 109, 129; **Six H (15 Six H):** 85, 89, 91, 94, 95, 109, 116, 129;
  SM: 126, 132, 136, 138, 140, 146; **Ten/10CV:** 62-67, 70, 74;
  Traction Avant: 71, 75, 80, (7&7C): 74, 75, 78, (11): 73, 78, 80, 89;
  (Super Modern Twelve): 71, 73, 77-79, 129; (Light 15): 78, 79, 81-86, 88, 91, 92, 95, 109, 138; (Big Fifteen): 78-81, 85, 89, 92, 109; (15): 78; (22): 93;
  Travellers Brougham: 58; **Twelve:** 65, 74; **Light Twelve:** 65, 66, 68;
  Big Twelve: 54-58, 61-67, 82; **Twenty:** 54-66, 68, 74;
  Visa: 141, 142, 143, 144; **XM:** 145, 146; **ZX:** 146, 147;
  7.5 h.p.: 13, 16, 23, 25, 35, 36, 39; **11.4 h.p.:** 15, 22, 25-27, 30, 31, 35-39;
  12-24 h.p.: 30, 35-39, 41-43; **13-30 h.p.:** 40-48, 50;
  2½ litre: 40, 42-45, 47, 50; **15CV:** 64
Clyno 22
Commer 61
Connaught Cars 121
Connolly leather 88, 120
Cord 71

Croisiere Jaune 53
Crossley Streamline 70

Daimler 67
Davies, Rupert 91
Delage 42
Delco Remy 46, 61
Delivery of vehicles 151, 152
Deux Chevaux (2CV) production 156
Diesel car 68, 81, 82
DKW 71
Double helical gear 7

ECO 2000 144
Eiffel Tower 11, 41, 95
Elizabeth, HRH Princess 84
Elizabeth, HRH Queen 84
Esparbes d', M. 12

Fairey Aviation 88
Fiat 500 96, 145; 501/509: 25
Floating Power 42, 61-63, 65, 77, 78, 79, 84, 115
Ford 37, 54, 61, 66, 93
  Anglia: 99, 107, 122, 123;
  BF: 65; Classic: 122, 124
  Henry: 6, 7, 54
  Model T: 7, 36
  Popular: 99, 103, 106
  Y: 70
  Zodiac: 121
Fordson 61

Garbe, Louis 129
Gaston 14-18
General Motors 94
George VI, HRH King 84
Goodyear airwheel 67
Grand Union Canal 22
Great Western Railway 22, 24, 87
Green Line Coaches 121

Haardt, Georges-Maries 7, 53, 55, 68
Hampton & Sons 21
Harbleischer, M. 7
Harrods 16, 17
Heat & Air Systems Ltd 120
Hillman 70, 88
Histoire Mondiale de l'Automobile 68
Hoyal 38
Humber 88, 121
H van 107

Ickx, Jacques 111
Inter Counties Ambulance Service 124

Jaguar 121
Javel, Quai de 8, 13-15, 22, 55, 68, 69, 72, 80, 86, 120, 138, 143
Jouets Citroën 84
Jowett Javelin 88

Kegresse 16
Kegresse half track vehicles 17-18, 21, 53
Kenlowe fan 121
King, Ben 41
Kirwan-Taylor, Peter 103

Lanchester 67
Lecot, Francois 75, 76
Ledwinka, Joseph 72, 75
Lefebvre, Andre 72, 74, 75, 97
LEP Transport 15-16
Levallois 13, 97, 98
Light Car and Cycle Car magazine 12, 16, 30, 63, 67
Lindbergh, Charles 38, 39
Lockheed, 72, 100
London General Cab Co 148, 150
London Rally 92
Lotus Elite 103
Lucas 44, 67, 88, 92, 120

157

MacPherson 143
Maigret 91
Marchand, Cesar 52
Margaret, HRH Princess 84
Maserati 132
Mauheimer, Charles 72
McKenna duty (taxation) 21
McLelland 47
Meccano 107
Mercedes Benz 82, 115
MG 66, 88
Michelat 42
Michelin 12, 14, 67, 76, 80, 84, 120
Michelin Superconfort tyres 84
Michelin X tyres 89, 94, 107, 119
Middleton Motors 121
Mini 81, 103, 107, 145
Monte Carlo Rally 75, 76, 114, 119
Montlhery racing circuit 40, 52, 74
Morris cars 37, 66, 67, 88, 103
Morris Cowley 16
Morris, Herbert 20
Morris Minor 70, 99, 107, 145
Morris Ten Four 70
Mors 7, 8
Moss, Stirling 121
Motor magazine 29, 37, 42, 43, 45, 46, 48, 67, 77, 82, 84, 88, 89, 92, 94, 95, 99, 103, 113, 122, 123, 140
Motor Industry (magazine) 87
Motor Sport magazine 101, 121

New Devonshire House 32-35, 37, 50, 65, 80, 81
Newton Bennett 88
NSU 128, 134
Nuffield Group 88

Panhard et Levassor 12, 24, 109, 110, 119, 130
Passenger coach (Citroën) 61
Petite Rosalie 69
Peugeot 7, 26, 29, 33, 37, 68, 72, 141, 143
Peugeot 203/403 122
Peugeot Bebe 25
Peugeut-Talbot-Citroën Group 38
Peugeot-Citroën 143, 144, 145
Pichon-Parat 130
Pilote wheels 84, 85
Porsche 109
Poxon, John 25
Pyrene 88

Quai André Citroën 76

Radford, Harold 125
Railton 70
Ranalah 66
Renault 21, 29, 33, 37, 68, 97, 141
  Celtaquatre: 72
  Dauphine: 122, 123
  Fregate: 122
  4L: 131, 145
  9/15: 25
  14: 141
Renault, Louis 8, 9, 12, 65, 68, 72, 74, 75
Ricardo Comet 82
Ridout, F. W. (Freddie) 30
Riley 67, 88
  Nine Kestrel: 70
Ritz Hotel 33, 34
Robri 95
Rolls-Royce 115
Rootes 61, 68
Rootes, Reginald 38
Rosalie Affair 52-54
Rosengart 71
Rover 65, 89, 121, 141
Rowe & Co 107
Royal Marines 103, 107
Ruben-Owen 88

Saab 109
Schilling, George 29
Schneider, Theophile 7
Scottish Cup 21
Sensaud de Lavaud, Robert Dimitri 74
Short Brothers 16, 35
Simca Aronde 122
Simenon, George 91
Singer Eleven Airstream 70
Slough, Borough of 28
  Trading Company/Estate 17, 21, 22, 24, 28, 49, 78
Societé des Taxis Citroën 149, 150
Societé Trans-Americaine de Jaute des Bois 76
Solex 42, 57, 61, 66, 121
Somerset-Leeke, J. 105
Somerset-Leeke, Nigel 103
Spirit of St. Louis 38, 39
Splintex 45
Standard 67, 88
Sunbeam 88
Sunbeam Talbot Ten 88
S U 121
Suresnes 13

Talbot 32, 67, 88, 97, 107, 141
Tatra 109
Taxis 148, 149, 150
Taylorisation 8, 13
T.P.V. 96-97
Traction Avant production 154, 155
Tractor unit 61
Trans African Expedition 53
Transports Citroën 44
Triplex 67, 88
Triumph 88

Vanden Plas 121
VariPower steering 133, 140, 141
Vauxhall 60, 61
  Cresta: 121
  Velox: 121
Voisin, Gabriel 12, 52, 72
Volkswagen 144

Wankel rotary engine 134
Weber 115
Westinghouse 37, 38, 41, 43, 44, 46, 48, 117
Weymann 16, 35, 45, 50, 51
White Cruise 68
Whitson, James & Co 106
Wilson epicyclic gearbox 67
Wolsley 88
Worthing Motors 20, 24, 25, 107

Yacco 52
Yellow Cruise 53

Photocredits

The majority of the photographs used in this book have come from material produced from publications by Citroën Cars over the years, and from the author's collection. Other people who have supplied material are:

Wendy Balkwill	5	National Motor Museum	21, 51, 59, 60, 70, 85, 92, 124
Citroën Car Club	110, 120 (both), 125	John A. Senior, courtesy Peter Harling	Dust jacket (all), title page, 2, 3
David Conway	101	Traction Owners Club	17, 55, 58, 63, 65, 67, 87 (both)
Brian Long	23, 31, 64, 69, 83, 119, 133		

Citroën Enthusiasts Clubs

CITROËN CAR CLUB. Founded in 1949, the oldest-established club for Citroën owners and enthusiasts. All models are catered for from the earliest to the present day including PANHARD. High quality monthly magazine, *Citroënian*, keeps members informed of events and provides valuable news and articles on Citroën matters. Membership Secretary: Derek Pearson, 'Alfriston', 61 Lakeside Drive, Bromley, Kent. BR2 8QQ.

TRACTION OWNERS CLUB. Formed to cater for the interests in particular for owners and enthusiasts of pre-1957 Citroën cars. Excellent bi-monthly magazine, *Floating Power*, with club news, events, cars of interest and archive material.
Membership Secretary: P. D. Riggs, 2, Appleby Gardens, Dunstable, Bedfordshire, LU6 3DB.

2CVGB. The Deux Chevaux Club of Great Britain provides events and gatherings for owners of 2CVs and derivatives. Many local groups have been formed. Members are kept informed of club news by monthly magazine, *2CVGB NEWS*.
Membership: PO Box 602, Crick, Northampton, NN6 7VW.

Acknowledgements

It is with deep appreciation that I record the tremendous help and encouragement received while writing this book. In particular I thank Peter Parker and Ken Smith, both now retired from Citroën U.K.; Julian Leighton of Citroën U.K. Publicity Department; LEP Transport, Epsom, Surrey; Brigadier Neville White of Slough Estates and to Slough Public Library.

The Citroën Car Club for allowing me access to their archives and photographic library, in particular, Joe Judt, Brian Drummond, David Evans and David Conway. The Traction Owners Club and Deux Chevaux Club of Great Britain; Brian Long for supplying archive advertising material and Mrs J. M. Somerset-Leeke for information concerning the Bijou.

To Lewis Balkwill, Walton Road Garage, Molesey, Surrey, and Wendy Balkwill for supplying archive photographic material. Appreciation is extended to the ex-staff of Citroën's Slough Factory, some of whom, sadly, have died before this book could be published.

To Alan Townsin who has undertaken the considerable task of layout for this book and, in the process, has offered much valuable advice and information, often asking pertinent questions. Alan's knowledge of motor transport and history of the automobile has been an inspiration as well as a source of invaluable research.

To John Senior and his team at Transport Publishing who have all offered help and advice and made writing this book an absolute pleasure.

Last but not least, to my wife, Jean, for her patience and understanding, continued encouragement and valuable assistance and comment.

Bibliography

Naturally, there is a far greater amount of literature upon the subject of Citroën, the man and the cars, published in French than in English. However the following provides further sources of information.

The definitive works can be considered to be PIERRE DUMONT'S *QUAI DE JAVEL, QUAI ANDRÉ CITROËN* in two volumes. The first volume, also marketed as *CITROËN — THE GREAT MARQUE OF FRANCE* has an English translation. Both volumes may be obtained from Editions E.P.A. 83, Rue de Rennes, 75006, Paris. *TOUTES LES CITROËN* is a masterpiece of a book compiled by RENE BELLU and lists every Citroën ever produced; the first half of the volume provides a graphic list of models in scale drawing form together with information and photographs in chronological order, a section is devoted to every year from 1919-1979. The second half of the book concerns prototypes and archive photographs. The book is in French and published by Editions Jean-Pierre Delville, 17, Rue des Grands Augustins, 75006, Paris.

The *CITROËNIAN*, monthly magazine published by the CITROËN CAR CLUB since 1949 gives a valuable insight to the history of the marque and, since the club's formation, has covered in detail every Citroën that has been produced. An antholgy of the Citroënian has also been published covering the years 1949 to 1959 and a second volume is due. Further information can be supplied from the Club Honorary Competition Secretary and U.K. Liaison Officer, Brian Drummond, 5, Bishops Close, Hurstpierpoint, West Sussex.

FLOATING POWER, magazine of THE TRACTION OWNERS CLUB is also another valuable source of information dealing with cars produced in the main from 1919 to 1957, the end of the Traction era. Further information can be obtained from the magazine editor, D. G. Gardner, 33, Austin Drive, Banbury, Oxon. OX16 7DL.

L'ALBUM DE LA TRACTION and *L'ALBUM DE LA DS*, published by E.P.A. have fine photographic records for the Traction Avant and the D Series of cars. Text is in French only.

ALMANACH DU CITROËNISTE is an annual publication compiled by FABIEN SABATES and is published by EDITIONS FRANCOIS REDER. Copious amounts of archive material are published with the text in French.

THE LIFE AND TIMES OF THE 2CV, by BOB MACQUEEN AND JULIAN McNAMARA, published by the GREAT OUSE PRESS and now out of print details the history of the 2CV and derivitives. Likewise, JAMES TAYLOR'S *THE CITROËN 2CV* published by MOTOR RACING PUBLICATIONS gives detailed information on Citroën's air-cooled cars.

CITROËN SM by JEFF DANIELS, published by OSPREY is an interesting account of this supercar.

RAYMOND BROAD'S book *CITROËN* is now out of print and gives a lighthearted account of the Citroën marque.

BROOKLANDS BOOKS road tests of the Traction Avant, DS and 2CV provide interesting reading and data concerning the cars.

CITROËN — L'HISTOIRE ET LES SECRETS DE SON BUREAU D'ETUDES published in two volumes and written by ROGER BRIOULT, published by LA VIE DE L'AUTO, 77303 Fontainebleau, details cars and prototypes that have led to the models of Citroën that have appeared. Text in French.

ANDRÉ CITROËN, LES CHEVRONS DE LA GLOIRE, published by E.P.A. Paris, written by FABIEN SABATES AND SYLVIE SCHWEITZER chronicles the life of Citroën. Text in French.

LES CAMIONS CITROËN, by FABIEN SABATES AND WOUTER JANSEN details Citroën's commercial vehicles. Published by MASSIN, 75014, PARIS. Text in French.

There are numerous other books from around the world, a full list and prices can be obtained from C.D. CONWAY, MODEL IMPORT COMPANY, REDLEES, 152, BARKHAM ROAD, WOKINGHAM, BERKS. RG11 2RP. (Mail order).